Śrī-yantra
and
the Geophilosophy of India

Śrī-yantra and the Geophilosophy of India

Niraj Kumar

With a foreword by
Dandiswami Paranand Tirth

DK PRINTWORLD
Publishers of Indian Traditions

Cataloging in Publication Data — DK
[Courtesy: D.K. Agencies (P) Ltd. <docinfo@dkagencies.com

Niraj Kumar, 1973-
Śrī-yantra and the geophilosophy of India / Niraj Kumar.
p. cm.
Includes bibliographical references (p.) and index.
ISBN 13: 9788124607268

1. Yantras. 2. Geography — India — Philosophy. I. Title.

DDC 294.537 23

ISBN 13: 978-81-246-0726-8
First Published in India, 2014

Printed and published by:
D.K. Printworld (P) Ltd.
Regd. Office : *"Vedaśrī"*, F-395, Sudarshan Park
(Metro Station: Ramesh Nagar)
New Delhi - 110 015
Phones : (011) 2545 3975; 2546 6019; *Fax* : (011) 2546 5926
e-mail : indology@dkprintworld.com
Web : www.dkprintworld.com

Dedicated to

Mātā Vaiṣṇo Devī

Foreword

Dandiswami Sri Paranand Tirth ji Maharaj

I WAS introduced to the author by Rashneek Kher, one of his favourite old boys. I went through his blog and was amazed at the depth and gravity of his creativity. This book was a spontaneous produce of rare blend of innovative thinking on the lines of ancient mysticism and also an exuberant feat of discursive scholarship. I received a mail from Niraj Kumar requesting me to write Foreword for his book. The other aspect of this book pertaining to Indian mysticism has been the topic of my specialization for a few decades but I wasn't as much familiar with Gilles Deleuze and Félix Guattari version of geophilosophy so there was no chance of ever trying to reconcile the two. Now I can thank to this laborious masterpiece of Niraj Kumar. I am sure most of the readers will also find this blend quite nourishing to their grey matter.

The concept of geophilosophy in Western thought evolved as late as in the 1990s, beginning from Edward S. Casey's vindication and Rene Descartes refutation of any such notion of "self and place" relationship. Martin Heidegger denies the continuation of this rejection by John Locke and evaluates this notion from the stand-point of qualia and thus delivers the planet as it were from the "ravages of calculative thinking".

A similar notion of philosophy with respect to geographic segmentation or to be more precise geo-metaphysics predates not only Deleuze and Guattari but even Descartes — the father of Western philosophy. Niraj Kumar with his stupendous knack of reconciliation has interpreted the arcane diagrammatic and phonetic encryptions in a contemporary verbiage to facilitate the comprehension of a modern man who might as well be more at home with Deleuze and Guattari rather than the discreet Śrī-Vidyā and Śrī-cakra cult.

Divine mother as the presiding deity of the power of consciousness and her semiotic depiction of universality along with various complimentary projections of a single holistic principle has been the most adorable entity of the theistic portion of Indian populace which is responsive and committed to the subliminal aspects of the faith of their ancestors. By Indian populace, I am not referring to their majority but authentic affiliation with the esoteric lineage through an unbroken chain of preceptors.

From a geophilosophic perspective, a multi-dimensional depiction of almost all areas of human cognitive faculties in time, space, substance and their interrelative reciprocation, is the most ingenious device of evaluating the space and self-rapport. Time, space and substantial conditioning are a three-dimensional limitation of the transcendental absolute. *Cakra* manifests as *deśa cakra* (formation in space) and *kāla cakra* (formation of consciousness in time) both in perfect unison transcend all names and forms, and lead to an insight into the universal substratum definable only in terms of *asti, bhāti* and *priyam* (existence, consciousness and bliss). This substratum provides a concrete and metaphysically consistent base for all coveted values of an advanced human society.

The evolution of human society's culture and thought from nomadic to agrarian and then to rural and urban sophistication is efficaciously encrypted in this mystic diagram. The psychological evolution of humankind, as Aldus Huxley puts it, culminates onto the point of collective word and meaning, the very point conceived within an isosceles triangle that signifies a perfect equilibrium of collective will, wisdom and work. A disturbed proportion of the three leads to deviation and thus an unruly dissipation of collective synergy. On the other hand, a well-balanced trio accelerates the pace of multifarious progress motivated by the synergy accumulated in the process of such orientation.

Śrī-yantra is an instrument of striking a balance between the gross subtle and causal dimensions of the macrocosmic and microcosmic phenomena. It syncs with the esoteric ontology of the cosmos, the individual body, the state, the nation in its geographic aspect, all creative and conducive societal values plus a grand unification of all existing dogmas, doctrines, creeds and commitments. A highly contributory configuration of conflicting philosophic thoughts has been interlaced within the complexities of this *yantra*. This mystic configuration does not work only in a discreet mystic way but the output of synchrony with a socio-ethical system and cosmic principle of righteousness is also expressible in a trans-modernist verbiage. *Collapse,* a journal of trans-modernism as the author puts it, introduced him to the concept of geophilosophy (*Collapse*, vol. VI on Geo/philosophy).

I am aware of what we can term as hypothetical Śrī-yantra, one of them is called *deśa cakra* or *cakra* of space. Space as such is just not a geographic segmentation in the tradition of Indian metaphysics that is calculable terms of area or span but an ideal notion with references of directions. Place or space is defined in terms of north, east, south, west, north-east, south-west, north-west, up and down. This antique tradition just falls in with the author's view on the effect of place on an individual or self. West is related with euphoria and hedonistic temperament whereas east pertains to piety and righteousness. North is peace and tranquillity whereas south is aggression and violence, south-east refers to vice and transgressions, south-west refers to cruelty and hostility. These directions are arranged on the periphery of *yantra*. One can also find such variations in the human temperament and the evolution of the society according to their locus. Highly sensitive mystics and thinkers can also perceive such difference in their temperaments if they face a particular direction for some time.

Niraj Kumar in his speculation of a "triangular" semblance of the Indian subcontinent has intuitively experienced certain ancient axioms of Eastern metaphysics. Patañjali, the exponent of Sanskrit grammar, has not only demarcated geographic boundaries but has also enunciated ideal and ethical variation if one went beyond certain regions. (Patañjali's commentary on the aphorism *eṁd prācāṁ deśe* in his compilation of the eight chapters on Sanskrit grammar.) This was conceptualized in the sixth century BCE by Pāṇini and was commented upon by Patañjali in 150 BCE.

Towards the end of his first chapter, the author leaves it to the reader to ascertain whether the once esoteric and now almost exoteric Śrī-yantra can still retain its crown position in

India. The answer, no doubt, is in affirmative. Śrī-yantra is a paradigmatic hallmark of completion that has ample room for innovations and creative ventures, experimentations and refinements without actually deviating from the underlying streamline of consciousness that comprises the substrata of almost all areas of human thoughts, actions, desires, so on and so forth.

In the consequent chapter named "What Is India", Niraj Kumar has given an exhaustive cache of facts and figures taken from various sources. The esoteric justification of certain Purāṇic inconsistencies has been the forté of Śrī-Vidyā cult which is why these concepts cannot be rejected straightaway as impossible. Four oceans with wine, *ghee*, syrup and milk filled in them do not exist in the real world so we do not just reject them as mythical. They are conceived as the four principal objectives of the human life — money, sex, religion and emancipation. All mythological descriptions have been esoterically deciphered by our hoary sages. It is only through their uninterrupted lineage that we can fathom the mysteries of "Śrī-yantra and Indian subcontinent analogy".

A topographic configuration of Indian thought ranging from atheists, Jainas, Buddhists, agnostics, obscurantists, sceptics and determinists, Vaiśeṣika, Nyāya, Sāṁkhya, Yoga, Pūrva- and Uttara-Mīmāṁsā schools all are arranged along various peripheries of the mystic diagram. Surprisingly their corresponding regions in the gross geographic realm can be easily traced for the collective mindset as influenced by those doctrines. We also have various Smr̥tis each with its root in a particular philosophy.

For example, Sāṁkhya (*likhita smr̥ti*) is based on Vaiśeṣika school of thought. Yājñavalkya's Āpstamba is based on the Pūrva-Mīmāṁsā school of thought. This geophilosophic variety accounts for the ethical and moral disposition of various geographic segments. Needless to say that all this is contained within a single unified domain of the conscious substratum of the entire universal phenomena.

Besides a valuable accumulation of various facts, figures and values from myriad canons of mystic revelations in one place this book also provides a type of interpolative vindication or justification of the two apparently conflicting ideologies of the oriental and occidental origins. Readers of more qualitative inclination than quantitative or analytical might as well skip certain details of highly quantitative and terse rational nature and resume reading the prose part of the book. All ontologies and diagrams are lucid and flawless. This book being a resultant of assiduous research must not be put aside as lacking "interest factor". It rather refines your taste as you proceed with reading. This type of work is just what we require after the phase of justification of spirituality in a scientific way or vice versa was over, i.e. in the late 1970s and early 1990s. Paradoxically the scientific justification came from the men of religion who had no science and the metaphysical vindication of science came from some scientists who had no religion. Evaluation and vindication of the Eastern metaphysics, methods and axiom from a socio-political, geographic and economic perspective were just what the literary world needed desperately.

Dandiswami Paranand Tirth
Yog Tantra & Āgama (YTA)
Shankaracharya Road, Delhi

Preface

FOR decades, I have been jotting down my bodily and dream experiences while on a quest for quintessence of Reality. Since childhood, I always felt that I was living in simultaneous worlds. First inkling of a beyond world came when I was six-year old. That was my birthday and suddenly a thought sprang — "Who Am I?" I went before mirror, saw my image and experienced the first rapture. I felt the vacuity. I was not That, then "Who am I?" The mirror became my virtual guide. The strange experience upon seeing duplication of myself in reflection has accompanied me till now. This has allowed me to peep through the mirror of wandering mind, India's civilizational structures.

I moved to Jammu in November 1983 to study in a Sainik School. My school was located in Nagroṭā right on the bank of river Tawī descending from the Śivālik hills. The Trikūṭa mountains lie just opposite the school campus and the illuminated pathway to the sacred shrine of Mātā Vaiṣṇo Devī held strong attraction for an incipient mind. The devotion to the divine Mother intensified. The three peaks of Trikūṭa appeared sentient. The mystery of triad intruded silently into my consciousness with an exciting event in 1988. One of my classmates often made fun of my interest in reading Swami Vivekananda's work. We were playing a cricket match in opposite teams. I was bowling and had taken consecutive wickets in two balls. My *bête noire* joined the batting. While turning back to bowl, I was facing the Trikūṭa hills. I prayed the Śakti to get off the "off stump", since in earlier two wickets, the leg stump and the middle stump had fallen. I ran, my eyes closed. Lo! The off stump was gone. It was a tremendous hat-trick. But, a serious question crept into mind, "How did the prayer to the three *piṇḍī*s worshipped in the cave in a three-peaked mountain, influence the three stumps in a cricket match?"

I was initiated by Swami Ranganathananda-ji Maharaj of Ramakrishna Mission/Order in June 1992. Certain mystical experiences led me to the wilderness and to abstain from competitive race for career. While engaged with certain practices, I encountered a transfiguration in my room in September 1993. This led me to rush to various spiritual luminaries seeking a way to reconnect with the unknown monk. I began to frequent cremation grounds at midnights and learnt to sit in meditation on the bank of the Ganges under the warmth of funeral pyres. That was how my fascination with the esoteric cults developed.

The quest to seek the rules of the multiplicity, morphological resonance, entanglement of the presences with absences, the mysterious attraction of the triadic things continued unabated. In this quest, I succeeded in perfect failures. I tried many things and accomplished nothing. And once while I was doing shopping in the year 2010 at Lajwanti Garden, Delhi, the thought popped up to purchase a copper Śrī-yantra as an auspicious wheel of fortune. Happily I bought one and told my kids and wife, "Good luck return!" Alas! That was not to be. But, I worshipped the *yantra* and recited *Lalitā Sahasranāma* for few days. I tried to visually pierce Śrī-yantra. In turn, I was pierced. It was a kind of non-intended consequence. There was *samāveśa* of the unknown presence.

I may merely say that this unusual book was never planned to write. It happened without expertise in the science or Śāstra,

Vedas or Tantras. Sometimes, the unknown is the best author. Much of the correlations and the connections in this book emerged on their own. The wandering mind has this unique charm of allowing democracy of ideas. When one builds up heuristic designs and work under paradigms, the hierarchical set-up disrupts the wonderland of ideas. By weaving the strange ideas, the work has taken the shape of a garland.

And a work was never intended that too on obscure subject of Śrī-yantra and Deleuzian geophilosophy. It emerged and is now in the hands of the readers to allow their minds to wander in the wonderland of chimerical ideas. Martin Heidegger wrote in the essay, "The Thinker as Poet" (1947):

> Three dangers threaten thinking. The good and thus wholesome danger is the nighness of the singing poet. The evil and thus keenest danger is thinking itself. It must think against itself, which it can only seldom do. The bad and thus muddled danger is philosophizing.

The present work is a complex battlefield of thinking itself. May God take each reader to the world without words!

Niraj Kumar

Contents

Acknowledgement

I AM grateful to my wife, Biak for bearing with me and supporting me to follow the wandering mind. Two kids, Nidhi and Priya, have been always helpful with their out-of-box queries that set the mind rolling with a child-like quest. My gratitude to my parents for bearing with me for so long with the hope that one day their son would start loving success as much as he enjoys failures. My brothers — Dheeraj and Pankaj — have been a constant source of encouragement. I salute all the great thinkers of ideas, known as well as unknown, who have made this world to be comprehended with greater clarity. I pay my obeisance to these great personalities for their contribution to the global wisdom: Gautama Buddha, Pāṇini, Patañjali, Bhartṛhari, Nāgārjuna, Abhinavagupta, Padamsambhava, Benoy Sarkar, Swami Vivekananda, Okakura, Sister Nivedita, Bhāskararāya, Gorakhnātha, Plato, Albert Einstein, Issac Newton and Charles Darwin. The highest salutation to the unknown maker of the first Śrī-yantra.

Each of the following friends and elders contributed in various ways: Rambahadur Rai, Priyadarshi Datta, Akhilesh Suman, Binod Singh, Vinay Purushottam, Rashneek Kher, Geetika Kaw, Dalip Singh, Iftikhar Gilani, Ajit Dobhal, Himanshu Shekhar, Bimal Singh, Govindacharya, Mahakal Bhairavananda Saraswati, George Fernandes, Lama Chosphel Zotpa, Pema Dorjee, Swami Shashankanand, Swami Amleshananda, Mahakavi Kashi Nath Pandey, Nita Rubbio, Antonella Cattaneo, Lallan Prasad, L.C. Singh, Shreedharan

Raman, S.S. Toshakhani, Lim Seng Guan, Nadarajah Ponnaih, Aneel Patil, Thomas Gallaghar, Rajiv Prasad, R. Venkatanarayanan, Baidya L.C. Sharmaji and Brajesh Pandey.

It is a great honour and divine blessing that Swami Paranand Tirth, an exemplary adept in Śrī-Vidyā, agreed to write the Foreword. My special thanks to Susheel Kumar Mittal, Director of the D.K. Printworld, for his constant encouragement, support and co-operation in publishing this bizarre work.

New Delhi, December 2013 **Niraj Kumar**

1

The Geophilosophy of India and Śrī-yantra

> The Superman is the meaning of earth. Let your will say: the Superman shall be the meaning of the earth. I conjure you, my brethren, remain true to the earth, and believe not those who speak unto you of superearthly hopes! [. . .] Once blasphemy against God was the greatest blasphemy, but God died, and therewith also those blasphemers. To blaspheme the earth is now the dreadfulest sin, and to rate the heart of the unknowable higher than the meaning of the earth.
>
> — Friedrich Neitzsche[1]

CAN there be a geophilosophy of India? Does geography influence thinking? How did Indian "self" evolve *qua* unique landscape that emerged through fusion of imaginative sacred geography and terrestrial topology?

The journal of transmodernism, *Collapse* in its sixth volume devoted to the concept of geophilosophy has raised a pertinent question:

> Is there nevertheless an enduring bond between philosophical thought and its terrestrial support, or conversely, is philosophy's task to escape the planetary horizon?[2]

---

1. Friedrich Nietzsche, *Zarathustra's Prologue in Thus Spake Zarathustra*, tr. Thomas Common, New York: Random House, 1954, pp. 6-7.
2. Robin Mackay, ed., *Collapse*, vol. VI: *Geo/philosophy*, Falmouth, UK: Urbanomic, January 2010.

Geographical Roots of Thinking

Every human being is situated in a "place", the surrounding of which is a product of historical, social, cultural and physical factors.[3] Edward S. Casey, the American philosopher of phenomenology, who got engaged himself with both Asian and Western thought, has devoted many years to investigate "the nature of human subject who is oriented and situated in place".[4] Space is the void in which things are positioned and "place" is the immediate environment of lived body. Casey ponders over how the place with its own qualitative, perceived, relational, landscape and historical features has been substituted by the concept of Cartesian space, characterized as empty, calculable, infinite and homologized. Modern Western philosophy is based on the inference that the human self is a function of consciousness and has no relationship with "place". This has roots in the works of early liberals. John Locke enunciated that there is no relationship between place and self. Place is merely a realm of space.[5] More

---

3 Edward S. Casey, "Between Geography and Philosophy: What Does It Mean to be in the Place-World?", *Annals of the Association of American Geographers* (2001), **91**(4): 683. Edward Casey has done tremendous enquiry on establishing difference between place and space. Also see, ibidem, *Getting Back into Place: Towards a Renewed Understanding of the Place-World*, Bloomington: Indiana University Press, 1993; ibidem, *The Fate of Place: A Philosophical History*, Berkeley: University of California Press, 1997; ibidem, "Cityscape and Landscape: Place and Site in Urban Life", special issue of *Sphinx* in 1998; ibidem, "Body, Self, and Landscape: A Geophilosophical Inquiry into the Place-World" in P. Adams, S. Hoelscher and K. Till (eds.) *Textures of Place: Exploring Humanist Geographies*, Minneapolis: University of Minnesota Press, 2001.

4 Edward S. Casey as in note 3, p. 683.

5 J. Locke, *An Essay Concerning Human Understanding* (1690), ed. P.G. Nidditch, Oxford: Clarendon Press, 1975.

or less, the trend defined modern philosophy. It was Martin Heidegger who espoused the cause of "place" and inspired a whole generation to rediscover "thinking" rooted in place. Heidegger elaborated at length his preoccupation with the issue.[6] He took up German poet Friedrich Holderlin's verse, "Full of Merit, Yet Poetically, Man Dwells on this Earth" to discuss at length the importance of place in human thinking. Heidegger later gave a call to reinvigorate poetic thinking as planetary thinking to rescue the planet from the ravages of the calculative thinking. The dwelling in a place is what gives mankind the power to engage in authentic thinking. Stephan Günzel mentions in his genealogical study of the concept of geophilosophy that for Heidegger,

> geography is prior to history. . . . Temporal descriptions originate in spatial facts. But the most important difference between Nietzsche and Heidegger, or, more exactly, between Nieztsche and Heidegger's reading on Nieztsche, is that Nieztsche's geographical reflections are based on virtual geography, Heidegger's geophilosophy, in contrast, takes the geographical issues in terms of real territories.[7]

Taking the cue from Heidegger, Gilles Deleuze and Félix Guattari, the two leading French philosophers, developed the concept of "geophilosophy" in their profound work, *A Thousand Plateaus*.[8] John Protevi, an expert on Deleuze and Guattari, has coined the term "Deleuzoguattarian geophilosophy" for the stream of thought emanating from

---

[6] Martin Heidegger, *Poetically Man Dwells in Poetry, Language, Thought*, tr. Albert Hofstadter, New York: Harper Collins, 2001 (reprint), pp. 213-29.

[7] Stephen Gunzel, "Nietzsche's Geophilosophy", *Journal of Nietzsche Studie* (2003), **25**: 87.

[8] *A Thousand Plateaus*, vol. 2 of *Capitalism and Schizophrenia*, 1980, tr. Brian Massumi, London and New York: Continuum, 1987.

this *magnum opus*.[9] Protevi boldly claims that *A Thousand Plateaus* constitutes a "geophilosophy", a neo-materialism, which, in linking the philosophical materialisms of Karl Marx, Nietzsche and Sigmund Freud with contemporary science, avoids the traditional bogeys of materialism: determinism and vitalism.[10] Deleuze and Guattari's concept of "geophilosophy", was introduced fully into philosophical discourse in 1991. Deleuze and Guattari raised the question of the status of a geographical paradigm within the positioning of philosophical problems. They did this specifically with respect to the meaning of landscape metaphors, descriptions of the sea and mountaineering analogies in philosophical texts. In their final book, *What Is Philosophy?*[11] Deleuze and Guattari called Friedrich Nietzsche the one who "founded geophilosophy". Nietzsche gave the teaching of Zarathustra:

> "The meaning of the earth" (*Sinn der Erde*) literally signifies a radical this-worldly orientation that includes the air, the sea, the mountains, and all sort of landscape, as long as their conception is connected to the surface and does not imply any form of transcendence.[12]

Geophilosophy can be summarized as the idea that philosophy or science in general needs a creative milieu to develop, and that this milieu event has to be localized in time and space. Geophilosophy is the philosophy of or for the earth that lies

---

[9] Mark Bonta and John Protevi, *Deleuze and Geophilosophy: A Guide and Glossary*, Edinburgh: Edinburgh University Press, 2004.

[10] John Protevi, *The Geophilosophies of Deleuze and Guattari*, Speech at November 2001 meeting of SEDAAG. www.protevi.com/john/SEDAAG.pdf (last accessed on 1 December 2012).

[11] Gilles Deleuze and Felix Guattari, *What Is Philosophy?*, tr. Hugh Tomlinson and Graham Burchell, New York: Columbia University Press, 1996.

[12] Gunzel, n. 7, p. 81.

at the root of synthesis of political, territorial, socio-cultural, historic, economic and spiritual thinking. Our thinking relates to the earth in which we dwell upon. Geophilosophy embraces the experiential, phenomenological fact of the absence of a transcendental outside and the rootedness of thinking in earth.[13] Human thinking after all is an "earthly thought".

This is how consciousness is characterized by geopiety not only towards human, but also for the flora and fauna. Geopiety in human beings expresses this reverential and emotional attachment to the native land, as history, myth, religion and sacred imagination fuse to create a symbolic soup "by exploring the fond memories people have for particular places and how reassuring those places become to people".[14] Heidegger discusses in *Being and Time*:

> Holy places and battlefields become forms of the transcendental conditions of history, such that they must be the transcendental conditions of Dasein as historical being-in-the-world.[15]

We will see futher how there is a sacred landscape of imagination that constitutes "What is India" through connecting various pilgrim places (*tīrtha*s). The state also constitutes its ideas through such network of sites. The loyalty to a particular group cannot be packaged, re-cycled and

---

13 Nicola Masciandro, "Becoming Spice: Commentary as Geophilosophy", *Collapse*, vol. VI: *Geo/philosophy*, 2010, p. 32.

14 Yi-Fu Tuan, *Space and Place: The Perspective of Experience*, Minneapolis: University of Minnesota Press, 1977; also see Yi-Fu Tuan's concept of geopiety in "Geopiety: A Theme in Man's Attachment to Nature and to Place", in David Lowenthal and Martyn J. Bowden (eds.) *In Geographies of the Mind: Essays in Historical Geosophy in Honor of John Kirtland Wright*, New York: Oxford University Press, 1976, pp. 11-39.

15 Gunzel, n. 7, pp. 86-87.

renewed without sanctifying certain places through history, legend or myth. The territory is the site of symbolic investment.

Deleuze and Guattari write in the introduction of the chapter "Geophilosophy" in the book, *What Is Philosophy*? (1994):

> Subject and object give a poor approximation of thought. Thinking is neither a line drawn between subject and object nor a revolving of one around the other. Rather, thinking takes place in the relationship of territory and the earth.[16]

Deleuze and Guattari, themselves, use the term "geophilosophy" to reorient philosophy from transcendental ideas — ideas that are deduced and elaborated above and beyond the contingencies of terrestrial reality — to concepts of immanence, whose intuition is entirely contingent upon the complex processes of earthly life. In place of a top–down vertical thinking that delineates being in higher to lower levels of categorical perfection, thinking becomes horizontal and experimental as Deleuze and Guattari articulate a virtually limitless connectivity between heterogeneous beings.[17] In geophilosophy, "geo" evokes multiplicity of "interconnecting geos" — geology, geography, geophysics and geopolitics, and emerging composites such as geophysiology, geomicrobiology, *ad infinitum*.[18] I will add many other geos currently in use in academic discourse like geosophy and geobody. In fact, the current geometrization of knowledge itself appears to be a connected tectonic shift in the terrain of knowledge.

---

16 Deleuze and Guattari, n. 11, p. 85.

17 Dianne Chisholm, "Rhizome, Ecology, Geophilosophy", *Rhizomes*, **15** (Winter 2007). http://www.rhizomes.net/issue15/chisholm.htmlaccessed (last accessed on 1 December 2012).

18 Ibid.

Deleuze and Guattari developed the geophilosophical framework by deploying the concept of "refrain" in their chapter "1827: Of the Refrain" in *A Thousand Plateau*. The refrain is a song that organized and fend off chaos, that draws from the earth a set of contingent meanings that lead to identity.[19] Deleuze and Guattari state:

> The role of refrain has often been emphasized: it is territorial, a territorial assemblage. Bird songs: the bird sings to mark its territory. The Greek modes and Hindi rhythms are themselves territorial, provincial, regional. The refrain may assume other functions, amorous, professional, or social, liturgical or cosmic: it always carried earth with it; it has a land (sometimes a spiritual land) as its concomitant.[20]

How is refrain born? How is territorial refrain created? From chaos, milieus and rhythms are born.[21] Every milieu is vibratory and constituted by the periodic repetition of the components. Rhythm is the milieus' answer to chaos.[22]

Deleuze and Guattari argue that the territory is in fact an act that affects milieus and rhythms, that "territorializes" them. The territory is the product of territorialization of milieus and rhythms.[23]

Deleuze and Guattari try to establish the primacy of territoriality. They write:

> We have gone from forces of chaos to forces of earth. From milieus to territory. From functional rhythms to the becoming

---

19 Bruce B. Janz, "The Territory Is Not the Map's Place, Deleuze and Guattari, and African Philosophy", *Philosophy Today* (Winter 2001), **45**(4): 395.

20 Deleuze and Guattari, n. 8, p. 344.

21 Ibid., p. 345.

22 Ibid.

23 Ibid., pp. 355-56.

> — expressive of rhythm. From phenomena of transcoding to phenomena of decoding. From milieu functions to territorialized functions. It is less a question of evolution than of passage, bridges and tunnels. Now we see that the milieus pass into the territory . . . the territory itself is a place of passage. The territory is the first assemblage, the first thing to constitute an assemblage; the assemblage is fundamentally territorial.[24]

Further, they depend upon the power of refrain for the territotial assemblage. For Deleuze and Guattari, refrain is "any aggregate of matters of expression that draws a territory and develops into territorial motifs and landscapes".[25] The refrain in Deleuze and Guattari's articulation is not merely sonorous, but it can be optical, gestural, motor, odouric. The privilege of sound has been taken away in this bridging and tunnelling of milieus that create territoriality.

Deleuze and Guattari deploy such concept to explain the rise of philosophy in Greece. For them, it is the location of Greece seemingly with a "fractal structure in so far as each point of the peninsula is close to the sea and its side have great length".[26] Greece had three necessary characteristics for the growth of philosophy, viz. immanence, friendship and opinion due to its geographical location which allowed Greece to develop like an

> international market organized along the borders of the Orient between a multiplicity of independent cities or distinct societies that are nevertheless attached to one another and within which the artisans and merchants find a freedom and mobility denied to them by the empires.[27]

---

24 Deleuze and Guattari, n. 8, 355-56.

25 Ibid., p. 356.

26 Ibid., n. 11, p. 87.

27 Ibid., p. 88.

These three possibilities could not arise in the empires, for empires are governed "arboreally", while Greece operated "rhizomically". Philosophy can appear only under the horizontal life of rhizomes. The "tree structure" of social life is not conducive to the emergence of philosophy. Deleuze and Guattari devolve the thought further to describe "Delian League likes the fractalization of Greece". Thus, they centre "the birth of Greek philosophy in a certain 'plane of immanence' created in the poleis that allows agon, philia and logos — competition, friendship and argument"; and how

> the Greek cities are able to sustain such a plane of immanence because they are close to, but separate from, the great empires of Egypt and Persia.[28]

Protevi describes in his paper on "Between Geophilosophy and Political Physiology", how geophilosophy includes any philosophical reflection on the role of the earth in social processes including even "geopolitics". Protevi considers the work of Karl Wittfogel on "hydraulic civilization" in the category of geophilosophy. Wittfogel tried to establish that the state was the origin of irrigation, rather than the overcoding force, that aridity is the key to irrigation and stratified societies. Similarly, Donald Worster showed in his work *Rivers of Empire*,[29] how the large-scale state and federal investment in irrigation in the American West could only produce stratified societies in arid conditions, where control of water grants a key power position.

---

[28] John Protevi, "Between Geophilosophy and Political Physiology", 3 October 2004. www.protevi.com/john/Geophilosophy.pdf (last accessed on 1 December 2012).

[29] Donald Worster, *Rivers of Empire: Water, Aridity, and the Growth of the American West*, New York: Oxford University Press, 1985.

Deleuze and Guattari further developed their theses on the relationship between thinking and territory in the plateau "1227: Treatise on Nomadology — The War Machine"[30] in the book, *A Thousand Plateaus: Capitalism and Schizophrenia*. They put forward two different forms of thinking in relation to geography. They took up the case of state and the nomads and showed how it is ultimately geography that has made nomadic societies into war-machine pitted against the state system. Deleuze and Guattari deploy the analogy of chess against the game of go to describe two different kinds of space and organizational thought. Chess is a game of state but game of go is fluid, implying perpetual movement like a nomad's movement. In chess there is a grid and the space of chess is "striated" and each piece possesses intrinsic properties and limited powers. These move according to fixed set of principles and the movement is not unexpected. This is the Order of State within which Deleuze and Guattari subsume religion also as this also presupposes some transcendental signifier thereby putting a break on the perpetual movement of the Being Nomads. By contrast, Deleuze and Guattari stress the war-machine moulded as in the game of go. The war-machine follows a guerrilla logic and

> it is a question of arraying oneself in an open space, of holding space, of maintaining the point of springing up at any point: the movement is not from one point to another, but becomes perpetual, without aim or destination, without departure or arrival.

There have been recent studies that show that the landscape does influence the thinking of the locals. Bernard Formoso conducted a study on minority community of Yi in China's Yunnan province and found how the terrace and the terraced landscape are significant symbols used in

[30] Deleuze and Guattari, n. 8, pp. 387-467.

traditional handicrafts, particularly in women costumes.[31] Pascal Bouchrey worked upon the Hanis in the Yunnan and discussed that how the

> cosmological conceptualization of the local environment is grounded in a practical experience of wet rice agriculture and irrigation management. The principles on which the irrigation system is based provide a conceptual framework facilitating various analogical transfers from which each village community constructs a religious interpretation of the surrounding landscape.[32]

Pascal argues that it is not the belief system that serves as a model for the irrigation system, rather there is a reverse process.

In the realm of geopolitics, geographical factors influence strongly the strategic culture of a nation state. The field of study on strategic culture has grown vast. There are many geopoliticians, particularly, Russian Eurasianists like Aleksandar Dugin who are re-examining the framework of international studies from the prism of geography. He delves into the origin of different forms of political system, *thalassocratia* (power by means of sea) and *tellurocratia* (power by means of the land). He emphasizes that the thalassocratic nations like the US and Britain have insular thinking, while the land-based civilizations have continental thinking.

While examining the political culture of Zomia, we have discussed how the terraced farming is a characteristic of Zomia

---

31 Bernard Formoso, "A Terraced World for an Armoured Body: The Symbolism of Women Costumes Among the Yi of Yuan Yang, 2006", *Research in Anthropology and Aesthetics*, **37**: 89-106.

32 Pascal Bouchrey, "Terrace Cultivation and Mental Landscapes in Southern Yunnan", in Marie Lecomte-Tilouine (ed.), *Nature, Culture and Religion at the Crossroads of Asia*, Hyderabad: Social Science Press, 2010, pp. 318-42.

. . . from India to Vietnam and China and possibly springs from imitating the adaptation of the hornbills habitat and physical characteristics.

> Terracing technology enters the cosmological world-view through analogous transfer. The terracing of hills to produce food grains has its equivalence in terracing pattern on handicraft that produces identity.[33]

It is certain that human life is not determined merely by the molecules/genes or nature. There is an inherent propensity to organize coherence. Without the integrative element, what to talk about organism, even proteins and cells could not have evolved. It is the coherence that organizes the biology from cellular processes to the organ integration. The lack of coherence leads to diseases like cancer where the cells continue to multiply bypassing the principle. The question that remains pertinent is whether this intrinsic propensity for coherence extends to mental processes? Do human beings seek to create a coherent belief system in which the society, ecology, geography, cosmology, all fit in neatly? And if human thinking is inherently coherent, how does one coherent belief system pave the way for another new system? What is the source of dynamic and evolving coherence? Why do we "think" to project coherence in place and space?

In a path-breaking work, *Neurobiology, Layered Texts and Correlative Cosmologies: A Cross-Cultural Framework for Premodern History* (2000), neuroscientist Steve Farmer, historian John B.

---

33 Niraj Kumar and C.N. Biak, "Zomi, Zomia, Nomadia: Landscape, Handicraft and Statecraft", 2011 http://epao.net/epSubPageExtractor.asp?src=manipur.Ethnic_Races_Manipur.Zomi_Zomia_Nomadia__Landscape_handicraft_and_statecraft_Part_1; http://ariseasia.blogspot.com/2011/09/zomi-zomia-nomadia-landscape-handicraft.html (last accessed on 1 December 2012).

Henderson and Indologist Michael Witzel have propounded how pre-modern societies were governed by correlative thinking,

> a general propensity to organize natural, political/social, and cosmological data in highly ordered arrays or system of correspondence.[34]

They discovered how the idea that reality consists of multiple "levels", each mirroring all others in some fashion, is a diagnostic feature of premodern cosmologies in general. The team traced the correlative thinking from its primitive origin to its modern decline in this work.

The first correlation was established between word and object and this was

> guided by matters of gross resemblance and intense etymological speculation; classical examples are found in early divinational treatises like the *yijing* or in the magical formulae of *Atharvaveda* and Egyptian funeral texts.[35]

The team found in their study that in most advanced traditions,

> repeated syncretic fusions of sources over long periods eventually led to the emergence of systems with highly exaggerated correlative properties (known in mathematics as "self-similar" or "fractal structures") in which every part of the cosmos was said to mirror every other.[36]

In India, this culminated in the sophisticated theory of *bimba–pratibimba* in both Vedic and the Āgama Śāstras. Śaṅkarācārya

---

34 Steve Farmer, John B. Henderson and Michael Witzel, "Neurobiology, Layered Texts and Correlative Cosmologies: A Cross-Cultural Framework for Premodern History", *Bulletin of the Museum of Far Eastern Antiquities* (Stockholm) (2000), **72**: 48-90.

35 Ibid., p. 49.

36 Ibid., p. 51.

conceptualized reflection of the transcendent unitary *Brahman* in the diversity of individuals, using the analogy of reflection of the sun in rippling water. His predecessor Bhartṛhari used the analogy of reflection of colours in a crystal to explain the changes in the meaning of words due to changing relationship with other words in different sentences. But, the best description of such a mutually reflected cosmos was developed by the Buddhists in the third century. The metaphor of Indra's net in *Avataṁsaka Sūtra* is a veritable reflecting universe.

> Far away in the heavenly abode of the great god Indra, there is a wonderful net which has been hung by some cunning artificer in such a manner that it stretches out infinitely in all directions. In accordance with the extravagant tastes of deities, the artificer has hung a single glittering jewel in each "eye" of the net, and since the net itself is infinite in dimension, the jewels are infinite in number. There hang the jewels, glittering like stars in the first magnitude, a wonderful sight to behold. If we now arbitrarily select one of these jewels for inspection and look closely at it, we will discover that in its polished surface there are reflected all the other jewels in the net, infinite in number. Not only that, but each of the jewels reflected in this one jewel is also reflecting all the other jewels, so that there is an infinite reflecting process occurring.[37]

The analogy of reflection describes the interconnectedness as well as interdependence of all phenomena.

Etymological correlation still characterizes Indian thinking and the pre-modern correlative thought has been revived by likes of phenomenologist bandwagon led by Heidegger, deconstructionists under Jacques Derrida, neo-materialists under Deleuze and Guattari, and speculative realists under Reza Negarestani.

---

37 Francis H. Cook, *Hua-Yen Buddhism: The Jewel Net of Indra*, University Park and London: Pennsylvania State University Press, 1977.

Whole Indian thinking itself is a creative exercise in correlation. French Indologist Louis Renou argued that the original meaning of Upaniṣad was "connection" or "equivalence". The aim of Vedic thought was to formulate Upaniṣads. Correlative ideas in Vedic traditions are often referred to as *bandhus*. Now, *bandhu* is also the blood relationship. *Bandhana* is bondage, a connection. The bridges are known as *bandha* which is built over the rivers to cross over. There is obsession with thread in Indian culture. *Sūta* or *sūtra* is ubiquitous. A person has to wear a scared thread, *janeu*. The marriage ceremony is solemnized only after the auspicious thread is tied. Sisters tie thread around brothers arm. In the temple, thread is offered. Trees are tied with sacred thread. The tying of threads and the knot from esoteric to exoteric realm is the overt manifestation of correlative thinking in India.

In India, moreover gods and demons, are

> systematically correlated with unique numbers, consorts, rituals, meters, directions, seasons, hours of the day, priestly orders, oblations, sacrificial animals, and similar phenomena.[38]

Farmer suggests that the universality of correlative thought can be traced to functional symmetries in brain processes known to neurobiologists as "topographic" maps. The extreme of the correlative thinking results into synethesia, pathological correlative thinking which is currently a growing area of curiosity for the neuroscientists in which stimulation of one sensory or cognitive pathway leads to involuntary experiences in another cognitive faculty. The authors argue that the deepest root of correlative thought lay in neurobiological processes.

---

[38] Witzel et al., n. 34, op. cit., p. 53.

Jean-Philippe Thivierge and Gary F. Marcus have unravelled the topography of human brain and were surprised to observe that

> vertebrate brain organization is an ordered topography, wherein sets of neuronal connections preserve the relative organization of cells between two regions.[39]

They have proposed that a key function of topography might be to "provide computational underpinnings for precise one-to-one correspondences between abstract cognitive representations". This perspective offers a novel conceptualization of how the brain approaches difficult problems, such as reasoning and analogy making, and suggests that a broader understanding of topographic maps could be pivotal in fostering strong links between genetics, neurophysiology and cognition.

The team suggests that

> understanding the role of neural topography in mental processes might only be the starting point of understanding how different types of neural organizations can bias humans against or towards different types of cognitive operations.

Thus, even beneath the visible surface, topography plays an important role in cognition. Is the internal topography of brain a by-product of external topography? Does the geographical feature determine the neural patterns inside the brain of the resident of a landscape?

The role of internal topography in cognition and memory has been unravelled in 2012 by Stuart Hameroff et al. They

---

[39] Jean-Philippe Thivierge and Gary F. Marcus, "The Topographic Brain: From Neural Connectivity to Cognition", *Trends in Neurosciences* (25 April 2007), **30**(6): 251-59, available on http://images.neuron.org/images/EdImages/Neuronthivierge_oct25.pdf (last accessed on 1 December 2012).

discovered how hexagonal tubulins inside neurons, stacked in hexagonal structures, play a role in memory. The neuroscientists are puzzled with how critical neurons representation maps are organized hexagonally and grid cells in cortex arranged in hexagonal patterns. Thus, hexagonal pattern is seen in human brain at varying scales. The team proposes that "scale-free" coherence implies self-similar information pattern repeating at different spatial and temporal scales and like fractal, these are very durable.[40]

Therefore, there is a strong case to argue for rootedness of thinking in landscape. There is growing research on the theme of cortical plasticity which suggests that the cortical maps inside brain are not "hard-wired" but highly plastic and these change patterns, with inputs from physical or cultural environments, are varied.[41]

How does external topography complement the brain cognition? In Indic tradition (including Buddhist, Jaina and other multiple sects sharing common milieu), higher degree of coherence has been achieved with the correlation of external and internal geographies. The imaginative sacred geography constitutes the landscape and this has been also internalized within human bodies through the concept of "*pīṭha* tradition" as well as the ubiquitous application of the concept of reflection (*bimba–pratibimba*). Internal topography correlates with external topography. This is unique and this is what constitutes the specialty of Indian thinking.

---

40 Stuart Hameroff, Travis J.A. Craddock, Jack A. Tuszynski, "Cytoskeletal Signalling: Is Memory Encoded in Microtubule Lattices by CaMKII Phosphorylation?", *PLOS Computational Biology* (March 2012), **8**(3): 1-16.

41 Bela Juilesz and Ilona Kovacas (eds.), *Maturational Windows and Adult Cortical Plasticity, Proceedings*, vol. XXIII, Sante Fe Institute, Readings: Addison-Wesley, 1995.

What is "thinking" in Deleuze and Guattari's geophilosophy? "Thinking consists in stretching out a plane of immanence that absorbs the earth."[42] Thinking is the "projection of transcendent on the plane of immanence".[43] Deleuze and Guattari put the *maṇḍala* diagrams used profusely in Indian tradition in the category of thinking:

> Chinese hexagrams, Hindu *maṇḍala*s, Jewish sephiroth, Islamic "imaginals" and Christian icons can be considered together: thinking through figures.[44]

We may reflect upon how Deleuze and Guattari view *maṇḍala*s to develop a geophilosophical perspective towards understanding Śrī-yantra in subsequent chapters:

> *Maṇḍala* is a projection on a surface that establishes correspondence between divine, cosmic, political, architectural, and organic levels as so many values of one and the same transcendence. That is why the figure has a reference, one that is plurivocal and circular by nature. Certainly, it is not defined by an external resemblance, which remains prohibited, but by an internal tension that relates it to the transcendent on the plane of immanence of thought. In short, the figure is essentially paradigmatic, projective, hierarchical, and referential.[45]

Thus, *maṇḍala*s have been counted as the subject of thinking by the founders of geophilosophy, Deleuze and Guattari. What is known as *maṇḍala*s in Buddhist practices, the Hindu *yantra*s slightly differ in constitution. *Yantras* are abstract and not filled with iconographic details, while *maṇḍala*s are veritable encyclopaedia containing images in all shades of colours.

---

42 Deleuze and Guattari, n. 11, p. 88.

43 Ibid., p. 89.

44 Ibid.

45 Ibid.

Deleuze and Guattari had in their mind, the geometric *yantras* only, but the indirect engagement with South Asian studies leads them to substitute one for another. Now, the issue at our hand is to find out a *yantra* which stands as the representative for geophilosophy of India. Can we discover the nature of Indian thinking and find a corresponding *yantra*, an abstract figure? Does Śrī-yantra have a chance to occupy the crown place in the geophilosophy of India? Is Śrī-yantra the Deleuzoguattarian refrain that emerged as an optical, geometric, territorial motif for India?

Locating Rhizomic Nature of Indian Thinking

There have been many works to explore the nature of Indian thinking. Hajime Nakamura's *Way of Eastern Thinking* (1964)[46] is a landmark in exploring the comparative nature of various thoughts across Asia — Indian, Tibetan, Japanese and Chinese. Nakamura sums up the characteristics of Indian thinking under the following themes: preponderance of abstract notion; abstract conceptions treated as concrete realities; fondness for the negative expression; grasping the Absolute negatively; attraction for the unknown; minimizing individuality and specific preferences; unity of all things; static quality of thought; lack of common-sense concept of time; continuity of one's self and other selves; consciousness of existence of self; lack of notion of order in the objective natural world; lack of historical consciousness; and introspective and metaphysical character of thinking.[47]

A.K. Ramanujan brilliantly explored the nature of Indian thinking using notions of grammar in the essay, "Is There an

---

46 Hajime Nakamura, *Ways of Thinking of Eastern Peoples: India, China, Tibet, Japan*, Honolulu: University of Hawaii Press, 1964.

47 Ibid., pp. 39-172.

Indian Way of Thinking?".[48] Highlights of the essay are reproduced so that the repetition is avoided while generating characteristics of Indian thinking, which others have not deciphered:

> In cultures like India's, the context-sensitive kind of rule is the preferred formulation. Manu explicitly says: "[A king] who knows the sacred law, must imagine into the laws of caste Utiti), of districts, of guilds, and of families, and [thus] settle the peculiar law of each" (Manu 7.41).[49]
>
> Or take Indian literary texts. No Indian text comes without a context, a frame, till the nineteenth century. Works are framed by *phalaśruti* verses — these verses tell the reader, reciter or listener all the good that will result from his act of reading, reciting or listening. They relate the text, of whatever antiquity, to the present reader — that is, they contextualize it. An extreme case is that of the Nāḍīśāstra, which offers you your personal history.[50]
>
> Scholars have often discussed Indian texts (like *Mahābhārata*) as if they were loose-leaf files, rag-bag encyclopaedias. Taking the Indian word for text, *grantha* (derived from the knot that holds the palm leaves together), literally, scholars often posit only an accidental and physical unity. . . . Not unity (in the Aristotelian sense) but coherence, seems to be the end.[51]
>
> In such a metonymic view of man in nature — man in context — he is continuous with the context he is in. In Peircean semiotic terms, these are not symbolic devices, but indexical signs — the signifier and the signified belong in the same

---

48 A.K. Ramanujan, "Is There an Indian Way of Thinking?: An Informal Essay", *Contributions to Indian Sociology* (1989), **23**(1): 41-58.

49 Ibid., p. 47.

50 Ibid., p. 48.

51 Ibid., p. 49.

context (Peirce 1931-58).[52]

One might say, from this point of view, that Hindu ritual (e.g. Vedic sacrifice, or a coronation; Inden [1978]) converts symbols, arbitrary signs (e.g. sacrificial horse), into icons where the signifier (the horse) is like what it signifies (the universe) and finally into indices, where the signifier is part of what it signifies: the horse is the Universe is Prajāpati, so that in sacrificing and partaking of it one is sacrificing and partaking of the Universe itself.[53]

We have a nature–culture continuum that cancels the terms, confuses them even if we begin with them. Such container–contained relations are seen in many kinds of concepts and images: not only in culture–nature, but god–world, king–kingdom, devotee–god, mother–child.[54]

Here is a *bhakti* poem which plays with many such concentric containments. Indian conceptions tend to be such concentric nests: The view of the "sheaths" (*koṣa*s), the different "bodies" (*kāyā*s) are examples.[55]

Even space and time, the universal contexts, the Kantian imperatives, are in India not uniform and neutral, but have properties, varying specific densities, that affect those who dwell in them. The soil in a village, which produces crops for the people, affects their character (as liars, for instance, in E.V. Daniel's village (1984); houses (containers *par excellence*) have mood and character, change the fortune and moods of the dwellers. Time too does not come in uniform units: certain hours of the day, certain days of the week, etc. are auspicious or inauspicious (*rāhukāla*); certain units of time (*yuga*s) breed certain kinds of maladies, politics,

---

52 A.K. Ramanujan, "Is There an Indian Way of Thinking?: An Informal Essay", *Contributions to Indian Sociology* (1989), **23**(1): 41-58. p. 50.

53 Ibid.

54 Ibid.

55 Ibid., p. 51.

religions, e.g. Kali-yuga. As hour, month, season, year, and aeon have their own properties as own texts, the arts that depend on time have to obey time's changing moods and properties. For instance, the *rāga*s of both north and south Indian classical music have their prescribed appropriate times.[56]

Thus, all things, even so-called non-material ones like space and time or caste, affect other things because all things are "substantial" (*dhātu*). The only difference is that some are subtle (*sūkṣma*), some gross (*sthūla*). Contrary to the notion that Indians are "spiritual", they are really "material minded". They are materialists, believers in substance (Marriott 1976, 1980): there is a continuity, a constant flow (the etymology of *saṁsāra*!) of substance from context to object, from non-self to self (if you prefer) in eating, breathing, sex, sensation, perception, thought, art, or religious experience.[57]

Such a pervasive emphasis on context is, I think, related to the Hindu concern with *jāti* — the logic of classes, of genera and species, of which human *jāti*s are only an instance. Various taxonomies of season, landscape, times, *guṇa*s (qualities) (and their material bases), tastes, characters, emotions, essences (*rasa*), etc. are basic to the thought-work of Hindu medicine and poetry, cooking and religion, erotics and magic. Each *jāti* (class) defines a context, a structure of relevance, a rule of permissible combinations, a frame of reference, a meta-communication of what is and can be done.[58]

In such a world, systems of meaning are elicited by contexts, by the nature (and substance) of the listener. In *Bṛhadāraṇyaka* 5.1, Lord Prajāpati speaks in thunder three times: "DA DA DA". When the gods, given to pleasure hear it, they hear it as the first syllable of *damyatai* (control). The

---

56 A.K. Ramanujan, "Is There an Indian Way of Thinking?: An Informal Essay", *Contributions to Indian Sociology* (1989), **23**(1): 41-58, esp. p. 5.

57 Ibid., p. 52.

58 Ibid., p. 53.

> antigods, given as they are to cruelty, hear it as *dayadhvam* (be compassionate). When the humans, given to greed, hear it they hear it as *datta* (give to others).[59]
>
> In "traditional" cultures like India, where context-sensitivity rules and binds, the dream is to be free of context. So *rasa* in aesthetics, *mokṣa* in the "aims of life", *saṁnyāsa* in the life stages, *sphoṭa* in semantics, and *bhakti* in religion define themselves against a background of inexorable contextuality.[60]
>
> Where *kāma*, *artha* and *dharma* are all relational in their values, tied to place, time, personal character and social role, *mokṣam* is the release from all relations.[61]
>
> In the realm of feeling (*bhāva*s) are private, contingent, context-roused sentiments, *vibhāva*s are determinant causes, *anubhāva*s the consequent expressions. But *rasa* is generalized, it is an essence. In the field of meaning, the temporal sequence of letters and phonemes, the syntactic chain of words, yields finally a *sphoṭa*, an explosion, a meaning which is beyond sequence and time.[62]
>
> In each of these the pattern is the same: a necessary sequence in time with strict rules of phase and context ending in a free state.[63]

Ramanujan's arguments can be summed up under following categories:

1. The thinking and culture are governed by rules of grammar. The rules are context sensitive.

---

[59] A.K. Ramanujan, "Is There an Indian Way of Thinking?: An Informal Essay", *Contributions to Indian Sociology* (1989), **23**(1): 41-58, esp. p. 53.

[60] Ibid., p. 54.

[61] Ibid.

[62] Ibid.

[63] Ibid.

2. Metonymic view of Reality: A concept is not called by its own name, but by the name of something intimately associated with that thing or concept. In a universe where there is intrinsic interrelationality, anything can be substituted for everything else.
3. The signifier is part of the signified in most of the dimensions of culture.
4. There is increasing densification of meaning, and any arbitrary symbol first becomes iconic and then an index. Thus, signifier appropriates the characteristics of the signified.
5. There is no black and white binary opposition between the binarized concepts. It is a continuum. The nature–culture, man–universe, this world–other-world all are part of a continuum with differing degree of "thingness". It's the degree of thingification and not any unalterable, antagonistic opposition between the binary opposites.
6. Indian conceptions are like concentric nests. There are sheaths beneath sheath like an onion.
7. Space–time categories are not neutral like Kantian categories. Space–time are as much contextual as different rules of behaviour (*dharma*). Space–time has varying levels of auscpiciousness–inauscpiciousness.
8. Indians are materialists. They believe in a continuous flow of substance from context to object, from non-self to self in eating, breathing, sex, sensation, perception, thought, art, or religious experience.
9. Indians perversely concern with *jāti* — the logic of classes, of genera and species. Human *jāti*s, taxonomies of season, landscape, times, *guṇa*s (qualities), tastes, characters, emotions, essences (*rasa*s), etc. are basic to

the thought-work of culture, cooking, religion, erotics and magic. Each *jāti* (class) defines a context, a structure of relevance, a rule of permissible combinations, a frame of reference, a meta-communication of what is and can be done.

10. Since the whole civilization is bound by context-sensitivity rules, the dream is to be free of context, to transcend contextual rules. So *rasa* in aesthetics, *mokṣa* in the "aims of life", *saṁnyāsa* in the life stages, *sphoṭa* in semantics, and *bhakti* in religion define themselves against a background of inexorable contextuality.
11. In each of the grammar of a particular cultural text, the pattern is the same: a necessary sequence in time with strict rules of phase and context ending in a free state.

Ramanujan and Nakamura throw lightening flash on the characteristics of Indian thinking, but the element of geophilosophy is missing in their deliberations. I would like to reflect over the impact of geography over Indian thinking first and thence to discover certain more characteristics of Indian thinking that impregnates Śrī-yantra, the condensed Indian thinking through singular abstract figure.

Note on Symbols[64]

Symbol/Symbolic: It is a sign in which the signifier does not resemble or imitate the signified but which is merely conventional. It is mediated through language. Word–word relationships are required to ascertain the meaning of a word without depending on a correlation in space and time between the sound of the word and its meaning. Meaning is derived through mental association with other symbols. The relationship is to be learnt. Traffic light, national emblems, national flags, language in general, code languages, etc. are symbols.

Icon/Iconic: It is a sign in which the signifier directly resembles or imitates the signified. It physically resembles what it stands for. The signal and meaning resemble. Simplest example can be that of the picture of face. Simple, everyday visible iconic signs are a cartoon, a scale model, onomatopoetic words, metaphors, imitative gestures; picture of a bottle containing alcohol with a diagonal bar across the picture displayed at traffic signals that directly forbids driving under alcohol. "Smoking? Don't do it."

Index/Indexical: It is a sign in which the signifier is not arbitrary but is directly and actually connected in some way to the signified in space–time. One can correlate using sense the implicit meaning. Smoke as a natural sign implies that there is fire. Limping gait is a sign that the person is physically impaired or injured. The whistling of pressure cooker is a sign that the food is cooked. A door bell is an indexical sign to imply that someone is standing at the door. Personal "trademarks" like handwriting are indexical signs that point to a particular person. Here, correlation need not be perfect.

---

64 Based upon Daniel Chandler, Semiotics for Beginners, available at http://www.aber.ac.uk/media/Documents/54b/semo2.ntml

2

What Is India?

WHAT is India? At first glance, the most important characteristic of Indian geography becomes manifest. India is a peninsula with a very clean triangular coastline. India is a triangle and she has been equated with a territorial Mother, Bhārata Mātā. The human life is governed by the presence of three celestial objects — sun, moon and earth. The influence of these three cosmic objects intermingles to produce human, all too human. But, the triadic influence seems to magnify in the peninsular geography of India which we will later unravel.

We live in geography, which is a "lived geography". Our landscape is constituted not only by topographical features and ecological niche but also by the mythical and religious imaginations. There is no point in our living space where we do not imbue some meaning and auspicious/inauspicious categorization. There is no pure abstract space in human geography. Living space is perceptual. Indian geography from ancient times has been an imaginary geography, mixed (churned out) with varying legends, myths, correlative thinking and Utopian world-view of transcendence.

Earliest imagination about Indian geography stems from the conception of the earth consisting of four *dvīpa*s (islands) — Bhadrasva, Jambu, Ketumāla and Uttarakuru.

Historian and epigrapher D.C. Sircar mentions how the older Purāṇas and the Pāli literature viewed the world as divided into four continents centred on Mount Meru.[1] The four continents were arranged in fourfold directions like the petals of lotus and of which Meru formed the pericarp. Four *dvīpa*-petal of the earth lotus are as follows: the Bhadrasva in the east, Jambu or Bhārata in the south, Ketumāla in the west, Kuru or the Uttarakuru in the north. This has been termed in the old Sanskrit literature as the *caturdvīpa vasumatī* concept.[2] Certain passages in the Buddhist texts like *Lalitavistara* and *Mahāvastu* have mentions of four *dvīpa*s as, Aparagodanīya Jambudvīpa, Pūrvavideha, and Uttarakuruand. The astronomical works of later centuries like the canonical *Sūrya-Siddhānta* also view earth as fourfold petals and Sumeru as the pericarp. I have discussed in the book how Indian civilization is twirled around the 3 + 1 structure where three parts belong to the world of immanence and the fourth is the transcendental part like in the *puruṣārtha* system or in *catuṣpāda* structure elsewhere. In the fourfold landscape, the fourth, Jambudvīpa, is the "actual" part, rest three parts are imaginary.

Interestingly, similar structure has been formulated for internal geography by Gorakhnātha in his classic text, *Amaraugha Śāsana*.[3] He describes minutely about *mūlādhāra* (the base of the esoteric energy) *kuṇḍalinī*. There is a four-petalled lotus with *kuṇḍalinī* lying coiled in the pericarp. *Kuṇḍalinī* rises from the base to the cranium through the spinal cord, which is also known as, *meru-daṇḍa*.[4] The two structures are

---

[1] D.C. Sircar, *Studies in the Geography of Ancient and Medieval India*, Delhi: Motilal Banarsidass, 1971.

[2] Ibid., pp. 17-26.

[3] Pandit Mukund Ram Shastri, ed. with notes, *The Amaraugha Śāsana of Gorakhnātha*, Bombay: Research Department, Jammu and Kashmir / Nirnaya Sagar Press, 1918.

[4] Ibid., pp. 9-10.

homological as well as correlated since *kuṇḍalinī* also alludes to the mythical Mt. Meru.

Epics like *Mahābhārata* moved beyond this fourfold division of Indian landscape. Bhīṣma-Parva describes in detail the sacred landscape of India. Jambu-khaṇḍa Nirmāṇa-Parva and Bhūmi-Parva of *Mahābhārata* are virtually treatises on the sacred geography of India. The Jambudvīpa island (rose apple island) has been described in detail by Sañjaya for the knowledge of the blind king, Dhṛtarāṣṭra. Sañjaya describes about six mountain ranges — Himavat, Hemakūṭa, Niṣāda, Nīla, Śveta and Śṛṅgavat.[5] These mountain ranges become important in later centuries for new pilgrimages after the advent of spiritual luminaries, since many of these mountains are translocated over different geographies. One sees how Śṛṅagavat mountain is in Karnataka where Śṛṅga Ṛṣi meditated and Śrī Śaṅkarācārya established the sect. There have also been many Himavats and Hemakūṭas in Tibetan tradition associated with the sect of Padamsambhava, the great tāntric master.

These six mountains were described as the abode of *siddhas*. The division between these mountain ranges is called *varṣa*. We reside in Bhāratavarṣa. *Mahābhārata* has a different location for Mt. Meru. Mt. Meru, the *axis mundi* of the cosmos/ earth is no longer in the pericarp of a lotus flower with the four-petalled structure. Meru lies between two *varṣas*, Mālyavat and Gandhamāl, both of which lie further beyond Harivarṣa. Meru is made of gold and it is like fire without smoke. The bird Sumukha left Meru since all birds on Meru were of golden colour and there was no difference between good and bad birds. The sun circumambulates Meru while the moon with the constellations does the same. It is the same principle that has been incorporated in calculating India's calendrical time and ancient astronomy like *Sūrya-Siddhānta*

---

5 K.M. Ganguli, tr., *The Mahābhārata*, Calcutta: Bharata Press, 1883-96.

and *Āryabhaṭīya*. Mt. Meru is also the abode of seven seers. Interestingly, Meru is not only the Mt. Meru of mythical imagination, it is redistributed across Indian geography in the form of gems and jewels. Meru distributes, Meru multiplies. Meru is there and yet everywhere. *Mahābhārata* describes how jewels and gems of all the mountains abounding in precious stones are of Meru. One-fourth of Meru's gold is enjoyed by the king of *yakṣa*, Kubera, while only 1/16th part is to be enjoyed by human beings. The Meru mountain is surrounded by earlier division of four islands, southern of which is Jambudvīpa, also known as Bhārata.

But, *Mahābhārata* also brings into account more complex description of the surrounding worlds like different oceans and more islands. There is a mention of the Sudarśana island which is circular and of the form of wheel (like *sudarśana cakra* of Viṣṇu). It is consisted of rivers, mountains and various cities. It is surrounded with salt-ocean (Lavaṇoda). The description of Sudarśana is equivalent to that of Jambudvīpa. Interestingly, Jambudvīpa is supposed to be surrounded by the ocean of salt water. Thus, Jambudvīpa is also like *sudarśana cakra*. But, here is another twist. As a person can see his own face in the mirror, Sudarśana island can also be seen in the lunar disc. Thus, the image of a *pīpal* tree and a large hare in the lunar disc is the reflection of the Sudarśana (Jambudvīpa) island.[6] What is Bhārata for the *Mahābhārata* protagonist is visible with naked eyes to a layman in the lunar disc as the "moon rabbit" and the sacred *pīpal* tree. Thus, the *bimba–pratibimba* concept has been deployed from the philosophical realm to unravel the geography of Bhārata. Even the Jātaka stories have employed the myth of hare on the moon, and these are inscribed in the monuments in earliest Buddhist structures at Goli (Guntūr) and Nāgārjunakoṇḍa, Andhra Pradesh.

---

6 K.M. Ganguli, tr., *The Mahābhārata*, Calcutta: Bharata Press, 1883-96. Section V of Jambu-khaṇḍa Nirmāṇa-Parva.

The description about Indian geography in *Mahābhārata* underwent further changes and the complex description of seven ring-shaped concentric continents as well as seven circumambient oceans emerged in the later Purāṇas. It is how the *caturdvīpa* conception of Indian geography transformed into conception of *saptadvīpa*. The most elaborate description of India is to be found in the last and the most extensive Purāṇa, *Brahmāṇḍa Purāṇa*.

The description of Bhārata is found in the sixteenth chapter of *Brahmāṇḍa Purāṇa*.[7] Interestingly, it is again the auspicious number 16 (a number that corresponds to the concept of immortality and youthfulness in Indian culture). What is Bhāratavarṣa? It is the mysterious subcontinent in the middle of the universe where the fruits of *karma*s are enjoyed whether auspicious or inauspicious. This is the special feature of Bhārata. Bhārata is the *karmabhūmi*. The subjects of Bhāratabhūmi are the Bhāratī (pertaining to Bhārata). Manu (the progenitor of people of this land) was called Bhārata because of his accomplishing maintenance and nourishment of subjects. So, in the land of Bhārata, every resident is to be nourished and maintained. *Brahmāṇḍa Purāṇa* also mentions that it is only Bhārata from where heaven and salvation can be attained.[8]

Tīrtha-Yātrā-Parva (section LXXX to CLXXX of Vana-Parva in the *Mahābhārata*) and the subsequent chapters of *Brahmāṇḍa Purāṇa* are encyclopaedias on different mountains, rivers, cities, flora and fauna as known during their times. Tīrtha-Yātrā-Parva declares:

> O thou best of the Bhārata race, sojourns in *tīrtha*s which are meritorious and which constitute one of the high.

---

[7] G.V. Tagare, tr., *Brahmāṇḍa Purāṇa*, part I, Delhi: Motilal Banarsidass, 1983.

[8] Ibid., p. 150.

These *tīrtha*s constitute the landscape of India. Harvard Professor, Diana L. Eck in her latest work, *India: A Sacred Geography,*[9] has summed up her three-decade study to understand Indian *tīrtha*s and the sacred imagination. The blurb rightly declares:

> *India: A Sacred Geography* tells the story of the pilgrim's India. In these pages, Diana Eck takes the reader on an extraordinary spiritual journey through the living landscape of this fascinating country — its mountains, rivers, and sea coasts, its ancient and powerful temples and shrines. Seeking to fully understand the sacred places of pilgrimage from the ground up, with their stories, connections and layers of meaning, she acutely examines Hindu religious ideas and narratives and shows how they have been deeply inscribed in the land itself. Ultimately, Eck shows us that from these networks of pilgrimage places, India's very sense of region and nation has emerged. This is the astonishing and fascinating picture of a land linked for centuries not by the power of kings and governments, but by the footsteps of pilgrims.[10]

She studies the "grammar of sanctification in the 'imagined landscape' of India, a landscape constructed of the pilgrimage places (*tīrtha*s) and pilgrimage networks that have long served to create a complex sense of place". She establishes the connections and significance of the similarity of events that took place at dispersed sites. In this elaborate work, she identifies the concepts of *avataraṇa* (divine descent), *svayambhū* (self-manifest destiny), *pratiṣṭhā* (sanctification by adhesion) and body language of godhead as the fourfold grammar of connected sacred landscape of India.

---

[9] Diana L. Eck, *India: A Sacred Geography,* New York: Harmony Books, 2012.

[10] Ibid., from the blurb.

Eck had developed the grammar of sanctification in her 1998 essay, "The Imagined Landscape: Patterns in the Construction of Hindu Sacred Geography".[11] Just like everywhere else, it is the image of the body that evokes the sense of unity. Even the Western philosophers have taken recourse to the body image to develop different political philosophy. The organic unity of any imagination is best described through the body image. The metaphor of the body as an analogue of the world continues to persist in Indian thinking. The genealogy can be traced to the Puruṣa-Sūkta of Vedas. The image of universe as *virāṭ puruṣa* is replete in texts and Indian art.

There is the body image of cosmic cow in which different *tīrtha*s are placed. Similarly, cultural geographers have unveiled various body patterns that define the contours of a *tīrtha* in India. But, the most elaborate work has been done with the distribution of *śakti pīṭha*s across the territory of India. D.C. Sircar is his study of *śakti pīṭha*s has traced the groupings of *pīṭha*s to the earliest tāntric texts during the eighth–ninth centuries. Even the ninth-century Buddhist tāntric text, *Śrīcakrasaṁvara Tantra,* has elaborate description of various *pīṭha*s, *kṣetra*s, *chandoha*s and their homologous body parts within the human body. Thus, even before the advent of the British, the idea of India as a scared land with a dismembered body distributed as *pīṭha*s was widespread. It is from this idea that the concept of Bhārata Mātā emerged and it is erroneous to suggest that the idea of Bhārata Mātā is the construction of modernity and nationalism in the Andersonian sense.

---

11 Eck, "The Imagined Landscape: Patterns in the Construction of Hindu Sacred Geography", *Contributions to Indian Sociology* (1988), **32**(2): 165-88.

Avataraṇa and *svayambhū* describe the non-terrestrial origin of many of the sacred spots. The twelve *jyotirliṅga*s are believed to be *svayambhū* without cause. Similarly, the holy rivers like Gaṅgā descended through mythical *avataraṇa* from the heavens. There are many sacred images believed to be naturally adhering to a particular place. One can retrieve various stories of how some devotee was carrying an idol of his *iṣṭa devatā* and when he put it at some spot to take rest or to attend to the call of nature, the idol adhered spontaneously to the spot and refused to be lifted or moved. That way, the place attained sanctification.

Eck narrates in detail India's sacred landscape. There are seven sacred cities (*sapta mokṣadāyī purī*) — Mathurā, Kāñcī, Ujjain, Ayodhyā, Dwārkā, Kāśī and Haridwar. There are seven sacred rivers — Gaṅgā, Yamunā, Sindhu, Narmadā, Godavarī, Kṛṣṇa, Kāverī; Gaṅgā being the paramount. There are four *dhāma*s — Dwārkā, Rāmeśvaram, Jagannātha Purī and Badrīnāth. There are four *kumbha*s — Prayāg, Haridwar, Nasik and Ujjain. There are *dvādaśa jyotirliṅgam*s (twelve *jyotirliṅga*s — *liṅga* of light) — Somnāth, Mallikārjuna, Mahākāleśvara, Oṁkāreśvara (and Amaleśvara), Kedārnāth, Bhīmaśaṅkara, Viśvanātha, Tryambakeśvara, Baidyanāth, Nāgeśvara, Rāmeśvaram, and Ghṛṣṇeśvara (Ellorā). The body of Satī, Lord Śiva's wife and the Ādi Śakti, is said to be scattered at fifty-one sites across India. Some put the figure at 108.

What is interesting about Bhārata is that

> the entire land of India is a great network of pilgrimage places — referential, inter-referential, ancient and modern. As a whole, it constitutes a "sacred geography". Everything is part of a living, storied and intricately connected landscape.[12]

---

12 Eck, n. 9, p. 2.

The system of meaning–significance is marked not by uniqueness, but by multiplicity. More important a thing is, greater is the chance of its duplication elsewhere. Eck finds:

> The landscape not only connects places to the lores of gods, heroes and saints, but it connects places to one another through local, regional and transregional practices of pilgrimages.[13]

But, most important is the idea of duplication and multiplication, and constituting a whole in the process. It is like spider weaving the web. The same pattern is being repeated and still the wholeness is kept intact. The sages of Upaniṣads compared Brahmā (the creator) with a spider only. The analogy suits the complex system of Indian landscape. Brahmā himself is derived from the root *bṛḥ*. *Bṛḥ* is something that grows and makes others grow. The universe emerged out of the cosmic egg, brahmāṇḍa.

Algorithm of Indian Landscape: Iteration

Brahmāṇḍa is the egg of Brahman (*brahma* + *aṇḍa*). The universe always grows and multiplies. The root *bṛḥ* points to the operation of plenitude. The words like *bṛhad* and *bṛhattara* are derived from the same root. We also know how pilgrims take vow (*vrata*) to visit *tīrtha*s and not to eat non-vegetarian food, not to indulge in sexual activity or similar vows. *Vrata* itself has double meaning. It is a double entendre. *Vrata* is also to connect. Thus, vows connect one to the sacred landscape as well as with the perceptual space and entities. We have seen in the earlier part how the whole Indian tradition is inscribed in formulating *bandha*s. Upaniṣad has the meaning of connection. *Bandhana* in the form of actual wearing of thread or tying thread in various rituals and various *tīrtha*s also signifies the "connectivity" aspect of our acts. Similarly, *parva*

---

13 Eck, n. 9, p. 5.

stands for various festivals. *Parva* is also the joint. *Parva* is the joint in epics like *Mahābhārata* where each chapter is a separate *parva*, which in turn consists of similarly joined *parvas*. It is from *parva* that *parvata* derived as a mountain appears as joined at intermittent intervals. *Parvata* is sacred and most of the holy sites of goddess are found on *parvatas*, the term from which the name of Goddess Pārvatī derived, whose body parts sprouted as *śakti pīṭhas*. *Parvas* also join the contextual times. The auspicious and inauspicious periods are joined with a *parva*. *Vrata* which a devotee takes on *parva* days also connects an individual to the larger community, microcosm to macrocosm; it connects the individual body with the cosmic body. *Vrata* is derived from *vṛt* (to move). This is the root of *vṛtta* (the circle). The wheel is also known as *vartana*. Buddha started *dharmacakravartana* at Deer Park, Varanasi, thereby setting in motion the wheel of *dharma*. India is also known as Āryāvarta, the land of Āryas, which is always on the move. Thus *parva, bṛh, bandha,* Upaniṣad and *vrata,* all connote duplication, multiplication and movement. Indian civilization has this renewing paradigm which makes it so vibrant in spite of centuries of unfavourable atmosphere.

One will be surprised to find so many stories and tales about demons and gods who multiply. The demon Raktabīja could not be killed because each drop of his blood would grow into another Raktabīja. Therefore, the goddess had to take the form of Kālī with a skull bowl in her hands to kill him finally by not letting his blood fall on ground. The miraculous powers of *siddhas* and holy men are often narrated with anecdotal stories of their multiplication of bodies and instant presence at multiple places. Yogananda has described in the popular work, *Autobiography of a Yogi*, such saints who could exist with multiple bodies.

Since correlative thinking and duplication are the root of Indian thinking, there is so much emphasis on the etymological relationship of different things and to explain through various tales and narratives how the seemingly disparate things are connected. In linguistics, similar aspect is termed reduplication. In fact, the earliest of the available written literature (Tripiṭakas) discloses the same aspect in Buddha's discourse. Buddha would repeat and repeat the same dialogue for different persons or places or condition and only in the last of the utterance enlighten with a connecting idea. The *mantra* which also defines the basic contours of the land of Bhārata has a high degree of alliteration. *Kathās*, *caritas*, *gāthās* and *nāmāvalīs* are exercises in repeatedly emphasizing same theme. Similarly, rituals involve repetition of the acts and *japas*, the repetition of *mantras*.

Eck argues how the pilgrims of India imagined landscape by "linking, duplicating and multiplicating places so as to constitute an entire world".[14] She discovers the way repetition of places, creation of clusters, groups — all these constitute vivid symbolic landscape not by exclusivity and uniqueness, but by polycentricity, plurality and duplication.[15] It is *tīrtha-yātrīs* (pilgrims) who create circuit of meaning and connection. She centres her argument around the theme of repetition and homologies which build the inter-referential landscape of Bhārata.

She takes up the case of Kāśī and discovers how "everything about this holy city seemed to be duplicated elsewhere, set amid a pattern of symbolic signification that made Benares not unique, but part of a wider landscape shaped by repetition". Kāśī is duplicated in the Himalayas as Gupta Kāśi. Gupta Kāśī has Kāśī Viśvanātha Temple and also Maṇikarṇikā Ghāṭ, and there are tales of how the pond in the Himalayas is connected through underground with the Maṇikarṇikā Kuṇḍa in Kāśī. Kāśī is also to be found in the

---

14 Eck, n. 9, p. 5.

15 Ibid.

south of Vindhyas. Many places in Deccan are called Southern Kāsī (Dakṣiṇa Kāśī). Anne Feldhaus who has done extensive work on geographical imagination in Maharashtra[16] discovers some of the Dakṣiṇa Kāśī places in Maharashtra like Dhom on Kṛṣṇā near Wai, at Karaḍ, Kolhapur, Nandikeśvara, Paiṭhan, Wai. The Saptapurī of Nasik is also known as Dakṣiṇa Kāśī. There is a Kāśī in Alampur, on the bank of river Kṛṣṇā in Andhra Pradesh.

Similarly, *cāra dhāma*s, the main abodes of God, duplicate at many places. Though *cāra dhāma*s are Badrī, Dwārkā, Rameśvaram and Purī, these are spread across the whole territory of India. There is a smaller *cāra dhāma yātrā* in the Garhwal Himalayas of Badrī–Kedāra–Gaṅgotrī–Yamunotrī. Kedārnāth is also the centre of one of the twelve *jyotirliṅga*s and one of the most sacred sites for Śiva devotees. Kedār itself multiplies into five Kedārs in the Himalayas. Pañca Kedārs — Kedārnātha, Tuṅganātha, Rūdranātha, Kalpeśvara, Madhyaveśvara — correspond well with the five Pāṇḍava brothers of *Mahābhārata*, who are believed to have visited and sanctified Kedārnāth. Śiva's *pañcākṣarī* mantra is homologized to five sounds of syllable *oṁ namaḥ śivāya*, thus correspondence is established across a wider spectrum. Not only that, there is another Gupta Kedār (secret Kedār) in the same region which is believed to be connected through the underground mechanism with main Kedār.

*Cāra dhāma yātrā*s can be replicated even at a smaller scale. There are popular *cāra dhāma yātrā*s at Citrakūṭa or Girnār. The *cāra dhāma yātrā* can be ritually performed within Kāśī.

One can similarly study India's geobody through the concept of seven streams. Vedas mention seven different

---

16 Anne Feldhaus, *Connected Places: Region, Pilgrimage, and Geographical Imagination in India*, New York: Palgrave Macmillan, 2003, pp. 127-184.

lineages that flow from the seven seers. The seven seers are found as a connected unit in the constellation Ursa Major as *saptarṣi* in the sky. The hot water stream at Rājgīr, which was a popular pilgrimage spot even during the time of Buddha, has seven streams named after each of the seven seers. There are seven streams of Sindhu in Vedas (Saptasindhu). The concept of *saptanada* pervades the Indian geographical imagination. The holiest river Gaṅgā emerges from the seven streams. There are narratives about recurring seven divisions of Gaṅgā. In *Brahmāṇḍa Purāṇa*, it is mentioned how Gaṅgā is a *saptanadī*. On being released, the river began to flow in seven channels out of which three flowed towards the east and three to the west. *Brahmāṇḍa Purāṇa* describes the streams Nalinī, Hrādinī and Pāvanī flowing towards the east. Sītā, Cakṣus and Sindhu flowed towards the west. Bhagīratha being the seventh channel flowed towards the south. This idea of Saptagaṅgā is all-pervasive. It is also mentioned in Purāṇas that when Gaṅgā was descending, first it reached the Dhruva Star (Pole Star) and then purified the seven planets near Dhruvaloka. Thus Gaṅgā before its mythical descent over earth had a journey of *sapta-graha*s.

Many rivers have seven tributaries or believed to have split into seven streams. Kāverī splits into seven streams. Thus, specific river may change, but the structure of duplication and resonance link these into an order. Why is the number seven intricately connected with the flow? We also know how the ritual of *piṇḍa-dāna* is done for the seven generation of ancestors. Wheresoever there is a downward flow, the structure of seven stream emerges. Even the sun is believed to be moving on a seven-horse chariot. *Sapta* (seven) and *śrīpata* (to creep) are derived from the same root. Due to this etymological connection, *śrīpata* becomes *sapta*. Thus, anything that creeps and meander like a snake is believed to have seven constituents. Just like rivers whose water streams nourish the

Table 2.1: Duplicated/Multiplied Gaṇgā

Location	*Name and Description*
Kashmir	Bāṇagaṅgā at Kaṭrā, Vaiṣṇo Devī Shrine: Kiśengaṅgā (Śāradā Pītha now in POK is situated on its bank); Gaṅgābal (lake near Harmukh peak considered as sacred as Prayāg); Gaṅgājaṭāṅ (in Baḍgām district where Gaṅgā Aṣṭamī is celebrated); Guptagaṅgā (adjacent to Nishat Garden); Gaṅgācoṭī (mountain peak in POK).
Mongolia	Saran Gaṅgā (Sajan-kang-ka at Dornod, Mongolia); Gaṅgā Nuur Lake (near Dariganga), Muharin Gaṅgā, Ulan Gaṅgā (mountain peak); Dzegestiyn Gaṅgā (Hill at Dornod).
South India	Gautamī Gaṅgā or Dakṣiṇa Gaṅgā (Godāvarī); Pañcagaṅgā that meets river Kṛṣṇā at Narsobawāḍī near Sāṅglī; Dakṣiṇa Gaṅgā (Kāverī, Narmadā, Tuṅgabhadrā).
Tibet	Gaṅgā Chuu stream that connects lake Mānsarovar with lake Rākṣaṣatal.
Human Body	*Nadī* (here "da" is third in the third series of Sanskrit consonants) and *nāḍī* ("ḍa" is third in the fourth series of consonants) have similar sounds. One is the subtle channel and another is the river. But, in Indian esoterism, two have fused. Just like river streams, there are confluences of different layers as well as directions of meanings. Iḍā is a subtle *nāḍī* that courses from the right testicle to the left nostril and corresponds to Gaṅgā River. It is believed to control all the mental processes.
Cosmos	Ākāśagaṅgā (Milky Way).

earth and the humans alike, the concept of seven seers and seven generations in *sapiṇḍa* continues to exist. In recent times, the idea has extended to sisterhood, since sisters like rivers nourish their children. Sets of seven goddesses are found throughout India. The riddles and the songs would mention about *sāta saheliyāṅ*. Similarly, geographically separate goddesses between Chenāb and Yamunā rivers connect through the category of seven sisters. Seven major pilgrimage centres of goddess Umā — Vaiṣṇo Devī, Kāṅgṛā, Cāmuṇḍā, Jwālājī, Cintapūrṇī, Nainā Devī, Manasā Devī — thus get conceptualized in imaginary holistic landscape.

The holiest river Gaṅgā duplicates and multiplies. Godāvarī is the Gautamī Gaṅgā/Dakṣiṇa Gaṅgā. Table 2.1 describes some of the duplicated Gaṅgās.

One can see transposition of the paradigm of sacred Gaṅgā at different levels from within body and beyond into the cosmos. From the microcosm to macrocosm, the river Gaṅgā becomes iconic signifier for sacredness of liquid flow. In fact, duplicating characteristics are incorporated in the myth of the origin of Gaṅgā itself, as discussed.

Similarly, one sees how mythical Mt. Meru duplicates. Though Tibetans and Hindus believe Mt. Kailāsa in the Himalayas as Mt. Meru, Meru is also found within the human body. The duplication mindset also influenced outsiders. Megasthenes wrote in *Indica* that when Dionysus came from the West and overran India, due to excessive heat on his soldiers suffered from a pestilence. Dionysus took his troops to the mountain of Meros where his troops were restored to health.[17] Vellingiri Hills near Coimbatore, Tamil Nadu, is known as Dakṣiṇa Kailāsa. But, it is not the only duplication. Like Mt. Kailāsa in the far north, there is Kataragama in the far south (Dakṣiṇa Kailāsa) in Sri Lanka and situated upon the same meridian as Mt. Kailāsa. The Murugan devotees throng there just as pilgrims visit the Kailāsa in the northern part of

---

17 Allan Dahlquist, *Megasthenes and Indian Religion: A Study in Motives and Types*, Delhi: Motilal Banarsidass, 1996, p. 47.

India. Kataragama is in the northernmost part of Sri Lanka and on same meridian. Thus, Sri Lanka is considered as a condensed India.

One can count and endlessly count such duplications of sacred places across the Indian landscape. Like Mathurā in the north, there is Dakṣiṇa Mathurā, Madura on river Kṛtamāla. The connection is established through the pair of eyes of the goddess that fell at these two places. Mathurā also duplicates at smaller level. There is a village in Medinipore, Bengal, with the same name. I will term this as "topophilic Sanskritization".

Tony Huber studied the Tibetan landscape[18] and found how Tibetan Buddhists were determined that sacred Indian places be "relocated" on Tibetan soil to "Buddha-ize the Tibetan landscape. In ancient geography, sites of *caritra*, southern port city on Orissa (Uḍra) coast, and Devīkoṭa, a place in the Dīnājpur district of Bengal, were real places which contained tāntric *pīṭhas*. One site as Caritra and four major sites as Devīkoṭas were claimed in Tibet. Tsa-ri in southern Tibet was said to be the site of Caritra or Devīkoṭa. Ti-se was taken to be Himavat and La-Phyi was identified as Godāvarī. Relocation process strengthened the Tibetan pilgrimage places. Like the Hindu imagination, Tibetan Buddhists developed the theory that certain places correspond to certain part of the body which are connected by a network of internal psychic channels or *nāḍīs*.

Odisha is famous for the Jagannātha Temple of Purī. But, Purī is also in Maharashtra across the river Godāvarī. Srinagar, the city of the Queen of Goddess, Lalitā, is not only in the

---

18 Tony Huber, "Where Exactly Are Caritra, Devikota and Himavat?: A Sacred Geography Controversy and the Development of Tantric Buddhist Pilgrimage Sites in Tibet", in A. McKay (ed.) *The History of Tibet*, vol. II: *The Medieval Period: c. 850–1895 — The Development of Buddhist Paramountcy*, London: Routledge Curzon, pp. 392-424.

state of Jammu and Kashmir, but also in the Garhwal Himalayas. Similarly, Nagroṭā *en route* to Kashmir Srinagar is also in the Garhwal Himalayas. It seems same symbolic structure has been translocated from Kashmir to the Himalayas. There is another Ayodhyā in Balasore, Odisha. There are many Tārāpurs in Odisha, Bengal and Bihar where temples of Goddess Tārā still exist. Lalitagiri–Ratnagiri–Udaygiri complex is found both in Odisha and Rājgīr, and probably in Maharashtra too.

One finds how the circumambulation of a sacred place has repetitive structure in India. There is *pañcakosī parikramā* with five stops, around a circumambulatory route in Kāśī. But, same *pañcakosī parikramā* can also be done in Ayodhyā, and around Narmadā, Mathurā, Oṁkāreśvara and Buxar. *Pañcakosa* and *pañcakosī parikramā* have homonymic connection. Human body is imagined as consisting of five concentric sheaths (*kośa*s), each grosser than the underlying sheath — *annamaya*, *prāṇamaya*, *manomaya*, *vijñānamaya* and *ānandamaya*. True self, *ātman* which is same as the cosmic *Brahman*, is *pañcakośātīta* (beyond the five sheaths). The *pañcakosī parikramā* is similarly performed to reach the true self. I was surprised to find *govardhana parikramā* in Vṛndāvana. One has to take a longer route of 23 km that covers Govardhana hills, Candrasarovara, Śyāma Ḍhāk, Ganthuli-grāma, Sūrya-kuṇḍa, Mukharai and Kilola-kuṇḍa. If one is not able to do the same, the same merit can be attained by doing *govardhana parikramā* within the city of Vṛndāvana. If even that cannot be performed, one can circumambulate around a small sacred stone placed in the Kṛṣṇa–Balarāma Temple near Bāṅke Bihārī Temple of Vṛndāvana. If one is not able to accomplish that even, it can be performed mentally also. Thus, it is seen that what duplicates is merely a ritual structure which is scale free. There is also endless inclusion of pattern within pattern replete with self-similar structures. The concentricity emerges as one of the important aspects of Indian imagination. Here, the elements have a degree of condensation. The matter extends from ether to metals. Everything is the manifestation of same entity. Different forms exist only due to the varying covering. It is how speech and matter get connected. Speech is only a subtler form of matter and gross matter is more manifest. *Vāc* has four layers of manifestation — *parā*, *paśyantī*, *madhyamā* and *vaikharī*. *Vaikharī* is the audible sound, but it is merely the grosser form of transcendental silence, *parā*. Grosser form of sound becomes matter. This is why it is believed that speech has propensity to influence the grosser universe. This has made India unique with its sonic theology where *mantra*s and rituals to apply *mantra*s are ubiquitous. India is the *guru* in exporting *mantra*s across Asia along with the faith that these sounds do influence the outcome in the material universe.

If the grosser universe is the manifestation of the subtler *vāc*, then there must be a grammar for sanctification of the landscape, since languages are governed by grammar and so do the *mantra*s. Feldhaus has developed *The Algebra of Place* for Indian geographical imagination like replication, comparison and containing other places. Eck has tried to further Feldhaus's work and she generated a grammar which gets enriched with examination of Indian civilization in the present work.

Mirror Reflection (Ābhāṣa) Generates Multiplicity

I am of the view that the mirror motif (*ābhāsa* is the reflection) itself is a very important strategy to generate the recurring sequence of signification. As we discussed earlier, how the patterns over lunar disc are believed to be merely the reflection of Jambudvīpa, the operation of this mirror-reflection strategy cannot be underestimated. The whole concept of phoneme emanation is based on this *bimba–pratibimba* strategy. The first vowel to emanate is *a*. When it reflected itself, it was *a* + *a* and *ā* emerged which gave the first *ānanda* (joy) to the creator, Brahmā. The universe, if, is a grosser manifestation of *vāc*, *vāc* itself is governed by the principles of reflection. We also find how in Indian languages and particularly in *mantras*, the palindrome sequences are found in abundance which also confirm the influence of mirror motif. Every ascendance simultaneously exists with descendance; rise with fall. Every *karma* has a *viparīta karma*. *Sṛṣṭi* and *saṁhāra* co-exist. Emanation and dissolution act in tandem. *Yantras* themselves are generated through superimposing a geometrical structure and its reflection. It is the reflection through which *Brahman* exists simultaneously in individual *jīva*. Man becomes microcosm of *virāṭ puruṣa*. Thus, *bimba–pratibimba* also adds to the duplication, multiplication, transposition as well as condensation of things and territories.

We know how the term *pratimā* is derived from the concept of *pratibimba*. The image of the deity (*pratimā*) connotes reflection as well as likeness. This is the crux of Indian thinking, brilliantly explained by Abhinavagupta in his *bimba–pratibimba* doctrine. In *Īśvarapratyabhijñāvimarśinī*, Abhinavagupta describes:

> How can what is unitary be a multiplicity? To this it has been replied: He who has the essential nature of consciousness is like a mirror. [In this way] there is the possibility of a diversity of appearances without contradicting his unity. What is the contradiction? Therefore, the essential nature of things, though unitary through the force of recognition (*pratyabhijñā*), accommodates within himself contrary divisions of his essential nature.[19]

---

19 K.A. Subramania Iyer and K.C. Pandey (eds.) *Īśvarapratyabhijñā-vimarśinī of Abhinavagupta: Doctrine of Divine Recognition*, Sanskrit text with Bhāskarī (2 vols.), Delhi: Motilal Banarsidass, 1986, repr., 2.1.1, **2**: 8-9.

Abhinavagupta posited that such reflections are not illusory and that the diversity of reflection is identical with itself. Abhinavagupta is so much enamoured by the reflection analogy that he proposed reflection as the surest and shortest way to the realization of ultimate unity with the godhead. He describes in the masterly *Tantrāloka*:

> The one for whom the entire, multitudinous collection of entities appears as a reflection within his Self, which is Consciousness — he is indeed the Lord of the universe.
>
> — 3.268, 2.598

Abhinavagupta also links the power of reflection with the preservation and sustenance (*sthitikaraṇa*), thus introducing a triad with emanation (*sr̥ṣṭi*) and dissolution (*saṁhāra*) (*Tantrāloka* 3.283-85, 2.608).[20]

Thus, an interesting proposition emerges that it is through reflection–duplication that something can be preserved. This aptly describes Indian civilization's perennial existence since the very structure is based upon the duplication through *bimba–pratibimba* model.

Duplication strategy creates pluralism. One manifests into many — self-same. It is like the Brahmā's act of *br̥ḥ*. The repetitive multiforms make the structure to thrive in spite of traumas inflicted upon its geobody from external or internal factors.

Structure of Indian thinking reveals that Indians believe in the underlying unity of everything. Everything is one and the same eternal *Brahman*. In such a world-view, one is assumed to become many. The non-dual becomes dual and thence the whole diversity of creation. But, just like the often-repeated metaphor of fire, which is assumed to be same in the sun,

[20] D.P. Lawrence, "Remarks on Abhinavagupta's Use of the Analogy of Reflection", *Journal of Indian Philosophy* (2005), **33**(5-6): 594.

moon or inside human body, the basic nature of many is same as what was contained in the first. This allows for proliferation of diversity and retaining unity at the same time. It is how India developed "unity in diversity". The different forms are only due to varying layer of manifestation. In such a world-view where there is endless repetition and bifurcation, dissipative structures emerge with strong centres of attractors. In case of Indian landscape, the sacred *tīrtha*s are like the basic attractor of the landscape and this makes it to maintain stability and continuity in spite of the rise and fall of political, religious and social authorities. Landscape, that emerges from scale-free imagination, attains autonomy of a sort. Thus, same Kāśī, same Kāñcī, same Kailāsa, same Prayāg remain the holiest site even after millennia of years.

How does geophilosophy that reflects India's unique triangular shape reshape the grammar of sanctification? How does Śrī-yantra emerge as the site for synthesis of varying thought-currents? Can we view Śrī-yantra as abstract encapsulation of the structure of Indian civilization?

3

Śrī-yantra
The Ultimate Code of Indian Civilization

WHILE exploring Indian civilization, we have dealt with the characteristics of Indian thinking. Hajime Nakamura propounded the following themes to characterize ways of Indian thinking: preponderance of abstract notion, abstract conceptions treated as concrete realities, fondness for the negative expression, grasping the absolute negatively, attraction for the unknown, minimizing individuality and specific preferences, unity of all things, static quality of thought, lack of common-sense concept of time, continuity of one's self and other selves, consciousness of existence of self, lack of notion of order in the objective natural world, lack of historical consciousness, and introspective and metaphysical character of thinking.

A.K. Ramanujan has further added how thinking and culture in India are governed by context-sensitive grammar, metonymic view of reality that makes it possible to establish far-fetched interrelationality in which anything can be substituted for everything else, signifier is part of the signified, densification of meaning from any arbitrary symbol to indexical scale, degree of thingification and a continuum of reality, concentricity, pervasive materialism, overemphasis on classification, and ultimate goal to transcend contextual rules. Anne Feldhaus developed an algebra of connectivity in geographical imagination upon which Diana L. Eck further developed a grammar of sanctification. Ramanujan had previously hinted how Indian culture has context-sensitive grammar. I have sheaffed different approaches and added how the model of reduplication maintains the stability of civilization. (Sheaffing is a mathematical condition which is both analytical and synthetical; it diversifies and glues thereby conjugating analysis and synthesis. The term has been popularized by the Colombian mathematician–philosopher, Fernando Zalamea.[1]) This model got derived from the analogy of reflection. I also added how there is a 3 + 1 structure which is ubiquitous, in which first three defines different layers of a thing and the fourth the transcending dimension. I have described how the relationality is deeply embedded in Indian thinking and this extends from discovering etymological relationship to structural relationship. We have also discussed rootedness of thinking in earth. Indian geography has this particular characteristic of having a perfect triangular peninsula. This has immense influence on Indian thinking.

Indian mind is encapsulated in a triadic thinking that possibly stems from the geophilosophical domain. Vedas are three and are termed *tri-vedas* — *Ṛk*, *Sām* and *Yajur*. *Atharvaveda* was a later development and still not debated along with the early *tri-vedas*. The reality is believed to be *tri-guṇātmaka* (composed of three *guṇas*) — *sattva*, *rajas* and *tamas*. Fires are three — Sūrya (sun), Soma (moon) and Agni/Vahni (fire). Fires in social world are three — *āhvaniyāgni* (sacrificial), *gārhapatyāgni* (household) and *dakṣiṇāgni* (crematory). There are three powers of *śakti* — *icchā* (will), *jñāna* (knowledge) and *kriyā* (action). Similarly, there are three *lokas* — *bhuḥ* (earth),

---

1 Fernando Zalamea, "Peirce's Continuum: A Methodological and Mathematical Approach", 2005 http://acervopeirceano.org/wp-content/uploads/2011/09/Zalamea-Peirces-Continuum.pdf; also, Zalamea, *Synthetic Philosophy of Contemporary Mathematics*, tr. Z.L. Fraser, Falmouth, UK: Urbanomic Sequence Press, 2013.

bhuvaḥ (space), *svaḥ* (heaven); three *padas* of Gāyatrī (Tripadī); three bodies — *sthūla* (gross), *sūkṣma* (subtle) and *akāraṇa* (causal); three states of speech — *paśyantī, madhyamā* and *vaikharī*; three states of consciousness — sleeping, dreaming and waking; three kinds of breath — *prāṇa, apāna* and *samāna*; three *nāḍīs* of the highest path — *suṣumṇā, piṅgalā* and *iḍā*; threefold classification of *kāla* — *bhūta* (past), *vartamāna* (present) and *bhaviṣya* (future).

Indian thinking is inherently triadic. This triadic thinking appeared to be the product of influence of the triangular topography. We will see how triangles also gained prominence in subsequent rituals.

Triadic Thinking and Iteration

The triadic nature of thought leads to philosophy of continuity. I am inverting Charles Peirce's meditations[2] on triadism as enunciated by his followers like Fernando Zalamea and Reza Negarestani, and the transmodernist bandwagon. While discussing Peirce's "Concept of Continuum", Zalamea writes:

> Peirce's triadic classification of the sciences extends also over a general continuum, which allows appropriate trifurcations of the neighbourhoods of the classification, encouraging translations, iterations and deiterations from one environment of knowledge to the other. The continuum not only supports the (possibility, actuality and necessity) of the transfers: deeper, it induces them, folding and unfolding systematically the unity and multiplicity of knowledge, considering polyvalent culture and philosophy as natural gradation problems over the continuum.[3]

He finds how triadic thinking encourages iteration and

---

[2] Charles S. Peirce, *Collected Papers*, Cambridge: Harvard University Press, 1931.

[3] Zalamea, n. 1, p. 64.

intertwined motion, the phenomenon discussed earlier about Indian civilization. The basic conception of Indian civilization is the existence of an open continuum where triadic classification leads to iteration of structures. The most appropriate logic to understand Indian civilization can be the Peircean logic. Zalamea writes:

> Peirce's Thirdness proposes a mediation beyond clashes, a third place where the "one" and the "other" enter in dialogue. It is the category of sense, representation, synthesis, knowledge.[4]

Thus, the interrelationality and the correlative thinking that characterizes India inadvertently lead to triadic thinking.

We can trace the strong connection of triad and triangles with the feminine from the earliest times of *Ṛgveda*. This too has resonances with correlative thinking. The power of feminine evoked awe due to the little understood power of generation. Since the female generative organ centres in a triangular space, the dot (*bindu*) at the centre of triangle came to represent the generative power of the creative *śakti*. India being triangular in shape was equated with a feminine *śakti*. Thus, India's geobody became the body of the Goddess. The worship of Mother Earth as Bhūdevī and Pṛthvī has its roots in *Ṛgveda*. But, what is surprising is that *Ṛgveda* also mentions about a set of *tri-devī* (three *devī*s).

Ṛgveda in IXth book mentions about the set of three beautiful goddesses to attend *soma* ceremony.

> Three beauteous goddesses Sarasvatī, Bhāratī and Ilā Mighty one attend. — 5.8[5]

---

[4] Zalamea, n. 1, p. 50.

[5] Ralph T.H. Griffith, tr., *The Hymns of the Rig Veda*, Benares: E.J. Lazarus, 1896.

Sarasvatī is invoked with Ilā and Bhāratī. The three — Ilā, Bhāratī and Sarasvatī — are the manifestation of Agni (Yajñāgni) and are tri-Sarasvatī. Bhāratī can be identified with later Goddess Pṛthvī who is also known as Lakṣmī or Śrī or Bhūdevī. I feel it is the set of the three goddesses which later evolved into the concept of Tripurasundarī. Alternatively, it might be the incorporation of the idea along with the ritual of drinking of *soma* in the earliest Veda to give credence to east Indian conception of the divine feminine and the wet nature of the subtle realm in contrast with the west-Aryan notion of fire-sacrifices.

The fascination with trinity is in abundance in ancient texts. There is simply a duplication of number 3 for afresh thingification. There are 33 *rudras*, 33 *devas* in the Vedas. There are 33 heavens and 33 teeth of Buddha in the Buddhist texts. In the Ādi-Parva of *Mahābhārata*, a significant number is mentioned to describe the generation of *devas*. It was thirty-three thousand, three hundred and thirty-three (33,333). Similarly, one can reflect how Tirumūḷar composed the great classic *Tirumantiram* in 3,033 verses and in all probability, 300 verses might be the "missing" verses or the secret wisdom which is transmitted only through oral tradition from a *guru* to a disciple.

We have seen merely the iteration of number three one after another. But, other complex operations like multiplication also emerged. Thus, numbers 6, 9, 27 became associated with the deity of triadic universe. Number 6 is the product of 3 x 2. It can be seen in a different way. When two triangles intersect, six-pointed hexagram is created. Thus, such a hexagram became sacred. Number 27 is an auspicious number of days to propitiate the Goddess Tripurā. But, it is the number 9 which became paramount as 9 is the product of iterative 3. Since nine lunar months are the gestation period for human species and there are nine holes in a human body, the numerical correspondences made the sages to imagine about an abstract system to represent the interlocking of nine layers within a triadic thinking.

Śrī-yantra as Sheaf of Indian Thought

Śrī-yantra is the sheaffing of triadic thinking. Śrī-yantra has unique characteristics that the interlocking of primary triangles also generates secondary triangles. There are three layers of trifurcation that lead to forty-three triangles. The triangle, which is the abstract representation of triadic thinking when fuses with its reflection (*bimba–pratibimba* being a causative mode of thinking in Indian tradition), the six-pointed hexagram is created. The reflection analogy is explained by the two primary concepts of *prakāśa* and *vimarśa*. While *prakāśa* is the Pure Consciousness and static Śiva, its reflection is *vimarśa*, the *śakti* that generates the "I" consciousness, and the differentiation of subject and object arises.

Many consider the hexagram itself as Śrī-yantra. While describing the Bhuvanapati-cakra (Tantra IV, verses 1309-13), Tirumūḷar established the correspondence with fifteen letters of Tripurasundarī with the double triangular *cakra*.[6] Lakṣmīdhara, the greatest commentator on Śrī-Vidyā and a Samayacārin, equates this structure with Śrī-cakra. This Star of David is the foundational structure of Śrī-cakra. In a complete Śrī-cakra, when nine triangles interlock, a beautiful structure emerges with iterative triangles. Thus, the structure becomes the signifier of Indian civilization as it is abstract with iterative triangles that are produced by the reflection, and interlocking of triangles with their own reflection. It is also a continuum and the continuum is described in two ways (mirror-image) — *sr̥ṣṭi karma* (from inner *bindu* to outer *bhūpar* /

---

6 Tirumūḷar Tirumantiram: *A Tamil Scriptural Classic*, Madras: Ramakrishna Math, 2002.

rectangle) or *saṁhāra karma* (dissolution, from outer to inner *bindu*). Thus, even though the primary triangles undergo multiple levels of operation, the structural characteristics do not change. Śrī-yantra is created by nine triangles and has nine sheaths corresponding to microcosmic as well as macrocosmic thingification. Like the evolution of many symbols into indexical signifier, Śrī-yantra also becomes indexical of Tripurasundarī. Verily, Śrī-yantra becomes the goddess.

Douglas Renfrew Brooks writes on Śrī-Vidyā and Śākta Tantrism in south India:

> Śrī-cakra not only represents the process of creative devolution but is its actual form. Put differently, Śrī-cakra is a symbol of the universe's primordial structure and, at the same time, the index of reality that forms its structure. Put theologically, the universe is a projection or reflection (*pratibimba*) of divinity's own self-reflection. Śrī-cakra, like the universe itself, is both identical to and different from its source. Just as a reflection creates an isomorphic image of its subject and yet is not its subject, so Śrī-cakra is both reality's form (*rūpa*) and its most perfect reflection (*bimba*). Śrī-cakra visually mimics its symbolic and indexical functions.[7]

Brooks reiterates what the Tantras mention:

> Microcosmically, Śrī-cakra is the human body, itself a "palace of nine gates", that is, with nine apertures.[8]

Why is Śrī-yantra the site to understand the sheaffing of India's civilization? One will be surprised that Śrī-yantra is the king

---

[7] Douglas Renfrew Brooks, *Auspicious Wisdom: The Texts and Traditions of Srividya Sakta Tantrism in South India*, Albany, NY: SUNY Press, 1992, p. 115.

[8] Ibid., p. 116.

of *yantras* both among Vedic and Āgamic followers. Śrī-Vidyā is as much pinnacle of learning among the yogic seers as the tāntric practitioners. Thus, it is the only site where the fusion of bifurcated trends can be realized. Śrī-Vidyā itself is enmeshed in triads. The goddess is the Mahā-Tripurasundarī, the beautiful ruler of three cities — earth, sky and heaven. There is a set of *yantra, mantra, tantra* to propitiate her. *Mantra* itself has three *kūṭas* (peaks) — Vāgbhava, Kāmarāja and Śakti. There are three seed syllables — *ka, aeṁ* and *hrīṁ*. Tripurasundarī has three aspects — *sthūla, sūkṣma* and *parā*. She is the Goddess of three stresses — *nāda* (sound), *bindu* (point) and *kalā* (digit). The ritual to worship her is also of three kinds — *kāyika* (bodily/*bāhyayāga*), *vācika* (by speech/*antaryāga*) and *mānasika* (by mind/*bhāvanā*). In Śrī-yantra itself, there are three layers of enclosures of different shapes — triangular, circle and line. The three concentric circles are — *tri-valaya* (*tri-vṛtta*) representing the triple world and the three lines (*tri-rekhā*) surround the ninth enclosure (*bhūpara*). There are three traditions — *kāḍi, hāḍi* and *kahāḍi*. The letters *ka* as well as *aeṁ*, which are the seed syllables in the *mantra*, have a triangular space in their shapes. The *trikoṇa* is the *yoni-maṇḍala* and the seat of the Goddess Tripurā. It is the triangular space as the creatrix that Indian religious flags are triangular, known as *patākā*. Śrī-yantra itself is known as *mahāpatākā* (the great flag). Indian civilization's triad-centricity is carried through these *patākās* in every procession, every holy place. Gandhi could realize the impact of triangular shape over Indian psyche. Therefore, his symbol of *carkhā* appeared as a triangle with the wheel at one end.

Tantrarāja Tantra and various Upaniṣads like *Bhavanopaniṣad* explain how human body itself is a Śrī-cakra with different points corresponding to different body parts and *cakras*. Thus, if Śrī-cakra on one hand is the Śiva–Śakti in union and the human body itself is a grosser Śrī-yantra, on the other hand, the identity of an individual with the cosmic principle is achieved, making one to transcend context-specific cultural grammar.

Within human body, Tripurasundarī is equated with the esoteric *kuṇḍalinī*. Now, let us see the description of the space where the Goddess is believed to be resting. Gorakhnātha, the most profound authority on *kuṇḍalinī*, has described it in his text *Amaraugha Śāsana*. Between the anus and the generative organ is *trikoṇa* (triangle) with three circles around it. In the triangle are perceived three knots of this root. In the three knots is the lotus in the centre of which *kuṇḍalinī* dwells in the middle of the triple path (*suṣumṇā, iḍā* and *piṅgalā*). *Kuṇḍalinī* is also known as *tripathagāminī* as it is led to the esoteric union with Śiva through the action of the set of three *nāḍī*s.

The triangulation does not end here. Gorakhnātha compares the rising of *kuṇḍalinī* with *mastaka* of the triangular fruit of the water-chestnut (*siṅghāṛā*). It is not a mere coincidence that while propitiating Durgā as Tripurasundarī, the flour of water-chestnut is consumed. Water-chestnut, that contains three local triangles (triad of triad) within a global form of triangle, came to signify the triad structures inherent in Indian tradition and Goddess worship. There is endless chain of homologization of triads. Since water-chestnut is perishable and seasonal Indian culinarists who always utilized emergent religious ideas to create new kind of dishes, created *samosā/siṅghāṛā* (fried food item), perhaps as a way to salute and appease the Mother Goddess. Eating *samosā* is a kind of ritual in India now. *Siṅghāṛā* is a *trikoṇaphalam* (fruit with three angles). Peanut (*mūṅgaphalī*) is *tribīja* (three-seeded). Cracking open peanut pods and consuming the nuts is the most popular pastime in India and that points to the inherent addiction of Indian mind towards the triadic things. *Kuṇḍalinī* is compared in *pañcastavi* with *trapuṣa* creeper which has a set of three leaves. *Bilva* leaves are found in bunch of three leaves, which is believed to represent three qualities (*sattva, rajas* and *tamas*). Three *nāḍīs* (*iḍā, piṅgalā* and *suṣumṇā*) are like the three eyes of Śiva. Popular custom of folding heart-shaped betel leaf into a triangle corresponds with the folding three energies of will, knowledge and action before internalizing.

Similarly, there is an obsession with *triveṇīs*. Anywhere if two rivers join, there are stories about an invisible third river merging at same point. Prayāg where Gaṅgā and Yamunā meet is the most sacred *triveṇī* as it is assumed that the invisible river Sarasvatī joins from the underground. Prayāg is also the king of *tīrtha*s described in detail in the Tīrtha Yātrā-Parva of *Mahābhārata*. The presiding deity of Prayāg is the Goddess of the Three Cities, Tripurasundarī, in the form of Lalitā. Prayāg is Lalitāpīṭha. There are three temples of Lalitā in Prayāg — Akṣaya Vaṭ is Kalyāṇī Lalitā, Jhūlā in Alopui and Lalitā Devī Temple in Meerapur.

Drawing a Sacred Triangle on India's Geobody

One can draw a triangle on the map of India to link three most sacred spots of the worship of Goddess of Three Cities, Tripurasundarī. Srinagar is the city established by Goddess Lalitā. The temple of Goddess Śārikā Cakreśvarī, the presiding deity of Kashmir at Hari Parbat in Srinagar city, is famous for the worship of the Goddess as Śrī-yantra in the north. The Śṛṅgerī-Śāradā Pīṭha on the bank of river Tuṅga and at the foot of Sahya mountain of the Western Ghāṭs in Chikmagalur district, Karnataka, is famous for the worship of Śrī-yantra in far south. Śaṅkarācārya himself had installed a Śrī-cakra here. The third vertex can be placed at the Udaipur Temple in the state of Tripurā where mother Tripurasundarī (Matabari, Kūrma Pīṭha) on a small hill near Radhakishorepur is worshipped in her fierce form. While Tripurā derives its name from the Goddess Tripurā, so do the places Srinagar and Śṛṅgerī. Thus, within India's geographical extant of triangle, there can be drawn various connecting triads between places and periods.

For me, the most exciting place to study the evolution of the Śrī-yantra worship appears to be the Wonder Triangle in Odisha — Lalitgiri, Udaigiri, Ratnagiri. These are the pilgrimage centres for the Buddhists, where massive excavation is being carried out by the Archaeological Survey of India (ASI). Lalitā is another name for the Goddess of the Three Cities, Tripurā. There are three rivers Gharghara (east), Sona (north) and Sindhu (south). There are three separate hills — Olasuni, Parabhadi and Landa. The ruins of Puṣpagiri University are being excavated here. The geographical location coupled with the fact that the region became famous for the cult of *siddhas* and entrepôt for the Nālandā monks to sail to South-East Asia make me to ponder over whether the Śrī-Vidyā cult originated in this perfectly triangular sacred space. I have some preliminary basis. The knowledge about Śrī-Vidyā appears to be simultaneous in Kashmir (through Śaṅkara's *guru*'s *guru*, Gauḍapāda), Tirumūḷar in south India as described in so detail in the seventh-century text *Tirumantiram* and South-East Asia, where Śrī-yantra diagrams have been found as far back as the seventh century.[9] It is during the same period that Bāṇabhaṭṭa wrote *Harṣacarita*. Since there is no mention about the visit of Xuanzang in Harṣa's court, the same may be presumed to be written during the first half of seventh century. In this work, Bāṇa wrote about the magical power of Śrī Parvata in Deccan. Śrī Parvata was also known for Siddha Nāgārjuna who appears to be a different person from the Mādhyamaka philosopher Nāgārjuna, also from the same region many centuries earlier. Thus, usage of terms *śrī* and *śrīṁ* can be traced to this period (seventh century onwards). The Śrī-Sūkta as an appendix in *Ṛgveda* appears to be a later

9 J.G. de Casparis, *Prasasti Indonesia* 2, Bandung: 1968, pp. 16ff.

insertion by the Siddha/Vedāntist masters only after the popularity of Śrī-Vidyā among Vedāntists, as the Ṛgvedic seers had no knowledge of the structure of written seed letters like *ae, ka, la, hrīṁ,* etc. which the Śrī-Sūkta eulogizes.

The riddle of simultaneous spread of Śrī-Vidyā to three different corners of Java, Kashmir and Śṛṅgerī can be resolved only if we centre the origin of Vidyā in the Wonder Triangle of Odisha. Moreover, in Odisha, triangular geography is a dominant theme. Purī–Cuttack–Bhubaneswar form another sacred triangle. Purī is also known as Śrīkṣetra in many old Tantras. In Jagannātha Purī itself, it is the triad of Jagannātha–Subhadrā–Balarāma which is the centre of holy pilgrimage for millions. The trade routes from Kaliṅga to Java and Bali have been explored by historians and everyone agrees that the popular cult of Śrī Devīs in the rice fields of Bali and Java originated from Kaliṅga. Śrīdevī itself is another epithet for Lalitā in her Lakṣmī aspect. There are also hints that Odisha was a major centre of Vajrayāna as well as Siddha tradition with so much emphasis on *maṇḍala* and *yantra* during the same period. The Śrī Kālacakra Maṇḍala of Buddhists originated somewhere in Odisha's Sambhalapur region which created the legend of Sambhala. The homonym, Śrī-cakra might have been created from similar sources and the diagram moved across the southern India and then to Java through navigation links as well as inland towards Nālandā and thence well-connected Kashmir, simultaneously.

Śrī-cakra and Śrī Kālacakra

Śrī-cakra and Śrī Kālacakra have structural similarity. Both are based on the nine-bodily hole theory and the assumption that body itself is a *maṇḍala/yantra*. It is Śrīcakrasaṁvara Tantra which is the progenitor of Śrī Kālacakra of Buddhists. Śrīcakrasaṁvara like Śrī-cakra is enclosed within three concentric circles (*tricakra*). David B. Gray has shown in his work *Shri Cakrasamvara Tantra: The Discourse of Heruka* (2007)[10] that it originated somewhere during the seventh century in eastern India since various botanical species mentioned in the text are found only in this region. Like Śrī-cakra, human body is the home of Śrīcakrasaṁvara and three bodies of Buddha — *dharmakāya*, *saṁbhogakāya* and *nirmāṇakāya* — each associated with a *cakra* of eight deity couples are imagined inside an individual body. Total twenty-four goddesses are correlated with twenty-four sacred sites scattered around India and internally with different body parts. The later-day Śakti Pīṭha tradition arising from Śrī-cakra has source in these Tantras. The term *saṁvara* denotes Supreme Bliss. (*Saṁ* is the bliss, *saṁ* is also to join, union. *Saṁvara* is to join the bliss of all Buddhas.) Hence, Śrīcakrasaṁvara is the techne to harness Supreme Bliss through the deployment of human body. It resonates so well with Śrī-cakra that both Śrī-cakra and Śrī Kālacakra can be seen as offsprings of Śrīcakrasaṁvara. In fact, Śrī Kālacakra was also known as Śrī-cakra and Arthur Avalon edited the Buddhist Kālacakra Tantra in vol. VII of his epic tāntric texts series with the title, *Shricakra Sambhara: A Buddhist Tantra*. The connections do not stop here. In the central triangle of Śrī-cakra, the practitioner believes that father figure Vārāhī and mother figure Kurukullā reside. Now, both of these are the father and mother figures in Buddhist Tantras also and associated with Śrīcakrasaṁvara or later Śrī Kālacakra. But, one cannot claim that these originated among the Buddhists only. There were plethora of sects including Śaiva (Kāpālikas, Kālāmukhas, Śākta) worshippers, Jaina, and many universities like Nālandā, Puṣpagiri, Vikramśilā and Odantipura which were emergent with fresh ideas for working out *sūtra*s (geometrical as well as syllabic) for cosmology. None of the

[10] David B. Gray, The *Cakrasamvara Tantra: The Discourse of Śrī Heruka*, New York: American Institute of Buddhist Studies, Columbia University Press, 2007.

twenty-four *pīṭhas* mentioned in Srīcakrasaṁvara Tantra is a Buddhist site. Thus, in all likelihood the text and practice were compiled from different sources of a common cultural milieu. The mention of places like Suvarṇadvīpa (Java), Kaliṅga, Oḍra and Kāmākhyā in the twenty-four holy sites corresponding to different deities further points out to the origin of this branch of Tantra in the Odisha region. Another interesting thing is that all these Tantras were classified as Yoginī Tantras among the Buddhists. The Yoginī cult was dominant in Odisha and even now ruins of many *cauṅsaṭha-yoginī* temples can be found there. Thus, I would pit for the origin of Śrī-cakra diagram to this triangular site of Buddhist learning in Odisha. In the ASI excavations at Udaigiri, a nine-enclosure sculptural *cakra*, constructed with bricks on an open ground, has already been discovered awaiting further researches by scholars.

Śrī or Tri?

Another interesting thing to happen was the substitution of *śrī* with *tri*. While *tri* is "three", the triad, and has etymological connection with the "crossing over", transcendence, so does *śrī*. Śrī-Vidyā is the science of engaging with triads to explore the path of transcendence. *Śrīṁ* is the seed syllable for the successful journey. *Śrīṁ* of Śrī-Vidyā is the phonetic *tīrtha*. *Tīrtha* is derived from *tri*. *Trāṇa* is derived from *tri*. Tārā is derived from *tri*. These terms connote salvation, so does the syllable *śrīṁ* of Śrī-Vidyā. There must be a phase when both terms co-existed and then later, *śrī* gained dominance and is now a universal honorific in India. I am reminded of the island of Sri Lanka whose northern coast is Trincomalee. Here, both *śrī* and *tri* were appropriated. At Kataragama in the region, there is a holy pilgrimage for Murugan. There a six-vertices star *yantra* is worshipped. The sacred geography of temples too is arranged in a six-vertices star pattern. Being in south and dominant Tamil-speaking region, the places should have been prefixed with Tamil *thiru* (derived from *śrī*), but the *śrī*/ *tri* prefix remains something to be explored. There is another interesting connection. The Vindhyavāsinī Shrine which lies on the same longitude and where the Goddess is worshipped as *bindu* — the central most dot of the inner triangle (Mahā-Tripurasundarī) — there are six holiest sites that also create double-triangle hexagons. Are these mere coincidences? Why is it that even outsiders like Megasthenes wrote about three-peaks mountain, Meros being one of these where Dionysus took rest along with his army for recuperation and which was a heavenly place? Was Megasthenes also influenced by India's triadic thinking whose highest conception is Śrī-yantra with its three-dimensional form as the Meru? What is the connection between Meru and Śrī-yantra?

4

Meru and Śrī-yantra

Śrī-yantra, the king among ritual diagrams, is also known as Meru. The three-dimensional Śrī-yantra is considered auspicious and the abode of Śiva. Śrī-yantra on the other hand is believed to be the diagrammatic representation of the sheaths of human consciousness arranged in the form of subtle *cakra*s at different levels. These *cakra*s are arranged in a linear order around the spinal cord. The highest *cakra*, *sahasrāra* at the peak of the crown, corresponds to the peak of Mt. Meru and to the central dot, the highest point in the three-dimensional Śrī-yantra. The spinal cord is also known as *meru-daṇḍa*. Śrī-yantra is the unfoldment of *kuṇḍalinī*. *Kuṇḍalinī* moved within Meru in *suṣumṇā nāḍī*. Within *suṣumṇā*, in *triguṇa nāḍī*, there are three sheaths. *Vajriṇī nāḍī* lies within *suṣumṇā* and *citriṇī* within *vajriṇī*. *Brahma nāḍī* is enclosed within *citriṇī* and it is what connects the Meru top, *sahasrāra cakra* with the triangular base where the coiled energy (*kuṇḍalinī*) resides in *mūlādhāra cakra*.

During the early stages of Indian civilization, Meru became synonymous with immortality. Indian thinking has this axiomatic formulation that the existence, though appears changing, has its foundation in the unchanging, immutable eternal *Brahman*; every being is supposed to be grounded on a solid foundation. This foundation is what holds the eternally moving cosmic cycle in space and time. The foundation is presumed to be elevated. Thus, mountains became sacred,

Śivaliṅgam became iconic representation of this reality, *kūrma* (tortoise) became sacred. The earth is believed to be carried on the back of a *kūrma*, a form of Viṣṇu's *avatāra*. It is one of the reasons that the image of Śrī-yantra is engraved on the image of tortoise to make it doubly auspicious. The tortoise not only lives in the nether world, below the terrestrial surface, but also is known for its longevity of life. The backbone in the human body which appears joined (*parva*) at knots like the *parvata* (mountain), became sacred as the Meru. The backside of human body where the spinal cord passes is also known as *pīṭha*. It is how the sacred centres of pilgrimage were created as various scales of *pīṭha* and *upapīṭha* across the Indian subcontinent.

Origin of the Concept of Meru

The exact origin of the term *Meru* may be found in the later Vedic period when the Aryans finally settled and a framework of geographical extant of the subcontinent was available with the thinkers. The first reference of Meru can be traced in the work of ancient Indian mathematician Piṅgala's *Candrahāsa*, where he discusses about Mt. Meru (Meru-Prastara) (*c.* 200 BCE, some also claim that he lived in 450 BCE, being the younger brother of the great grammarian Pāṇini). In *Chandaḥsūtras* (verses 8.23-27 while classifying poetic metres of long and short syllables), Piṅgala presents Mt. Meru (Meru-Prastara, "steps of Mount Meru").[1] This is better known as the Pascal's triangle though Piṅgala should be credited with the discovery of the summation rule for the arithmetic progression.

This is how a commentator on Piṅgala's *Chandaḥsūtras*, Halāyudha, explains (*fig.*1):

---

[1] A.N. Singh, "On the Use of Series in Hindu Mathematics", in *Osiris: Studies on the History and Philosophy of Science and on the History of Learning and Culture*, The David Engene Smith Presentation Volume, ed. George Sarton, vol. 1, January 1936, Amsterdam: Swets and Zeitlinger N.V., 1969, p. 623.

1

1 2 1

1 3 3 1

1 4 6 4 1

1 5 10 10 5 1

1 6 15 20 10 6 1

fig. 1: Mt. Meru

The sum of the series will be 2^n. Thus, Indian mathematicians had the knowledge of summation of series long back. Arithmetic and geometric series have been found in the earliest Vedic literature. Arithmetic series have been found in *Taittirīya Saṁhitā*. In *Vājasaneyī Saṁhitā*, there are *yugma* (even) and *ayugma* (odd) arithmetic series. A geometric series has been found in *Dīgha Nikāya* like 10, 20, 40 . . . 80,000.[2]

By the fifth century BCE, Indians had the knowledge of calculating the sum of series of natural numbers. *Bṛhaddevatā* (500–400 BCE) was composed by Śaunaka as a catalogue to Vedic deities. He put the sum of the series of natural numbers up to 1,000 as 5,00,499. 2 + 3 + 4 + . . . 1,000 = 5,00,499.[3]

In *Kalpasūtra* of Bhadrabāhu (350 BCE), the sum of geometric progression up to number 8,192 is correctly calculated.

1 + 2 + 3 + 4 + . . . 8,192 = 16,383.[4]

Thus, it is not that Piṅgala worked the method to calculate sum of the series for the first time. The series and its progression were held in awe, both in progeny of cows and the geometry of fire-altar (*yajña* place). The technical term for

---

2 A.N. Singh, n. 1, pp. 607-08.

3 Ibid., p. 608.

4 Ibid.

progression "series" was known as *średhī*.[5] This is derived from *śreṇī* — the series of distinct things. *Śreṇī* implied growth, progression of wealth and anything else. It is how the seed phoneme, *śra*, was used in Śrī-Sūkta, the appendix of *Ṛgveda*, to depict the Goddess of wealth, prosperity and fertility. Śrī-Sūkta later became hymn to Goddess Lakṣmī.

How close this numerical series is connected with the cultural concept gets clearer once we realize that Sanskrit term for "series" is *dhana* also. *Dhana* is the term for wealth. The first term in the series is called *ādi-dhana* and in a finite series, the last term is called the *antya-dhana*.[6] The increment from one unit to another in the numerical series is *vṛddhi*. *Āya* has been used as a term for natural numbers. *Āya* (income) and *vṛddhi* are the terms deployed for prosperity, growth in wealth and any positive growth.

It is interesting to see this connection even in the history of Indian economic system. Commerce was carried by the guild, known as *śreṇīs*. *Śreṇīs* always aimed for *vṛddhi* in *dhana*. So, the terms which were being limited to the mathematical treatises spread like a Foucauldian techne across other realms like economics, philosophy and spirituality. This may be the reason that *śra* which stands for progressive growth, began to be widely used as prefix before proper names. *Śrī* as prefix might have begun to be used as an auspicious term for everlasting infinite growth. The climax was reached with the art of constructing Śrī-yantra where there is a series of auspicious triangles which further generate self-similar auspicious structures.

When Piṅgala developed the Meru-Prastara, it is likely that the term Mt. Meru was already in vogue. The *Mahābhārata*

---

5 A.N. Singh, n. 1, p. 608.

6 Ibid., p. 609.

theme had been discussed in Patañjali's *Mahābhāṣya*, a commentary on Pāṇini's grammar, in second century BCE. Thus, *Mahābhārata* must have been composed by the time Piṅgala developed his Meru-Prastara. Piṅgala found the formula of calculating number of variations of a metre containing *a* syllables as 2^a. The great aesthetician Bharat Muni (who gave the concept of eight *rasas*/savouring) used the concept of Meru-Prastara involving six and twenty-six syllables in his *magnum opus, Nāṭya-Śāstra*. Caraka, the court physician of Kuṣaṇa ruler Kaniṣka, deployed the same method to arrive at total number of combinations to sixty-three out of six substances, in his treatise *Caraka Saṁhitā* (first century CE).

The idea of Meru became so popular that it became a favourite theme for Purāṇic composers to describe the geography of India. Meru became the centre of the earth. Meru became the spinal cord of earth. We will see the description of Meru in *Mahābhārata* and Purāṇas in next section.

Āryabhaṭa and Meru in Mathematics

Meru came for serious scrutiny by mathematicians from the fifth century onwards. Āryabhaṭa, India's greatest mathematician, who is credited with the discovery of zero, Pythagoras Theorem, and who recalculated *nakṣatra cakra* and fixed *ayaṇāṁśa* (astronomically, it is the amount of precession and astrologically, the longitudinal distance between tropical (*sāyana*) and sideral (*nirayaṇa*) zodiacs) as zero in CE 499, elevated Meru as the astronomical place. In the masterly work, *Āryabhaṭīya* (CE 499), Āryabhaṭa describes Meru as follows:

> Meru is exactly 1 yojana in height. It is light-producing, surrounded by the Himavat mountains, situated in the middle of the Nandana forest, made of jewels and cylindrical in shape. —Gola section, verse 11

> The heaven and the Meru mountain are at the centre of the land, the hell and the Baḍavāmukha are at the centre of the water. The gods residing at the Meru mountain and the demons residing at the Baḍavāmukha consider themselves positively and permanently below each other.[7] —verse 12

This sums up the astronomers' perspectives on Meru. The earth was viewed in two parts — half full of ocean and half full of land. The centres of them were the poles. Meru was the mountain at the North Pole and the Baḍavāmukha, a pit (*mukha*/mouth) at the South Pole. Meru was the heaven, Baḍavāmukha, the hell. Meru was the city of gods and demons lived at the South Pole. Meru mountain was viewed as 1 *yojana* high, i.e. approximately 8 km, which is very similar to the high peaks of the Himalayas. It was viewed as circular in shape (*sarvato vr̥tte*), full of gems (*ratna*) and light emanating (*prabhākaro*). Possibly, Indian astronomers were not aware of the land beyond the impregnable Himalayas. Though, there were certain routes to Central Asia or to south-west China, no one could have imagined that there was a land beyond the impregnable Himalayas. Thus, Mt. Meru, even for the astronomers, was located amidst the Himavat. That was the highest latitudinal point.

This becomes clearer from two verses in *Āryabhaṭīya*. The Indian prime meridian was marked passing through Ujjayinī, the capital of Avantī. The prime meridian intersected the equator at Laṅkā. Thus, Laṅkā in *Rāmāyaṇa* is not the Sri Lanka

---

7 Āryabhaṭa, *Āryabhaṭīya*, ed. Kripa Shankar Singh, New Delhi: Indian National Science Academy, 1976, pp. 121-22; also see, Walter Eugene, tr. *The Āryabhaṭīya of Āryabhaṭa*, Chicago: University of Chicago Press, 1930; Satya Prakash, *Founders of Science in Ancient India*, New Delhi: The Research Institute of Ancient Scientific Studies, 1965; B.S. Yadav and Man Mohan, eds., *Ancient Indian Leaps into Mathematics*, Birkhauser: Springer, 2010.

beyond Rāma-Setu, but the astronomer's Laṅkā at 0° latitude and 0° longitude. Prime meridian itself is a kind of *meru-daṇḍa* for the moving earth. It is the assumed centre of earth. The prime meridian or *meru-daṇḍa* linked Laṅkā to Meru mountain at the northernmost point and the Baḍavāmukha at the southernmost point.[8] In fact, Āryabhaṭa caused much debate among the coming generation of astronomers with his precise earmarking of different cities. If at the equator, Laṅkā is the city at prime meridian (0° longitude), Yavakoṭi is at 90° east on the equator, Romaka is at 90° west of Laṅkā and Siddhapura is at 180° from Laṅkā and hence diametrically opposite to Laṅkā. I am of the view that Yavakoṭi is Java (Java was known as Yava) and Romaka is for Roman empire, which lies west to India. Since the known world at the time extended from Rome to Java and the Himalayas to Laṅkā, the extreme places were thus marked for a complete description of *bhūgola*. Siddhapura lying at the equator and opposite Laṅkā may be the source of the mythical land of Sambhala among Tibetan Buddhists or Siddhapura among the Hindus that still evokes awe and inspiration for hundreds of seekers after the truth. These myths also spawn plethora of stories about sages living in Siddhapura/Siddhāśrama who continue to meddle with human affairs.

Thus, Āryabhaṭa has to be credited for elevating Meru as an astronomical concept for geographers and giving credibility to the conception of Meru that began to flourish by this time. This had to do with two events. First, the Buddhist calendar observed the first millennium sometimes between late fourth century and middle fifth century CE. *Sahasra* was considered the maximum attainable terrestrial number. Second, the *nirayaṇa* (fixed) and *sāyana* (moving) zodiacs coincided in the

---

8 Āryabhaṭa, *Āryabhaṭīya*, ed. Kripa Shankar Singh, New Delhi: Indian National Science Academy, 1976, pp. 123-24.

year CE 285 (20 March) when *ayaṇāṁśa* was zero. The completion of precession followed by the millennium point in the popular calendar that determined rituals was enough to have fuelled the millenarian movement which we find cropping up in the concept of *avatāra*, Kali-yuga and proliferation of Purāṇas and deities, both among the Hindus and Buddhists. Āryabhaṭa evoked literati's interests in mathematics.

Āryabhaṭa also worked on Piṅgala's Meru-Prastara and expanded the work. Āryabhaṭa created *citighana* (pile-cubes) which means "the solid content of a pile in the shape of a pyramid on a triangular base".[9] He derived rules for the summation of squares and cubes in this work using *cidghana* (like Meru-Prastara):

$$1^2 + 2^2 + \ldots + n^2 = \frac{n(n+1)(2n+1)}{2}$$

$$1^3 + 2^3 + \ldots + n^3 = (1 + 2 + \ldots + n)^2.$$

Citighana, involving a pyramid made up on a triangular base, was an advancement over Piṅgala's Meru-Prastara.

Varāhamihira, a contemporary of Āryabhaṭa and who lived in Ujjain, mentions in *Pañca-Siddhāntikā*, particulary, *Sūrya-Siddhānta* about Mt. Meru to be at the North Pole.[10] It was Varāhamihira's disciple, Brahmagupta, who wrote lengthy criticism of *Āryabhaṭīya*. Āryabhaṭa's famous disciples like Bhāskara I (CE 629), Deva (CE 689), Lalla and the commentators on their work created a vibrant discourse about geography and astronomy and all of these added to the popularity of the concept of Meru.

---

9 A.N. Singh, n. 1, p. 617.

10 G.S. Pandey, ed., *A Study in the Mathematical Contributions of Varahamihira and His Heritage*, Shimla: Indian Institute of Advanced Study, 2010.

Meru in Mahābhārata and Purāṇas

Since *Mahābhārata* is older than Piṅgala's *Chandaḥsūtras*, Piṅgala might have appropriated the concept of Mt. Meru to describe his method to sum up a series in popular parlance. Book VI of *Mahābhārata*, also known as the Bhīṣma-Parva that contains the famous *Bhagavad-Gītā*, has preceding section on Jambu-Khaṇḍa, describing the geography of India. There are six *varṣaparvas* (mountain ranges dividing the continent). Those are Himavat, Hemakūṭa, Niṣāda, Nīla, Śveta and Śṛṅgavat. Sañjaya said to Dhṛtarāṣṭra, the king of Kauravas, that the Kauravas and other characters in *Mahābhārata* lived in Bhāratavarṣa, and in its north is the Himavat. Beyond the Himavat is the Harivarṣa. Between Mālyavat and Gandhamādanavarṣa lays the mountain Meru made of gold. Meru is like a *maṇḍala*, a globular mountain. Sañjaya narrates how, the sun, moon and all *nakṣatras* (asterisms) always circumambulate Meru.[11] This also points to the conception of Meru as the terrestrial North Pole. The myth of Meru covered with gold has been narrated in detail. Everything is golden — birds, peaks and even the juice of the fruit *jambu* (rose-apple); whatever it touches turns into gold. The jewels and gems, and all the mountains abounded in precious stones are part of Meru. *Mahābhārata* mentions that a fourth of the gold and *ratnas* available at Meru is enjoyed by Kubera, the guardian deity of wealth. And only a sixteenth part of that wealth is available for mankind. Many Purāṇas narrate how Laṅkā became the city of gold by weaving the story that when Meru was being carried from the celestial world, a part of it fell down in Laṅkā. Since, parts of Meru are believed to be scattered as precious gems and minerals, the myth of *pārasa* stone, which can transmute anything into gold, has connection with this story in *Mahābhārata*. The quest for *pārasa* stone set

---

11 K.M. Ganguli, tr., *The Mahābhārata*, Calcutta: Bharata Press, 1883-96.

many a journeys in medieval India and the term entered the vocabulary of the *siddha*s as well as *bhakti* poets to describe the effect of grace and touch of a *bhakta* by the *guru*/divinity.

Sañjaya describes further how Vedic sages of lore like Nārada and Viśvāvasu, and many unheard sages like the Hāhās and Hūhūs, living at Meru and composing diverse hymns. Paśupati sports with Umā over there and the sacred river Gaṅgā, also called Bhāgīrathī, falls on the delightful lake of Candramas. Sañjaya then describes about the ageless human beings living in the vicinity of Meru. On the western side of Meru, lies Ketumāla and Jambu-Khaṇḍa. The human beings are long-lived for 10,000 years and they too bear golden complexion. There is neither sickness nor old age nor sorrow. *Mahābhārata* describes Kailāsa as the huge mountain of Hemakūṭa, thus differentiating it from Mt. Meru.

Mt. Meru is the *axis mundi* of the earth, in various Purāṇas like *Bhāgavata Purāṇa* and *Viṣṇu Purāṇa,* composed during the later Gupta period. Purāṇas narrate how on the summit of Mt. Meru, Brahmā built a city where there is no death, the city of Amarāvatī (immortality). The reference is also found about Amarāvatī as the city of immortals on Meru peak in the Āraṇyaka-Parva in *Mahābhārata*.

Padma Purāṇa mentions Meru mountain has the configuration of a *dhatūrā* flower and a bell. Both are cylindrical in shape, and in one way resonates the shape of Śivaliṅgam. *Vāyu Purāṇa* mentions that Meru mountain has colours on its sides: white on the east, black on the west, red on the north and yellow on the south. *Bhāgavata Purāṇa* mentions Meru mountain to be abundant with *jambu* tree (*Syzygium jambos*). These break open and the juice runs like rivers in the southern area of Ilāvartta that transmutes clay into gold and creates the Jambunada. One must remember that Buddha had his first *jñāna* experience under a *jambu* tree. Thus *jambu* tree is also significant as a bliss-providing tree and as a representative of the Meru complex. The *jambu* fruit is regarded as a tonic for the brain and liver. The flowers of *jambu* tree are believed to be anti-pyretic. The seeds are anti-dysentery. Seeds have anaesthetic property too. The powdered leaves can be rubbed on the bodies of those infected of smallpox, which was quite rampant in India, and it produces a cooling and soothing effect. In one way, *jambu* tree is a single-window source for effective treatment of most of the common diseases. This might be the reason for linking *jambu* with Meru, the Utopia of immortality. And India, believed as to be the only *karmabhūmi*, was named as Jambudvīpa.

One of the eighteen major Purāṇas, *Brahmāṇḍa Purāṇa* that contains every available knowledge about the geography of India and cosmology narrates in detail the characteristics of Meru mountain. *Brahmāṇḍa Purāṇa* also contains *Lalitā Sahasranāma*, composed as a hymn to Lalitā, the goddess of Śrī-yantra in the 36th chapter titled Lalitopākhyāna. Thus, the description of Meru for which Śrī-yantra is the indexical representation, in this important text, is highly significant. *Brahmāṇḍa Purāṇa* 1.2.15 describes Jambudvīpa as well as Meru.[12] Meru is the most beautiful mountain with four colours. The shape of Meru is circular and it originated from the umbilical cord of Brahmā, thus born of the unmanifest one. It is thus on par with Brahmā himself. Meru, the golden mountain, is in the middle of two circles.

Brahmāṇḍa Purāṇa describes how Sumeru shines like a midday sun.[13] The entire mountain is surrounded by golden world and is the abode of the groups of *deva*s, *gandharva*s, *nāga*s, *rākṣasa*s and *apsarase*s. Meru is the earthly heaven indeed.

---

12 G.V. Tagare, tr., *The Brahmāṇḍa Purāṇa*, part I, New Delhi: Motilal Banarsidass, 1983, pp. 141-49.

13 Ibid., p. 146.

It is the ultimate Utopia for Indian mind where there is neither sorrow nor old age, disease, or lack of any splendid thing.

Meru Goes Asian

The Purāṇic period witnessed the spread of idea from compositions to constructions. The climax of this phase was the construction of the Angkor Wat Temple in Cambodia. The Khmers ruled the state during the medieval period. In CE 1000, Sūryavarman, ascended the throne of Kāmboja and ruled for over fifty years. He laid the foundations of the city of Angkor. Angkor Wat, the city of temple, is located near the capital city of the ancient Khmer empire. The temple is a representation of Mt. Meru, and dedicated to Viṣṇu and later to Buddha. There are strong reasons to believe that this was built to duplicate Mt. Meru, as a way to declare the Khmer capital as the *axis mundi* of the world. The name Khmer itself contains the root *mer*. Meru — building by the emperors of Kh-Mer empire reveals the working of harmonies in Asian history.

Another world famous Buddhist temple is the Borobodur. Dating between CE 750 and 842 it is located near the city of Yogyakarta in central Java. It was built in three tiers and the aerial view clearly establishes Śrī-yantra pattern, the Meru. The complex was built by the Śailendra dynasty to illustrate the different phases of the soul's progression towards *nirvāṇa* and episodes from the life of Buddha. But, the stylistics appear to be taken directly from Amarāvatī in India. We should keep in mind how Amarāvatī finds reference in *Mahābhārata* as the city on top of Mt. Meru. Since, Buddhists and Hindus shared common cultural matrix, and much of the symbols, representations, myths, *kathā*s were common, appropriated through interaction with each other, Mt. Meru also entered the Buddhist imagination. It would not be improper to say that *stūpa* building which was undertaken at a large scale under Aśoka was merely a belief in duplicating the mountain of immortality, Meru. *Stūpa*s are semi-hemispheric and correspond to the shape described for Mt. Meru. For the first time *stūpa*s were built at Sāñcī, Bharhut and Gayā. But, by the first century, Sātavāhanas who ruled from Andhra built the *stūpa* at Amarāvatī. Close to Amarāvatī in the Guntur district is the *stūpa* at Nāgārjunakoṇḍa, for the famed Buddhist saint, Ārya Nāgārjuna. The Nāgārjunakoṇḍa Hill is the famed Śrī Parvata, whose mention one often finds in the literature of the Gupta period. Now, Śrī Parvata and Amarāvatī are the terms also associated with the mythical Meru. In all possibility, Amarāvatī *stūpa* was built to merely duplicate Mt. Meru, the *axis mundi* for the Sātavāhana kings.

The Borobodur complex with its stylistic debt to Amarāvatī and architectural pattern resembling a Śrī-yantra has much to do with the propagation of Śrī-Vidyā cult. *Śrī* as a honorific is very popular in Bali, Indonesia. Add to this an interesting fact that in each rice field of Bali, there is a small shrine to Śrīdevī, the goddess of Śrī-Vidyā which is believed to be inhabited by this goddess of bounty of harvest and prosperity. Thus, the Borobodur complex in Bali as a human construction to replicate Mt. Meru seems certain.

It is not that the idea of Meru spread only towards the east. The depiction of Meru has been discovered in the Dunhuang. Scenes of the heavens above Mt. Meru have been discovered from the Mogao Cave Complex, Cave No. 285 near Dunhuang. The images date back to CE 538-39.

Buddhists like Hindus, believed Meru to be the centre of the universe, the *axis mundi*. The Pāli canon records the historical Buddha mentioning about it, some canons also mention that Buddha visited Meru. Vasubandhu provided description of the Meru-centred universe in *Abhidharmakośa* at the same time when Āryabhaṭa and Varāhamihira were debating over it. The Buddhist conception of cosmos as

Cakraval as the flat disc rotating like a wheel has Meru in the axle hole. Finally, Buddhists like Hindus settled for Mt. Kailāsa (Kang) as the abode of Gods by the eighth century. It is amazing that Mt. Kailāsa does have a Meru (spinal cord)-like structure on its back. And this adds to the ingenuity of unravelling Meru.

Śrī-yantra and Meru

There is no literature about Śrī-yantra or Śri-Vidyā before sixth century CE. Even if we take into account the belief that Śaṅkarācārya inherited the knowledge about Śrī-cakra from his *guru*, Gauḍapāda and he in turn from Govinda, that does not take us beyond the sixth century. Śaṅkarācārya composed *Saundarya-Laharī* as a devotional hymn to the goddess of Śrī-cakra and also Tārā-Prabhr̥tikā for Mother Tārā,[14] a closely associated deity with Śrī-cakra where Kurukullā, the red form of Tārā, is the mother principle and lords over the innermost triangle.

I would like to point out that Śrī-yantra, as an indexical representation of mythical Meru, emerged only after the debates that Indian mathematicians engaged during the fifth and sixth centuries. It was Meru-Prastara of Piṅgala, which when advanced by Āryabhaṭa in the form of *citighana*, entered social space. Since, the trigonometry too was developed by Āryabhaṭa, triangle with its unique properties and simplicity and the fact that even mythical Meru mountain was supposed to have a triangular base, emerged as the front runner among different geometric shapes.

Śrī-yantra emerged as a result of Meru-Prastara of triangles. But, Śrī-yantra emerged only under the influence of

[14] S.K. Ramachandra Rao, *The Tantrik Practices in Srividya*, Bangalore: Kalpatharu Research Academy, 1990, p. 179; also see S.K. Ramachandra Rao, *Srividya-Kosa*, Delhi: Sri Satguru Publications, 2005.

mathematicians. This might be the reason that Piṅgala who discovered Meru-Prastara has been immortalized by naming a major *nāḍī* associated with Śrī-yantra/Meru within the human body. *Piṅgalā* is the solar *nāḍī* and one of the three *nāḍī*s — others being *suṣumṇā* and *iḍā* — in the *kuṇḍalinī* psycho-anatomy. But, there appears to be various astronomical facts behind the emergence of the diagram/structure. Śrī-yantra emerges from the interlocking of nine triangles. There is a symmetric pattern generated by this interlocking of isosceles triangles. The nine prime triangles have twenty-seven points. The triangle represents three fires — sun, moon and the earthly fire. Astronomically, triangle represents the close relationship between three cosmic bodies — earth, sun and moon. Nine triangles correspond to nine planets in Hindu astronomy and twenty-seven points to the twenty-seven asterisms (*nakṣatra*s). The knowledge of *nakṣatra cakra* involved the highest mathematics. Āryabhaṭa and his successors developed sophisticated mathematics for *nakṣatra* movement upon which Indian ritual calendars were based. In the conception of Meru, the mention of *nakṣatra* revolving around Meru is a certain mention.

Śrī-yantra resolved the different knowledge traditions through an abstract representation. One can see how the sixteen outer petals correspond to sixteen vowels as well as sixteen digits of the moon, with sixteenth as *ṣoḍaśa kalā*, the Tripurasundarī. Similarly, one can see how 16 + 8 points of lotus petals of two outer enclosure and 27 (9 x 3) points of the prime triangles add to 51, a sacred number in Tantras, the sacred pilgrimage as well as Sanskrit grammar. The vowels and consonants add to 50 and taken with *kṣa* (the sum of the consonants and the grossest manifestation of *vāc*), it becomes 51, which is the total number of *śakti pītha*s.

Śrī-cakra is a representation of Meru, but Meru is also deployed to describe its inner principles. There are three ways to create Śrī-cakra. When it is drawn on a flat surface, it is the *bhū-pṛṣṭha*. When *yantra* is inscribed on a tortoise shell type elevation, it is *kacchapa-pṛṣṭha* (tortoise). But, when it is built on an elevated platform with a peak and *cakras* at different elevations, it is *meru-pṛṣṭha*. Even the lay out of Śrī-yantra is known as *meru-prastara* like the Pascal triangle discovered by Piṅgala. Meru-Prastara of a Śrī-cakra is the pattern of *cakras* arranged in Meru form and this is meant to describe the universe as emanation from the central point (*sṛṣṭi karma*).

Śrī-yantra is believed to bestow the devotee enormous wealth, long life and good health. These are the properties of mythical Meru like abundance of gold, deathlessness and joy. There is an interesting correlation between Śrī-yantra, Meru and the metal gold. Gold does not rust and this symbolizes its property of agelessness, hence immortality. Gold always glitter that manifests the eternal *lāvaṇya* (charm) of a Ṣoḍaśī (Goddess of Śrī-cakra worshipped in the form of sixteen-year old young maiden corresponding to the sixteenth digit of the moon, i.e. the digit of immortality). Gold is used as *rasa par excellence* in Ayurvedic formulations in the Indian medical system. Gold has the property to heal someone even on the deathbed. Gold ash (*suvarṇa bhasma*) makes one charming and younger. So, even the therapeutic of gold has this property of anti-ageing effect. The golden Mt. Meru is believed to be the abode of the young, charming and immortals.

In Śrī-Vidyā *sādhanā*, there are various levels of practices. But, the most supreme is the inner meditation in which one's own body is imagined to be the Śrī-cakra, the *axis mundi* of the universe. Since, in a moving cosmos, it is the centre that does not move and hence not prone to change and the associated decay, death, old age; by assuming oneself as the Meru, a practitioner, in fact, tends to generate anti-ageing processes through self-actualization. The centre always transcend the circle and not bound by the law of the centre. The practitioner thereby creates a short cut path towards transcendence.

Meru is the imaginative landscape that quenches the human quest for a terrestrial plane of immortality and transcendence; a centre that is unbound, changeless, ageless and eternal. Indian civilization has strived constantly to duplicate and actualize this landscape in art and architecture. Śrī-yantra is the synthesis of different routes to apprehend Meru, the peak of immortality. Śrī-yantra is the most abstract representation which combines the Hindu and Buddhist belief systems; Āgama and Vedic systems; art and architecture; algebra and geometry; recursion and singularity; cosmology and geography; ritual and wisdom; grammar and arbitrary images; *mantra*s and visualization; skill and intellect; devotion and perfection. It is constructed upon the use of combinatorial mathematics. In my understanding, Śrī-yantra is the combinatorial matrix of Indian civilization. It is the Meru of Indian civilization. It holds in its inner enclosure the nectar of continuity and immortality of the Indian civilization.

5

Śrī-yantra
Structural Properties

ŚRĪ-YANTRA is a double diagram. It is at the same time a *yantra* as well as a *maṇḍala*. *Yantra* is a pure geometric configuration without iconographic representations, whereas *maṇḍala* is a filled space with various deities representing various aspects of reality. Śrī-yantra can be utilized for meditation and studies by secular psychologists as well as the esoteric practitioners. It is context sensitive, depending upon visualizer's own perspective. It is like looking at the moon. Just as the shadow over the moon appears to some as hare, to others as deer and to many as tree, Śrī-yantra appears differently to different observers.

Tantrarāja Tantra[1] mentions about 940 *yantra*s but, Śrī-yantra holds the crown position among *yantra*s. I would term it as the acme of Indian civilization.

Śrī-yantra is drawn of nine triangles, four pointed upward and five pointed downward, that intersect and interlock to form forty-two small triangles around a central small triangle. Such interlocking of triangles that produce many times more the number of primary triangles is extraordinary. Triangle itself holds a very important position in Eastern civilization, particularly in India which has the geographical extension of

---

[1] Lakshmana Shastri, *The Tantraraja Tantra*: Tantrik Texts, vol. VIII, ed. Arthur Avalon, London: Luzac, 1919.

a triangle (peninsula fits neatly in a triangle). The generative organ of a woman is placed inside a triangular space and, in India, triangle became an iconic signifier of the *śakti* principle, the dynamic force of creation. Śrī-yantra though involves different geometrical shapes like circle and square, it is the triangular shape which is predominant.

Number 9 is another important number in the scaling of number 3. It is to mention that how the idea of Meru-Prastara (Pascal triangle) and Mt. Meru as the mythical *axis mundi* of the world gained currency after Āryabhaṭa's work in the fifth century CE. Āryabhaṭa also worked on the series involving square as well as cube of the numbers. Thus, in all likelihood number 3 and its square number 9, gained sudden prominence after his classic work. Moreover, the body-centricity emerged to shape the iconographic and sculptural boom during the Gupta period when idols were being installed in temples and homes, *mudrā*s were being discovered to propitiate divinities and the psycho-anatomy of *kuṇḍalinī* was being debated among proliferating esoteric sects. The practitioners observed that there are nine holes in the human body. They also imagined about the manifestation of the universe from subtler to grosser and the concentric sheaths one after another like the onion peels. The audible sound emerges as the grosser form of *parā vāc*, so did laughter from the unmanifest to the audible guffaw and finally the whole universe was supposed to follow the same path of graded revelation. In fact, Indian thinking was inherently fractal. Similar patterns recur in different sheaths. And the tendency to correlate analogous and homologous structures is found across the full spectrum. It was assumed that the understanding of even a single layer can open the understanding of the subtlest eternal, immutable *Brahman*. *Yantra*s emerged as the cosmic diagrams to understand the singularity underneath the plurality of phenomena.

Śrī-yantra: An Enneagram of Human Body

Nine holes in the human body correspond to nine wheels. These became *cakra*s as enunciated in verse 2 (*tena navarāndhrarūpo dehaḥ*) and verse 3 (*navacakrarūpam śrīcakram*) of *Bhavanopaniṣad*.[2] The human body with its nine holes itself was imagined to be the ultimate *guru* in the sixth verse of *Bhavanopaniṣad*. Śrī-yantra is believed to be a geometric form of the human body. Now, the correspondence of number 9 with nine orifices in human body (in women, though it is ten, in the patriarchal esoteric world, they could never unravel the secret of women's body and assumed the women's orifices to be the mirror images of man's body) was a significant discovery. Add to this fact that the gestation period in human beings is nine lunar months. The discoverers linked the individual gestation growth with the form of a Śrī-yantra. [The gestation period from the time of conception to birth is 266 days or nine lunar months. Doctors calculate 280 days from the first day of the Last Menstrual Period (LMP).] Śrī-yantra emerges with the intersection of nine triangles, but it has also been constructed with nine concentric sheaths. Thus, number 9 was employed to its fullest while constructing Śrī-yantra.

Five downward pointing triangles representing *śakti* intersect with four upward pointing triangles representing Śiva, forming forty-three triangles. Interestingly, the design crops up with only eight triangles, four upwards and four downwards. The ninth triangle does not interlock with any triangle. It is independent. It is the fifth Śakti triangle with apex pointing downward. Heinrich Zimmer mentions in the *Myth and Symbols in Indian Art and Civilization* (1946):

---

2 Sitaram Shastri, *Kaula and Other Upanishads with Commentary by Bhaskar Raya*, Tantrik Texts, vol. XI, ed. Arthur Avalon, London: Luzac, 1922, pp. 37-40.

> The Absolute is to be visualized by the concentrating devotee as a vanishing point or dot, the drop (*bindu*), amidst the interplay of all the triangles. This *bindu* is the power-point, the invisible, elusive centre from which the entire diagram expands. And now, whereas four of the Śakti triangles link with their represented *vāhinī*-counterparts, the fifth or innermost triangle, remains over, to unite with the invisible point. This is the Primal Śakti, consort of the transcendental Śiva, creative energy as a female manifestation of the pure, quiescent *Brahman*, the Great Original.[3]

Thus, the fifth triangle is supposed to interlock with *bindu*.

This central equilateral triangle has played the most interesting role in the evolution of Śrī-yantra into a crown-*maṇḍala*. I have my own take. In human body, eight holes are in symmetry. Two eyes, two ears, two nostrils are in bilateral symmetry. The mouth and the organ of evacuation are in transversal symmetry, with mouth being the upper orifice for the intake of food and the downward orifice its mirror image for evacuation of the waste. But, it is the ninth hole which is not interlocked with its other in human body. The ninth orifice interlock with external "other", that creates *yamala*, conjugal pair. Thus, the interlocking of eight triangles, leaving aside ninth triangle, does correspond to the orificial position of human body. Interestingly, this ninth circle is the source of creation, both in the male and the female body. The ninth triangle as the creatrix became the emanation triangle in Śrī-yantra.

The ninth triangle is an equilateral triangle and at the centre of it is *bindu* (dot), the abode of the goddess of Śrī-yantra, Lalitā Tripurasundarī. *Bindu* is the in-centre also since this is also the centre of the circle which encloses the bunch of

---

3 Heinrich Zimmer, *Myths and Symbols in Indian Art and Civilization* (1946), ed. Joseph Campbell, Princeton: Princeton University Press, 1992, p. 147.

triangles. *Bindu* contains the potentiality of the universe within itself. *Bindu* too is believed to be consisting of three aspects, called *nāda, kāla* and *bindu*.

At the centre of the *bindu* is Kāmakalā, which has three *bindus*. One is red, one is white and one is mixed. The red *bindu* is Kurukullā (the female form), the white *bindu* is Varāhī (the male form), and the mixed *bindu* is the union of Śiva and Śakti, within our own human body as Śrī-cakra. Varāhī, the father-form, gives four *dhātus* to the child and Kurukullā, the mother-form, gives five *dhātus* to the child. These represent the nine *dhātus* of the human body (seven *dhātus* of human body in Ayurveda are chile/plasma (*rasa*), blood (*rakta*), flesh (*māṁsa*), fat (*meda*), bone (*asthi*), marrow (*majjā*), semen (*śukra*)). Hair and skin were added since these two also grow from the food and support body. These are also known as nine gems (*navaratna)* and described in chapter V of *Tantrarāja Tantra*.[4]

Varāhī's four triangles are twelve (4 x 3) *kalās* of the sun or the twelve zodiac constellations. Kurukullā's five triangles are the fifteen (5 x 3) *kalās* of the moon constituting fifteen lunar *tithis*. Triplication in caused by three *guṇas* of *sattva, rajas* and *tamas*.

Basic Structure of Śrī-yantra

Now, the whole structure can be looked differently, as stated it is context-specific. Let us have a cursory look at the different enclosures first, before we delve into its mathematical properties.

The fourteen-sided polygon is formed with the intersection of eight triangles (as stated, ninth is independent) which contains forty-three triangles. It is enclosed within a circle. The circle may signify the *cakra*, the eternal movement of *kāla* (time) under which the whole manifestation is bound. There

---

[4] Avalon, Introduction, n. 1, pp. 20-21.

is an eight-petals enclosure on the circumference of the circle. Surrounding the eight-petal sheath is a sixteen-petal circle. Then there is another trinity, concentric three circles (*trivalaya*) and at the outermost part, there are three lines forming a square called *bhūpura*. Each side of *bhūpura* has a gate.

There are two ways to understand Śrī-yantra — from inside to outside (*sṛṣṭi karma* — emanation hierarchy) or from outside to inside (*saṁhāra karma* — dissolution stages). We are taking here the outer to inner progression.

Nine *cakra*s are:

1. *Trailokyamohana cakra* — space between outer square (*bhūpara*) and three concentric circle (*trivalaya*)

2. *Sarvasaparipūraka cakra* — sixteen petals
3. *Sarvasaṅkṣobhana cakra* — eight petals
4. *Sarvasaubhāgyadāyaka cakra* — fourteen triangles (*caturdaśa koṇa*)
5. *Sarvārthasādhaka cakra* — ten triangles (outer *dasara*)
6. *Sarvarakṣākara cakra* — ten triangles (inner *dasara*)
7. *Sarvarogahara cakra* — eight triangles (*aṣṭa koṇa*)
8. *Sarvasiddhiprada cakra* — inverted primary triangle
9. *Sarvānandamaya cakra* — *bindu* — full of all bliss.

It is interesting to observe that the whole geometric figure is encapsulated within trinities. The central diagram is determined by the triangles, but other sheaths are also following the rule of three. The outer square has three lines, the outer concentric circles are three. Thus, even though different geometrical figures are involved, three as a number determines their positioning. I would like to further add that this trinitarian system extends to the tradition as a whole.

Vidyā	*Krama*	*Yoga*	*Sect*	*Tradition*
Kāḍi	Kālī	Kuṇḍalinī	Samayācāra	Dakṣiṇamūrti
Hāḍi	Sundarī	Haṁsavidyā	Kaulamata	Ānandabhairava
Sāḍi	Tārā	Samavarodhinī	Miśra Mārga	Hayagrīva

Trailokyamohana cakra: Field between three layered *bhūpara* and three layered circle enclosure (*trivalaya*)

Sarvasaparipūraka cakra of sixteen petals

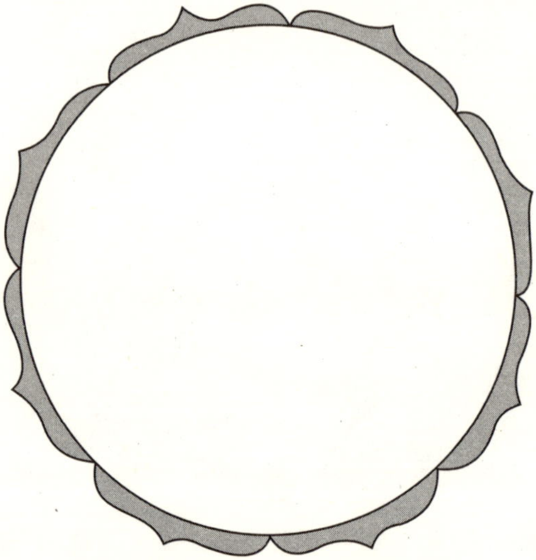

Sarvasaṅkṣobhana cakra of eight petals

Sarvasaubhāgyadāyaka cakra of fourteen triangles

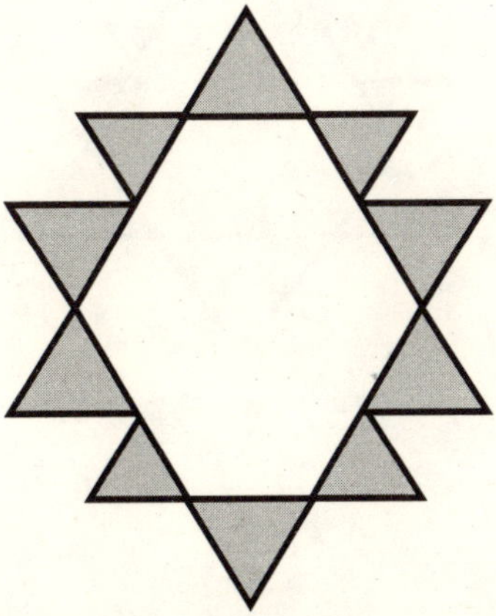

Sarvārthasādhaka cakra of ten outer triangles

Sarvarakṣākara cakra of ten inner triangles

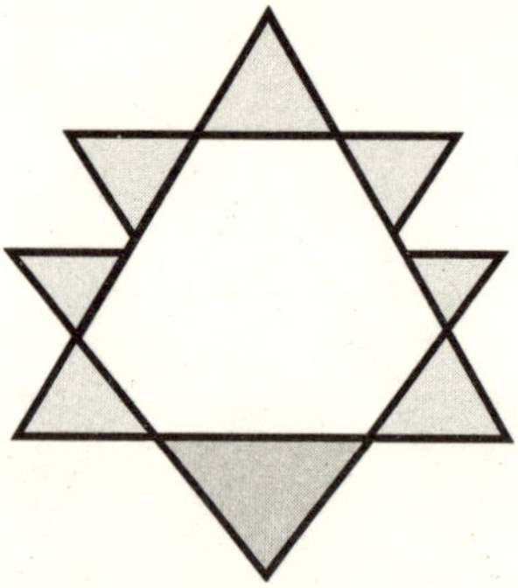

Sarvarogahara cakra of eight triangles

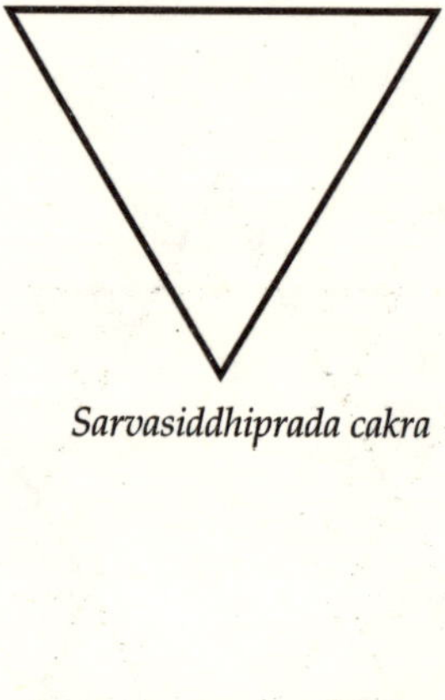

Sarvasiddhiprada cakra

Bindu: Sarvānandamaya cakra

There are other trinities like *yantra–mantra–tantra* or *guṇa* trinities. But, I am certain that the play of trinity emerged after observing the relationship between the three closely-related celestial *piṇḍa*s — sun, moon and the earth. Even in *Yoginī-Hṛdaya*, it is mentioned that the three *bindu*s, known as *kāmakalā* (digit of sexual desire), are the root potential of the sun, moon and fire. It is like the sun and moon coming together in an eclipse, or the seed from which the human being grows like a plant. Thus, it is basically an extension of astronomical and mathematical knowledge without which this *yantra* might not have emerged.

Mathematical Properties

Śrī-yantra appears as a bilaterally symmetrical geometrical figure. It is composed of nine interwoven isosceles triangles, five downward and four upward. The central triangle is an equilateral triangle. The two largest up and down triangles are drawn such that these touch the circle. There are eighteen three-line crossing points. Apex of every primary triangle touches the base of another triangle, while the two biggest triangles, one up and down, each touch the circumference of enclosing circle at three points. Equilateral inner triangle brings inner asymmetry, though equilateral triangle itself is highly symmetric. Rest of the primary triangles are isosceles triangles, but these bring the symmetry of the fringes. This is quite paradoxical. There is no diameter, but they diameter appears by linking all the apexes of nine triangles. Across the diametric division passing through the apex, it is symmetric; else in all kinds of division, it is asymmetric.

In my opinion, this reveals another esoteric aspect that symmetry is established only at the peak points. Whatsoever is the level, or the sheath, the peak makes the way for equanimity, one can see the world with equanimity and poise, and the cycle of *karma* ceases. Śrī-yantra is thus both symmetric and asymmetric. It is a kind of aperiodic ordering. Śrī-yantra is a visual koan, as per John Fudjack and Patricia Dinkelaker.[5]

C.O. Evans and J. Fudjack, further wrote in *Consciousness* (1976):

> The visual gaze at the array of triangles provides perception of depth since triangles seem to shift to one either larger and seemingly closer or smaller and seemingly farther. The symmetric fringe of Śrī-yantra and asymmetric centre provide in-built illusion in the diagram.[6]

The fact that it is the symmetry breaking that causes a phenomenon to emerge, the central asymmetry of Śrī-yantra represents the creatrix centre, appropriately represented by the unstable *bindu* enclosing within three *bindus* which emanate

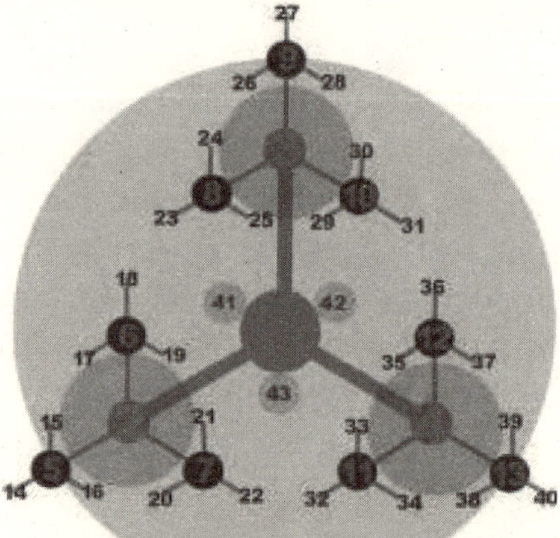

The ternary tree of 43 triangles
Source: http://hans.wyrdweb.eu/tag/sri-yantra

---

5 John Fudjack and Patricia Dinkelaker, "The Enneagram as Classic Double Mandala", April 1999. http://tap3x.net/EMBTI/j4selfcc.html (last accessed on 4 December 2012).

6 C.O. Evans and J. Fudjack, *Consciousness: An Interdisciplinary Study* (1976) available at www.mentalstates.net/consciousness.html

the graded existence. On the other hand, Śrī-yantra also appears as symmetric at macro level. Thus, it is a cosmogram that represents orderly universe with a creative, active centre, from where new phenomena continue to emanate.

Śrī-yantra has a central vertex. Nine triangles have twenty-seven vertices, that correspond to *nakṣatra cakra* (twenty-seven *nakṣatra*s). Number 27 itself is significant as it is obtained by another multiplication of 9 by 3. Total number of points in the figure comes out to be 51 (27 vertices of primary triangles + 24 points of the petals). This corresponds to 51 *pīṭha*s, 51 alphabets and 51 Gaṇeśas in *Yoginī-Hṛdaya.*

Though, the triangles form a regular fourteen-sided polygon, the total number of triangles that emerge is forty-three. This number falls in the series of Metallic Mean, which will be discussed later.

Forty-three triangles themselves bring to the fore the perfect trinitization of the geometrical figure as depicted above.

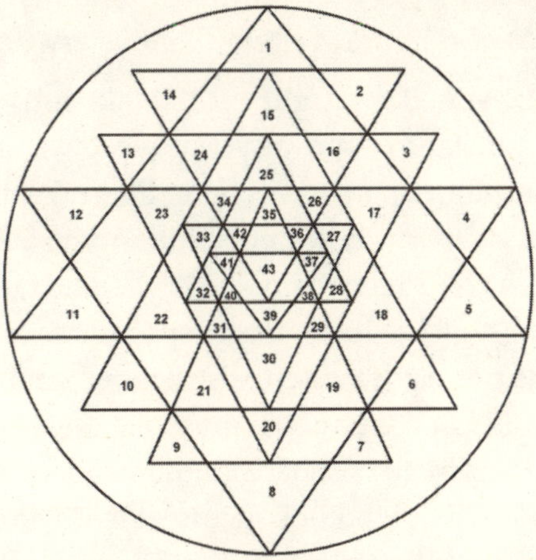

Forty-three triangles in Śrī-yantra
(source: http://aspenmoonart.com/sriyantra-explored/sri-yantra43count)

A single triangle undergoing three layers of trinitization creates forty-three triangles.

1

|>3 *first trifurcation*

4

|>9 *second trifurcation*

13

| > 30 (9 x 3 + 1 x 3) *third trifurcation*

43

Such progression as "balanced ternary-tree structure" in algorithm. Now, engineers are trying to use this algorithm in computer programming. The ternary-tree representation for efficient parallel computation on binary trees has been successfully simulated by the Japanese computer engineers and they are claiming that the ternary logic will replace binary logic in the central processing units (CPUs) in future. Number 43 is being recognized with the infinite potentiality, not only in technology but also in unravelling the mystery of the universe.

The finite speed of light *c* (300,000 km/second) is a fundamental constant of our physical world. There will be no causation if the information flow is faster than *c*. Without causality, nothing exists, neither physics nor philosophy. Second, there is no time before the Planck time (10^{-43} seconds). Planck scale (1.616199 (97) x 10^{-35} m), is the smallest space–time and herein it is not continuous but have a discrete structure, similar to ordinary matter, which is not continuous at atomic scales but instead is composed of discrete atoms. Space is inhomogeneous and discreet at smallest scale. What kind of structure it is? In a recent research led by Dmitri Krioukov et al., it has been suggested that the structure of a relativistic space–time is almost fully determined by its causal structure alone and the team applied the causal set approach to quantum gravity. Once the research team applied the simulation exercise, they were baffled to find similarities of emergence of geometric structures in complex dynamical system ranging from universe to human brain and then the internet and are optimistic that a common law governing the complex causets (causal sets) across the vast spectrum can be discovered.[7]

No doubt, the surprise discovery of hexagonal structures, concurrency of the number 43, the nested nature of the universe and the fact that the intelligence of varying nature pervades the universe, all point towards the plausibility of mathematics of Śrī-yantra as the gateway to the ultimate secrets of the world, since Śrī-yantra possesses all such characteristics.

Śrī-yantra has a very high level of concurrency. Dick Tahta, the famous mathematician who taught Stephen Hawking and who was instrumental in establishing the branch of ethno-mathematics concluded:

> The central design of Śrī-yantra consists of nine isosceles triangles, intersecting in a surprisingly complex pattern of collinearities.[8]

Alexander Kulaichev, who was the first to work on the mathematical properties of Śrī-yantra in 1984, concluded:

> The whole Śrī-yantra seal may now be described by a system of algebraic non-linear equation. From the geometrical nature of the system, it may be presumed that there is at least one real solution (root), which may be calculated by some iterative method.[9]

---

7 Dmitri Krioukov et al. "Network Cosmology", *Scientific Reports* 2, Article number 793, doi:10.1038/srep00793 Published 16 November 2012.http://www.nature.com/srep/2012/121113/srep00793/full/srep00793.html.

8 Dick Tahta, "On the Geometry of the Śrī-yantra", *The Mathematical Gazette*, March 1992, **76**(475): 49-60.

9 Alexander Pavalovich Kulaichev, "Śrī-yantra and Its Mathematical Properties", *Indian Journal of History of Science*, 1984, **19**(3): 279-92.

Kulaichev tried to describe the Śrī-yantra seal by a system of algebraic non-linear equation from second to sixteenth power of variable.

He was surprised that what "sort of representational means and knowledge had been used for the reproduction of Śrī-yantra seal during centuries?" and "how the idea of nine triangles consolidating in such a polygon with precise matching of numerous points of intersection arose?" Kulaichev posits for the "possibility of existence of unknown cultutral and historical alternative of mathematical knowledge, e.g. highly developed tradition of the special imagination"[10] in India after his thorough study of the mathematical properties.

The traditional method to construct Śrī-yantra is to first draw the diameter (across which all the apex of nine triangles get connected) and then to divide it into forty-eight equal parts. This partition itself is significant as it is the trinitization of number 16, which represents Ṣoḍaśī, Goddess Tripurasundarī, who abides at the centre along with fifteen *nityas* (the digits of the moon) and the goddess whose aspect is immortal. The central *bindu* itself is known as Kāmakalā. *Kāla* in *Ṛgveda* represents the sixteenth fraction. Thus, the traditional method steeped into the cultural understanding about the trinal aspect of Ṣoḍaśī guides the priest to draw the complex Śrī-yantra seal so accurately, which Kulaichev considers as an extremely tough drawing with all its collinearities and concurrency. The traditional priest draws horizontal lines of polygon on the level of subdivision 6, 12, 17, 20, 23, 27, 30, 36, 42.[11]

Interestingly, Śrī-yantra can be visualized from three perspectives — laterally, vertically and perception of depth. Thus, even in a two-dimensional flat picture, three-dimensional perception arises. The arrangement of smaller and larger

---

[10] Alexander Pavalovich Kulaichev, op. cit., p. 292.

[11] Ibid., p. 285.

triangles also causes oscillation of perception. This may be responsible for inducing oscillation in neural network and activation of bigger chunk of the brain. Each arrangement in Śrī-yantra comes in a surprisingly new way and makes human mind to explore new meanings which are context-sensitive.

The circle can be seen as the circumambulation of *bindu*, a pattern seen in the temples where *garbha-gṛha* (*bindu*) is the focal point for various *parikramā*s at the sacred places of pilgrimage. *Bindu* is like the centre of the universe, the *axis mundi*, across which the whole manifestation circles in time.

The triangles themselves can be seen as twofold — primary triangles and secondary triangles — which are created due to the combinatorial properties of interlocking primary triangles. The recursiveness of triangles appears as if all triangles are constructed separately, though it is only the result of the interlocking. Thus, in one way, though there are fractal properties of recursion of same pattern, it is not the exact fractal of determinate dimensions, since the triangles appear out of intersection and are not the drawn images. Here, smaller triangles are secondary repetitions generated by interlocking of primary repetitions of similar shape. Thus, forty-three smaller triangles can be termed as cognate triangles in mathematical terms.

Patrick Flanagan (1991)[12] discovered another interesting feature in the diagram. The first up-triangle in Śrī-yantra is the exact cross-section of geometry of the Great Pyramid of Gaza. If ½ its base is one unit, its height is equal to the square root of the Golden Section, phi (ϕ). Golden Section itself is half the $\sqrt{5} + 1 = 1.618$. The two sides of the triangle are

---

12 Patrick Flanagan, How to Draw a Sri-yantra, 1991, http://www.sri-yantraresearch.com/Construction/Flanagan patrick_flanagan _method.htm.

equal to ϕ, since all primary triangles are isosceles triangles. ϕ is a rudimentary fractal and causes inter-nesting and recursion in innumerable phenomena, particularly in biology like phyllotaxis and tissue arrangements.

Śrī-yantra contains forty-three triangles. This number emerges in the series of Bronze Mean. One must remember how ϕ, the Golden Mean that emerges as the solution in the Fibonacci sequence, a continued fraction itself, is also associated with Śrī-yantra. Bronze Mean is a generalization of the sequence of Fibonacci based on trinity.

Śrī-yantra and Higher Algorithm of Algebra

Various mathematicians are trying to use the Metallic Mean algebra to describe the recursiveness in Śrī-yantra.

In a general linear equation $X^2 - X - 1 = 0$, ϕ is the real solution. This ϕ is the Golden Ratio, discussed above. It is the solution of the Fibonacci sequence which emerges by adding previous two integer numbers. The Fibonacci sequence was already discovered and described by Piṅgala in *Chandaḥsūtras* during third century BCE and termed as Meru-Prastara. Thus, emergence of ϕ in the construction of Śrī-yantra, a cosmic diagram which represents the Meru, the *axis mundi* of the cosmos, is not unprecedented.

The recursiveness that emerges in Śrī-yantra could not have been constructed without the active participation of mathematicians during the Gupta period. The mathematical series were being solved by the early mathematicians. The Meru-Prastara itself was a kind of solution to the problem of the continued fraction, an iterative process in geometry and algebra. In fact, every series is a continued fraction.

In *Āryabhaṭīya* (CE 499), Āryabhaṭa developed the solutions of indeterminate equations using continued fractions. A continued fraction is an expression obtained through iterative process of representing a number as sum of its integer part and the reciprocal of another number, then writing the other number as sum of its integer part and another reciprocal and so on. Śrī-yantra also appears as geometrical representation of some kind of continued fraction and the method that Indian mathematicians adopted remains unknown.

In recent years, the Metallic Means family has been developed by the Argentinean mathematician, Vera W. de Spinadel[13] and this is being helpful in various emerging fields. What are these Metallic Means?

When in the quadratic equation, $X^2 - pX - q = 0$, the solutions of this formula are called Metallic Means. When $p = q = 1$, the Golden Mean emerges (ϕ). The Golden Mean is connected with the "trinitarity" (Alexey Stakhov).[14] When $p = 1$, the Silver Mean emerges which has been of use recently in bioinformatics. Similarly, there are Copper Mean, Bronze Mean and Nickel Mean as solutions of various equations with differing p and q values. These "means" are important in the study of onset of chaos and emergence of fractal like structure which have been found ubiquitous at various scale of the universe.

All the members of Metallic Mean family are positive quadratic irrational numbers that are the positive solutions of quadratic equation. The members of Metallic Mean family expand into continued fractions.

---

13 Vera W. de Spinadel, "The Metallic Means Family and Art", *Journal of Applied Mathematics*, 2010, **3**(1): 53-64; also see, ibidem, "The Metallic Means and Design", in *Nexus II: Architecture and Mathematics*, ed. Kim Williams, Fucecchio (Florence): Edizioni dell'Erba, 1998, pp. 141-57; ibidem, *The Metallic Mean Family and Renormalization Group Techniques*, 2000 available at http://www.tex.imm.uran.ru/tom6/spinadel/

14 Alexey Stakhov, *The Mathematics of Harmony*, Singapore: World Scientific Publishing Company, 2009.

Spinadel has explained this beautifully with the simplest example. If $p = q = 1$, then $X^2 - X - 1 = 0$

or,

$$X^2 = X + 1$$

$$X = 1 + 1/X.$$

If one replaces iteratively the value of X of the term, one obtains

$$X = 1 + \cfrac{1}{1 + \cfrac{1}{1 + \cfrac{1}{\ddots}}}.$$

This is a purely periodic, continued fraction that defines the Golden Mean,

$$\phi = [\bar{1}] = \frac{1+\sqrt{5}}{2}.$$

One can observe the beauty of the continued fraction and shift one's mind to the continuing triangles, emerging out of the interlocking in Śrī-yantra to realize how there is a similar pattern, one in algebra and another in geometric shape.

If $p = 3$ and $q = 1$, one gets the Bronze Mean

$$\sigma_{Br} = \lim_{n \to \infty} \frac{G(n-1)}{G(n)} = [\bar{3}] = \frac{3+\sqrt{13}}{2}.$$

This too is a purely periodic continued fraction. These metallic means which are higher-order relatives of the Golden Mean are being used by scientists to analyse the behaviour of non-linear dynamical systems in going from periodicity to quasi-periodicity.

The Bronze series that appears has the following series:

$$\frac{1}{1}, \frac{4}{1}, \frac{13}{4}, \frac{43}{13}, \frac{142}{43}, \frac{469}{142}, \ldots.$$

Bronze Mean can be written in continued fraction with 3 as primary integer.

Bronze Mean = 3 + 1/3 + ...

The solution is

$$\sigma_3 = \frac{3+\sqrt{13}}{2} = [\bar{3}].$$

Bronze Mean like Golden Mean is linked with different symmetries and fractal patterns. Bronze Mean is a generalization of the sequence of Fibonacci based on trinity. One can just observe how each part of the continued fraction of the Golden Mean once tripled generates the Bronze Mean. Thus, Bronze Means' connection with Śrī-yantra packs up another dimension of trinitization.

Bronze Mean generates quasi-crystal. Crystals are the most symmetric, regular and periodic object. At the opposite end of the scale, there is disordered or amorphous substances, like the "glasses". Crystal can be modelled by putting an atom or a molecule at all the vertices of a regular triangular, quadrangular or hexagonal lattice. These lattices have symmetries of order 3, 4 and 6. But, in 1982, an Israeli scientist Dan Schechtman discovered pentagonal symmetries of order 5, wholly impossible in a crystal since it is not, obviously, allowed to fill the plane with regular pentagons. After much controversy, he was awarded Nobel Prize for Chemistry in 2011 for the discovery of new state of matter.

These configurations, that possess a quasi-periodic spatial structure, were called "quasi-crystals". Quasi-crystals are found in the collagens inside our tissues and play a vital role in the electro-magnetic stimulation of muscular tissues. Quasi-crystals are ordered and not ordered. Roger Penrose discovered Penrose tiling on this pattern. Though, it appears to be symmetric, it is not. I have seen Penrose tiling in the

Penrose tilings

ceiling murals in the Taj Mahal and its adjoining complexes. I noticed the abundance of similar murals also at Humayun Tomb in Delhi. Śrī-yantra too has this peculiar property of seeming to be ordered, and yet not ordered. It is asymmetric at the centre but ordered at the fringes. Like Penrose tiling, it is self-similar but it is not completely symmetric.

According to de Spinadel, these Metallic Means are fundamental in the actual research in every type of design, on the stability of micro- and macro-physical systems, going from the DNA's geometrical internal structure to the astronomical galaxies, or even on the search of universal roads to chaos in the analysis of non-linear dynamical systems and so on.

Since, the Metallic Means have only recently been discovered, the presence of these families not only in Śrī-yantra but the tiling in ancient and medieval architecture in India, presents one with the only conclusion that Indian mind looked at the universe as a continuity, as emanation of a unity into plurality, with the micro- and macro-containing similar properties. The continued fraction is the field in which India gave the greatest genius in mathematics, Srinivas Ramanujan. He worked on the partition numbers, the same as the continued fractions and interestingly, he used to state that all these formulae got revealed to him in dreams by the blessings of Namagiri, Goddess of Namakkal. Thus, connection of continuous fraction with spirituality in India opens new vista to explore contemplative minds of our ancients.

Fractal and Śrī-yantra

Fractal is a property of self-similar repetitions, discovered in recent times by Benoit Mandelbrot (1924–2010). Fractal comes from *fractus* in Latin meaning irregular, broken. Indian civilization engaged with understanding of the self-similarity between macro- and micro-cosm for eons and it is how Piṅgala, Āryabhaṭa and other mathematicians worked on the mathematics of series. The infinite repetition of the whole in individual is condensed in *mantra, aham brahmāsmi* (I am the universe). This is what is sought to be depicted in the Śrī-yantra diagram — the identity of human body with Mother Sakti.

The fractal perspective of Indians is getting clearer day by day with the study of recursive patterns in Hindu temples. One can find the fractal-like spires (*śikhara*s), and other parts of the architecture which are self-similar to the unity of the whole in the famous Kandarīya Mahādeva Temple at Khajurāho. Recently the fractal properties of this temple were discovered by a Korean team of researchers. The purpose of the temple structure is to lead from a broad base to a single point where all lines converge. It is the same schemata in Śrī-yantra where whole geometry is a graded step towards the centre or from out of the centre. Another correlation is the term for the peak of the temple *śikhara,* also known as *śr̥ṅga* and the seed syllable *śr̥ṅga* for the central point of Śrī-yantra, the peak. Śrī-yantra reiterates the structure of mythical *axis mundi,* Mt. Meru and it is interesting to observe that there is a Śr̥ṅgavan at Mt. Meru as described in *Mahābhārata*. Śr̥ṅgaparvata, Śr̥ṅga R̥ṣi (sage), Śr̥ṅgerī where Śaṅkarācārya credited with spreading Śrī-Vidyā knowledge in south India, had placed a Śrī-yantra; all have similar syllabic root.

I would like to argue that just as human geography is governed by the law of fractal, the imaginative geography too is governed by a similar law.

Yanguan Chen[15] has worked on the filling pattern of central places in human settlements. The central places are recognized as the market centres, administrative centres, etc. in which certain products and services are available to consumers/citizens/subjects. He found that though traditionally the central places were presumed to be regular with complete space filling, in the empirical observation, it is not so. He found how there is intermittency of space filling in central-places which gives rise to the fractal central-place model. There is no complete space filling. It is why consistent with fractal system, concepts of self-similarity, scaling laws and self-organizations come into play. "A central-place system appears as both a hierarchy with cascade structure and network with self-similar properties." Traditionally, it was assumed that the central place makes the best use of geographical space, hence it ought to be a close-packed system. But, Chen found that empirically it is never seen, rather there is always "interspace representing the place which cannot or should not be occupied by human beings despite the compact distribution of urban places".

Since, Śrī-yantra is believed to be the iconic representation of Meru, the *axis mundi* of cosmos, we find how here also there is intermittent space. The primary triangles that intersect also create such space which is not inhabited by any deities in the maṇḍalic representation of Śrī-yantra. This also confirms that Śrī-yantra has a fractal structure of unknown dimensions.

---

15 Yanguan Chen, "Fractal Systems of Central Places Based on Intermittency of Space-filling", *Chaos, Solitons & Fractals*, 2011, **44**(8): 619-32, http://arxiv.org/ftp/arxiv/papers/1105/1105.0589.pdf

Śrī-yantra and New Genetics

In my opinion, just as the DNA helix finally affirmed what ancient sages knew about the male and female principles within human body and often depicted in art and sculpture as two coiled snakes, and the new bioinformatics of genetic code would establish that the genes prefer a Meru arrangement. Śrī-yantra has properties of quasi-crystal in being ordered and yet inherently unstable, and the genetic bases have been found to be encoded by "covalent bondings on an aperiodical crystal".

The principle of "recursive genome function" has been developed by Andras J. Pellionisz,[16] who has revolutionized the biological sciences with "geometrization of neuroscience and genetics". This has been achieved by the application of recursion algorithms, based on the principle that each state of the system is deduced from its previous states just like in algebraic series. The working by ancient Indian mathematicians on famous sequence of Fibonacci numbers, where each subsequent integer is the sum of the previous two, has already been discussed.

Now, scientists have confirmed that the folding of DNA strands is fractal. The science adviser to the US President, Eric Lander, and his team published a path-breaking work with the magazine cover page of *Science* magazine showing Lander appealing "Mr President, the genome is fractal!" (2009).[17] They stated that DNA can be read not only serially,

---

16 Andras J. Pellionisz, Graham, Roy, Peter A. Pellionisz, Jean-Claude Perez, "Recursive Genome Function of the Cerebellum: Geometric Unification of Neuroscience and Genomics"; in *Handbook of The Cerebellum and Cerebellar Disorders*, ed. Mario Manto et al., vol. 3 pp. 1381-1424, New York: Springer, 2013.

17 Erez Lieberman-Aiden et al., "Comprehensive Mapping of Long-Range Interactions Reveals Folding Principles of the Human Genome", *Science*, October 2009, **326**(5950): 289-93.

from one end of the thread to the other, but because all segments of DNA are in maximal proximity to one-other, they can also be read in parallel. This characteristic is also found in Śrī-yantra with the additional perception of depth attribute.

As the bioinformatics bridge between genomics and mathematics emerged, J.C. Perez another leading interdisciplinary scientist, has declared: "In single-stranded DNA, human genome, codons population are fine-tuned in Golden ratio proportions".[18] The frequencies of sixty-four codons in the whole human genome scale are a self-similar fractal expansion of the universal genetic code. The original genetic code kernel (universal genetic code) governs not only the micro scale but the macro scale as well. It predetermines global codons proportions and populations.

Thus Perez is the leading voice in establishing that living substances have their own forms of creating order and that these forms are connected with special algebras. A new field of biomathematics has emerged where the Metallic Mean family is ingrained fully, which needs to be unravelled further. These algebras are related to special multidimensional geometries.

Russian scientist S.V. Petukhov has developed such a new mathematics to understand human biology. Even he proved that Golden Mean is a base of genetic code. In a recent book, Petoukhov writes:

> The new theme of Golden Section in genetic matrices seems to be important because many inherited physiological systems and processes are connected with it. It is known that proportion of a Golden Section characterized many physiological processes: cardiovascular processes,

---

[18] J.C. Perez, "Codon Populations in Single-stranded Whole Human Genome DNA Are Fractal and Fine-tuned by the Golden Ratio 1.618", *Interdiscip. Sci.*, 2010, **2**(3): 228-40.

> respiratory processes, electrical activities of brain, locomotion activity and so on. . . . Matrix relation between Golden Section phi and significant parameters of genetic code testifies in favour of a molecular genetics that provides such physiological phenomena.[19]

In recent years, the attention towards the continued fraction and the Golden Section has even enamoured many physicists and chemists to engage in understanding the nuclear and galactic structure afresh with the number theory tool. Jan Boeyenes and Demetrius Levendis found that the ratio of protons to neutrons in any nuclide is a simple rational fraction, and this quantity, in relation to mass number, is the important factor that determines the stability of nuclides against radioactive decay.

For light nuclei the ratio is $Z/N = 1$ and, for heavy nuclides, it converges to the Golden Mean ($\tau = 1/\Phi$), as shown by geometrical construction.

He concludes:

> Convergence to the Golden Ratio probably relates to the geometry of the cosmos, as a balance between general curvature and the overall size of the universe, as measured by Hubble's constant. The observation that spiral galaxies display the structural Golden Ratio in the same way as biological growths, implies aspects of self-similarity and evidence of the general curvature of space.[20]

Śrī-yantra contains innumerable properties which are in the realm of contemporary research. The Golden Mean and the Bronze Mean are found in Śrī-yantra. Śrī-yantra contains the

---

19 S.V. Petukhov and Mathew He, *Mathematics of Bioinformatics: Theory, Practice and Applications*, New Jersey: Wiley, 2011.

20 Jan C.A. Boeyens and Demetrius C. Levendis, *Number Theory and the Periodicity of Matter*, Berlin: Springer verlag, 2008.

properties of quasi-crystals in appearance and this should not be seen as an exception, since in monuments across India, such quasi-crystal tilings have been engraved on the walls, floors and domes. Śrī-yantra is a geometric matrix of Indian thinking with its various properties like recursion, order and asymmetry, trinities, mathematical progression, context-specific grammar of meanings. Śrī-yantra is not only a diagram but also an active principle with the property to induce neuro-biological changes. In Indian thinking, the correlation between similar structures and the transference of action from one structure to another has been a pet theme. If the new matrix of genomes discovers the Śrī-yantra pattern within genetic code, that might be a breakthrough discovery to further establish influence of meditation over a Śrī-yantra upon genetic programme of the body. Next decade of research in bioinformatics, mathematics and neuroscience of visualization will 11throw fresh light on this gift from the ancients to our generation.

6

Śrī-yantra and Quest for Higgs Boson

THERE is a global celebration after the European Council for Nuclear Research (CERN) announced preliminary results in the search for the Higgs particle. CERN stated in a press release that the two experiments conducted to search the elusive Higgs particle have observed a new particle in the mass region around 125-26 GeV (almost 134 times heavier than proton). This is the weight of the Higgs Boson as predicted by the Standard Model. The CERN press release mentioned:

> We observe in our data clear signs of a new particle, at the level of 5 sigma, in the mass region around 126 GeV. The outstanding performance of the LHC and ATLAS and the huge efforts of many people have brought us to this exciting stage, but a little more time is needed to prepare these results for publication. . . . The results are preliminary but the 5 sigma signal at around 125 GeV we're seeing is dramatic. This is indeed a new particle. We know it must be a boson and it's the heaviest boson ever found.[1]

Indeed, it is a remarkable feet, but it is not what the media entrenched in fabricating "simulated reality" is propagating at an alarming speed. Indian media went ballistic with anchors declaring how "God" has been found. This is an interesting journey of an idea in postmodern age. The God-particle is a

---

1 CERN press release, "Observation of a New Particle with a Mass of 125 GeV CMS Experiment, CERN", 4 July 2012. http://cms.web.cern.ch/news/observation-new-particle-mass-125-gev

moniker for the Higgs Boson, a mathematical proposition. When CERN declared the preliminary result with lot of reservation that something akin to the Higgs Boson has been found, it never intended to declare the end of hunt for "God" or some metaphysical God-particle. Just as in Peircean semiotic, an arbitrary term, first turned into an index and then into an iconic signifier, the Higgs Boson itself has been turned into the God! Many channels invited *sādhus* and *mullāhs* in their studio and pooh-poohed them that now that God has been found, what is left for religion. Some even declared the ultimate victory of science over religion. Very next day, the newspapers published the picture of statue of Naṭarāja kept in the residential block at CERN compound. So, why this contradictory positioning? If the physicists at CERN are hell bent on destroying the only pillar of religion, why should they install a Śiva statue for inspiration?

There are misconceptions that once the existence of Higgs Boson is confirmed, science will reach its ultimate end. Higgs Boson is the elusive particle in the jigsaw puzzle of the Standard Theory only. Physicists are already working on physics beyond Standard Theory. What does Standard Theory argue?

There are two basic constituents of the universe — matter and force. While matter is built up with particles like electron, proton, neutron, the force is carried through force-particle. There are four kinds of elementary force: gravitation, electromagnetic, strong and weak. All these forces exist in some kind of field and the fields operate through the particles with different characteristics than the matter particle. These are known as bosons. Bosons have no density problems and infinite number can coexist in space. The electromagnetic force is mediated by photon, strong force that keeps the nucleus intact by gluon, the weak forces that cause radioactivity through W and Z bosons. Many physicists predict that graviton is the boson for the gravitational force. But, that is the story beyond the physics of Higgs Boson.

Maxwell unified electric and magnetic forces into single electromagnetic force. Similarly, Pakistani Nuclear Laureate, Abdus Salam and Steve Weinberg unified weak force and electromagnetic force. The next generation of theoretical physicists unified the strong force with the weak and electromagnetic force. This is known as the Standard Model. But, as evident, there is still a long way to go to unify the three forces with that of gravity. The confirmation of Higgs Boson will only give a direction to physicists for further higher level of unification. They will have to account for the Standard Model in any further Theory of Everything (TOE).

Is Higgs Boson Ṣoḍaśī?

Higgs Boson has been elusive for two decades. The top quark was discovered in 1995 and it was heavier than the preliminary report on Higgs Boson. So, if the top quark was discovered in 1995, why did it take so much effort and time to have a glimpse of Higgs Boson? The elusive nature of this particle makes me to coin another moniker for it, Ṣoḍaśī.

What is Ṣoḍaśī? In Indian civilization, it stands for the fullness. It is the part which is not visible and yet present everywhere. It is the sixteenth digit of the moon and is also called "Soma", conjunction of Sa and Uma, the God and the feminine *śakti* together. It is stated that on the new moon, the sun and moon dwell together; God and Goddess dwell together, and the nectar of immortality is produced feeding, nurturing and sustaining the universe. "Soma" is the immortal essence of the moon, the immortal digit which is present in all fifteen digits.

Jan Gonda has discussed in his classical study, *Change and Continuity in Indian Religion*,[2] the importance of number 16 in

[2] Jan Gonda, *Change and Continuity in Indian Religion*, Hague: The Mouton, 1965, pp. 115-30.

Indian tradition. Since 16 stands for perfection and completion, Indian rituals are replete with sixteen stages. Tripurasundarī, the goddess of Śrī-yantra, is also worshipped as the goddess who is beautiful in three realms. She is assessed to be sixteen years old.

Bṛhadāraṇyaka Upaniṣad I.5.14 identifies *ātman* with the sixteenfold Prajāpati:

> स एष संवत्सरः प्रजापतिः षोडशकलः, तस्य रात्रय एव पञ्चदश कलाः, ध्रुवैवास्य षोडशी कला; स रात्रिभिरेधा च पूर्यतेऽप च क्षीयते; सोऽमावास्यां रात्रिमेतया षोडश्या कलया सर्वमिदं प्राणभृदनुप्रविश्य ततः प्रातर्जायते; तस्मादेतां रात्रिं प्राणभृतः प्राणां न विच्छिन्द्यात्, अपि कृकलासस्य, एतस्या एव देवताया अपचित्यै ॥
>
> *sa eṣa saṁvatsaraḥ prajāpatiḥ ṣoḍaśakalaḥ, tasya rātraya eva pañcadaśa kalāḥ, dhruvaivāsya ṣoḍaśī kalā; sa rātri-bhiredhā ca pūryate 'pa ca kṣīyate; so 'māvāsyāṁ rātrimetayā ṣoḍaśyā kalayā sarvam idaṁ prāṇabhṛdanu praviśya tataḥ prātarjāyate; tasmādetāṁ rātriṁ prāṇabhṛtaḥ prāṇā na vicchindyāt, api kṛkalāsasya, etasyā eva devatāyā apacityai* | |
>
> This Prajāpati (Hiraṇyagarbha) has sixteen digits and is represented by the year. The nights (and days) are his fifteen digits, and the constant one is his sixteenth digit. He (as the moon) is filled as well as wasted by the nights (and days). Through this sixteenth digit he permeates all these living beings on the new-moon night and rises the next morning. Therefore on this night one should not take the life of living beings, not even of a chameleon, in adoration of this deity.[3]

The *ṣoḍaśa-kalāḥ prajāpatiḥ* is the Creator. Full incarnations of God are sometimes endowed with sixteen powers — *ṣoḍaśa-*

---

[3] Swami Madhvananda, ed., *Bṛhadāraṇyaka Upaniṣad* with the commentary of Śaṅkarācārya, Madhu Kāṇḍa, chapter 1.5.14, Almora: Advaita Ashrama, 1950, p. 225.

kalā-mūrti, like Kṛṣṇa is supposed to possess. The fifteen digits are visible but, the sixteenth is beyond our visibility.

In Āgamaśāstra (Tantras), the sixteenth *kalā* is the transcendental and fifteen *kalā*s, the *nitya*s. In Śrī-cakra, the most abstract diagram, which is the epitome of Indian civilization, fifteen *nitya*s are present in the innermost circle, but the Supreme Goddess is the sixteenth digit at the centre. It is the central *bindu* which abides in all and completes unto itself. The sixteenth digit or the transcendental *sadakhya* is latent in all fifteen *kalā*s (digits).

Higgs Boson acts like a Ṣoḍaśī, the sixteenth digit in the Standard Model.[4] Higgs Boson holds the key to the origin of particle mass. In the Standard Model, as discussed earlier, three fundamental forces are unified into one system. It involves interaction of sixteen kinds of particles. Higgs Boson is the elusive sixteenth that gives the other particles mass. The concept of Higgs Boson was propounded by the British physicist Peter Higgs after the electro–weak unification was achieved. It was found that in order for electro–weak unification to work mathematically, it requires that the force-carrying particles have no mass. But, experimentally it was not correct since bosons carried mass. Peter Higgs, Robert Brout and François Englert suggested that all particles had no mass just after the Big Bang. But, once the universe cooled and the temperature fell below a critical value, an invisible force field called the "Higgs field" was formed together with the associated "Higgs Boson".[5] The field prevails throughout

---

4 CERN, The Standard Package available at public.web.cern.ch/public/en/science/standardmodel-en.html (last accessed on 4 December 2012); also see, Dave Fehling, *The Standard Model of Particle Physics: A Lunchbox's Guide*, Johns Hopkins University www.pha.jhu.edu/~dfehling

5 CERN, "Missing Higgs" available at http://public.web.cern.ch/public/en/science/higgs-en.html

the cosmos like the sixteenth digit of the moon. Particles that interact with it are given a mass via the Higgs Boson. The more they interact, the heavier they become, whereas particles that never interact are left with no mass at all. Thus, photons and gluons remained massless but all other particles gained mass. It is like a porridge sea. Heavier the particle, greater will be the drag by the Higgs field. Thus, Higgs Boson constitutes the invisible cosmic sea which pervades other particles.

Interestingly, Higgs Boson is also the sixteenth particle in the Standard Model. The matter particles are of two basic types — quarks and leptons. Each group consists of six particles, which are related in pairs or "generations". Thus, there are three generations of particles. Lightest are the most stable and the first generation particles. All stable matter in the universe is made from particles that belong to the first generation like electron, proton and neutron. Heavier particles of second and third generations quickly decay to the most stable level.[6]

The six quarks are paired in the three generations — the "up quark"/"down quark" (first generation), the "charm quark"/"strange quark" (second generation), the "top quark"/ "bottom quark" (third generation).

Similarly, six leptons are arranged in three generations — the "electron"/"electron-neutrino", "muon"/"muon-neutrino" and the "tau"/"tau-neutrino". The electron, muon and tau all have an electric charge and a mass, whereas the neutrinos are electrically neutral with an unknown insignificant mass.

Three fundamental forces in the Standard Model have own corresponding boson particles which mediate force —

---

6 Particle Data Group of Lawrence Berkeley National Laboratory (LBNL), Project History Under Supervision by Michael Barnett and Andria Erzberger. "The Particle Adventure", *Fundamentals of Matter and Force*. www.particleadventure.org/fermibos.html

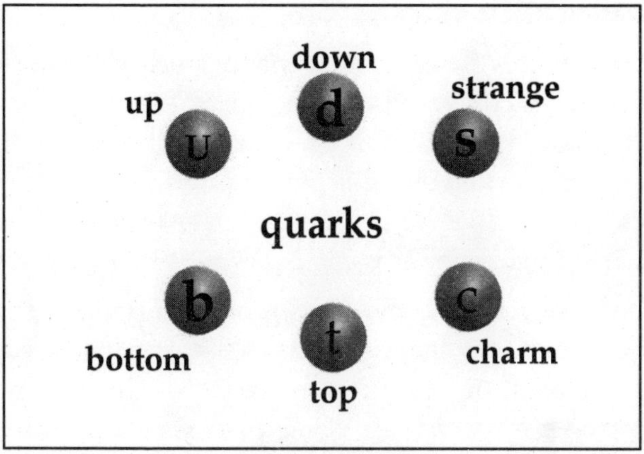

fig. 1: The quark family

the "gluon" for strong force, photon for the electromagnetic force, and the "W and Z bosons" for the weak force. All these constitute fifteen particles in a 4 x 4 box. The last box in the Boson column is the Higgs Boson. All fifteen types of particles that include three types of neutrinos, six quarks, heavy W and Z bosons had been earlier discovered. The preliminary results pointing to the existence of Higgs Boson will make the sixteen-box model complete.

Generation		I	II	III		
Fermions	Quarks	Up	Charm	Top	Gluon	**Bosons**
		Down	Strange	Bottom	Photon	
	Leptons	Electron	Muon	Tau	W (80 GeV) & Z (91 GeV) Boson	
		Electron-neutrino	Muon-neutrino	Tau-neutrino	Higgs Boson (125 GeV)	

chart 1: Sixteen box standard model

Triadization of Universe

Indian tradition is based upon a triadic view of the universe. The universe is composed of three *guṇas* — *sattva, rajas* and *tamas*. It is based upon this fundamental triadization that Indian thinking is dominated by Trika philosophy and etymologically connected terms like *trāṇa* (crossing over or the salvation), *tīrtha* (sacred places for crossing over) and *yātrā* (pilgrimage).

If one looks around the development in particle physics, one is surprised how more than 200 sub-atomic particles have been discovered, but they are the triads of electron, proton and neutron only, which are stable particles and which make up the material universe. One can look through the prism of the Standard Model and describe it at lepton–quark level by the observation that all the matter around us is composed of electrons, and up and down quarks. Why did nature prefer only three particles or at deeper level three fermions, to maintain stability? Physicists also postulate twenty-six-dimensional, ten-dimensional or five-dimesional universe, it is assumed that something which is mathematically feasible is existentially feasible; that mathematical existence and physical existence are equivalent, so that all mathematical structures exist physically as well.[7] But, it is the three-dimensional universe in which we grow and our intelligence flourish. Why is the three-dimensional universe the only visible stable known-universe? And why does this three-dimensional visible universe contain matter only in three natural states — solid, liquid and gas?

Now let us reflect over the Standard Model. There are only three generations of fermions discovered so far. Why do the fermions have only three generations? Each succeeding

---

7 Max Tegmark, "Parallel Universes", in J.D. Barrow, P.C.W. Davies, and C.L. Harper, eds., *Ultimate Reality: From Quantum to Cosmos*, Cambridge: Cambridge University Press, 2003.

generation is more unstable than the preceding one. Thus, generation I that contains two quarks up and down — and two leptons — electron and electron-neutrino — constitute the stable visible universe. Physicists have experimentally observed that the first generation fermions have second and third generation partners, with identical charges to the first but larger masses. The second generation partner to the electron is the muon, and the third generation partner of electron is the tau. *Chart* 1 on page 115 shows the second generation and third generation partners with similar charges but increasing mass and instability of the stable four fermions. Fermions have different masses due to interaction with the dragging Higgs field mediated through Higgs Boson. But, the existence of only three generations of fermions has perplexed the scientists and the philosophers alike!

Let us see how the triad operates in the Standard Model. There are matter particles and force particles. Matter particles are fermions and force particles are bosons. Fermions can be either quarks or lepton. While proton, neutrons and such particles inside nucleus consist of quarks, electrons and their neutrinos are leptons. We can have a triad here of leptons, quarks and bosons.

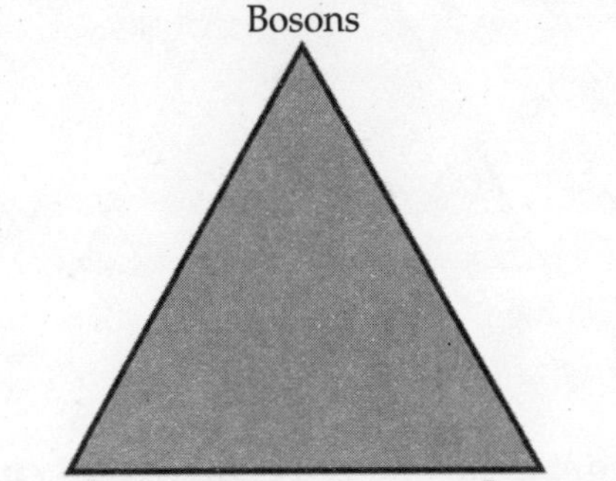

fig. 2: Triad of the force and matter particle

Similarly, one can construct triads of quarks and leptons as their resembling particles appear as the second generation and third generation particles in high-energy physics.

For the up quark, the series is up, charm and top, and for the down quark, the series is down, strange and bottom.

In the triangular representation, we have following figures:

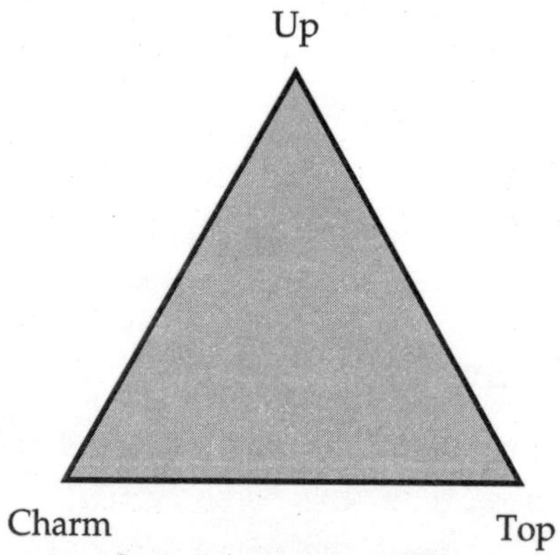

fig. 3: Series of up quark

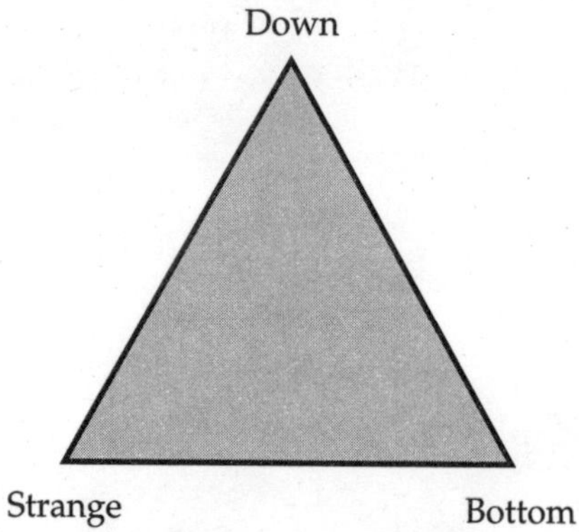

fig. 4: Series of down quark

It is known that up and down quarks also pair. These can be seen as mirror images with opposite isospin. Now, one can superimpose the two triangles and construct a beautiful hexagon.

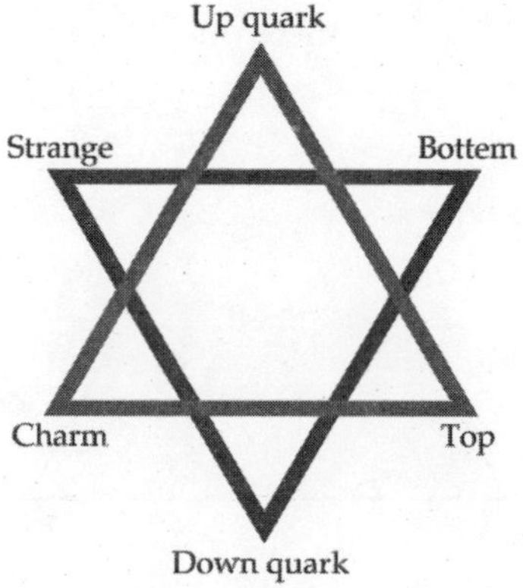

fig. 5: The hexagon maṇḍala of quark family

This is a beautiful diagram which is generated by the intersection of a triangle with its mirror image. It is the all-pervasive hexagon that builds Śrī-yantra. This design is found in abundance in nature and is the best lattice-packing design. In fact, if the universe itself is filled up with matter — exotic and normal — the hexagonal packing will appear to be the predominant characteristic of the universe. If quantization is applied to space–time, the universe will consist of discrete space–time at Planck length just as matter at smaller scale consists of discrete atom. And once we realize that in nature, hexagon is the preferred combinatorial geometric design, the quantized space–time is expected to be constituted by the similar hexagonal characteristic. It is also interesting to find that Deuterium ions are found in abundance in early universe. Deuterium ion is nothing but the geometrical design of two interesting opposite triangles discussed above, since protons and neutrons merely differ in isospin and can be seen again as a mirror image.

One can take up similar exercise for the lepton family too. The electron with its second and third generation partners, muon and tau, can be fitted into a triangular relationship and

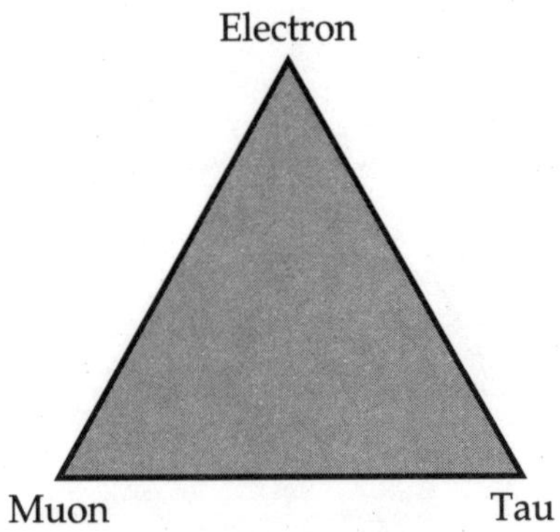

fig. 6: Electron series in the lepton family

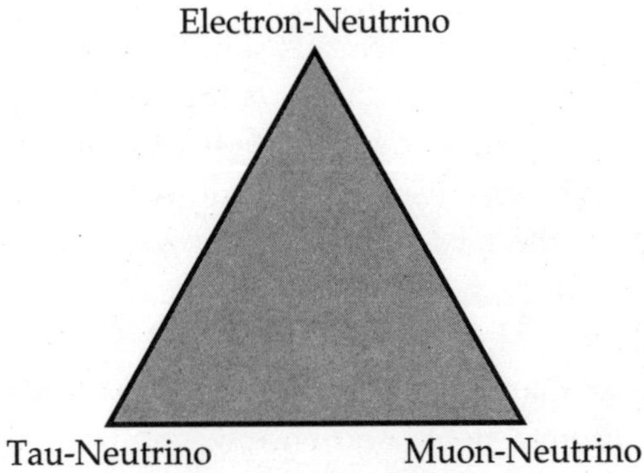

fig. 7: Neutrino series in the lepton family

so do the three neutrinos — electron-neutrino, muon-neutrino and tau-neutrino.

We also know how electrons and neutrinos do interact through weak interaction. One can build-up a hexagonal *maṇḍala*, the Meru of Śrī-yantra with the two triangles, one upward facing and one downward facing as in *fig*. 8.

It is not that only fermion can be built into the hexagonal Śrī-yantra configuration. One can take bosons also and build

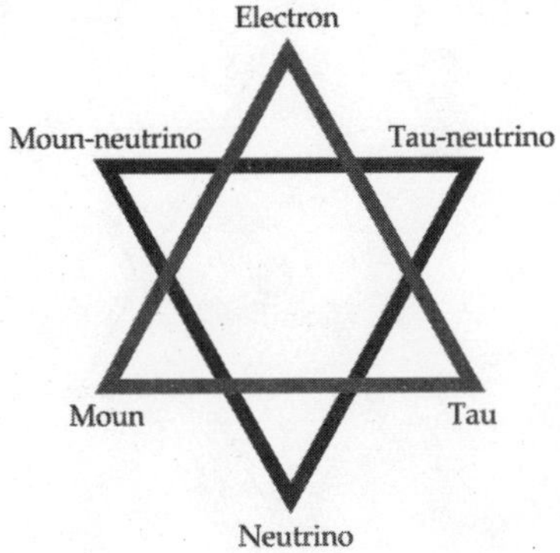

fig. 8: Hexagon Maṇḍala of the lepton family

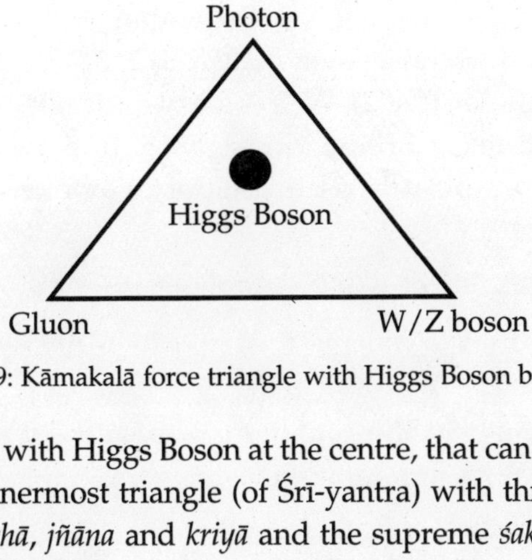

fig. 9: Kāmakalā force triangle with Higgs Boson bindu

up triangle with Higgs Boson at the centre, that can correspond with the innermost triangle (of Śrī-yantra) with three primary *śakti*s of *icchā*, *jñāna* and *kriyā* and the supreme *śakti* of Ṣoḍaśī as the central dot.

The central dot will be the Higgs Boson due to its anticipated centrality in the interaction of forces and massification in the Standard Model.

We can generate another Śrī-yantra model with Higgs Boson at the centre. Two triadic linkages are feasible in the model. The fermions with three constituents — quark, electron and neutrino forming a triangle and three bosons — photon, gluon and W/Z boson forming another triangle. Since, bosons

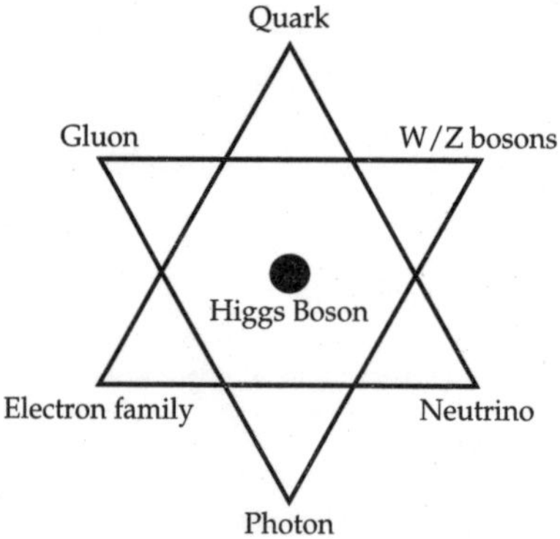

fig. 10: Haxagon maṇḍala of the standard model

and fermions too have mirror relationship at the level of spin (fermion with fractional spin of 1/2, 3/2, 5/2 . . . and boson with integral spin, 0, 1, 2). We get the two triangles — one with upward vertex and the other with downward vertex intersecting to explain the relationship of the fermions and bosons in the Standard Model.

The arrangement will be as follows:

Upward triangle — quark at top, neutrino and electron family at base.

Downward triangle — photon at downward vertex, and gluons and W/Z bosons at the base.

Central bindu — Higgs Boson.

Interestingly, Higgs Boson too is expected to be in the triadic aspect. If Higgs Boson has its own second and third generation partners in the family, that may resolve the crisis before the new physics. Scientists are puzzled that less than 5 per cent matter is the luminous matter. More than 95 per cent of the universe is still composed of exotic matter. Many are postulating that the exotic matter might be composed of neutrinos which has been observed to possess some mass. But, it appears unlikely that neutrino mass can exert such a powerful gravitational effect over the structure and geometry of space–time. It is known that dark matter constitutes 27 per cent of total energy in our universe and dark energy 68 per cent. The concept of dark energy arose during 1990s after the measurement of large-scale structure in the universe like superclusters of galaxies. Physicists had anticipated that the cosmic expansion should decelerate. But, observations confirmed that the universe's expansion was accelerating. Nobel Prize for Physics was given for this discovery to Saul Perlmutter in 2011 for the discovery of cosmic acceleration. This could not be explained by the earlier cosmological models and now it is widely believed that cosmic expansion is fuelled by the presence of dark energy. The motion of stars in galaxies or the motion of galaxies observed shows that these move faster than what the presence of visible matter in the neighbourhood can be attributed with. Here arose the idea of dark matter which is believed to exert gravitational force and since it does not interact with light (electromagnetic particle), it escapes observation. We have thus another triad of matter, dark matter and dark energy, and the triad of Higgs Boson may explain the three constituents of the universe, in future.

The least unstable Higgs Boson might contribute to the massification of leptons, bosons and quarks, while other generation of Higgs Boson would explain the mass of dark matter and gravitational effect due to dark energy.

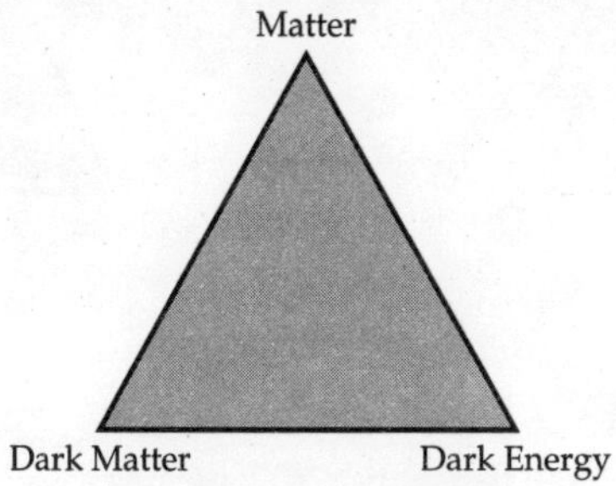

fig. 11: Triad of "presences" in the universe

Why am I certain about the three generations of Higgs Boson stem from the simple observation of nested hierarchy in the universe? Just as the cosmos consists of nearly 30 per cent of matter and 70 per cent of dark energy, we find the same proportion in the ratio between land and ocean surface on the planet earth where intelligent design, human being with same proportion of tissue and water, emerged to explore the darkest secret of the universe. Dark energy would thus correspond to a mega presence of fluid energy which is what physicists are guessing. The hierarchical presence of constants is also seen in the Standard Model. All these must stem from the deeper layer of symmetry and unification. Recently network cosmologists under D. Krioukov have postulated that similar laws appear to operate in dynamic complex systems as different as human brain, internet and the universe.[8]

Triadization and the interaction of geometrical models with its mirror image seem to be the underlying secrets of our universe. Triplet of quarks constitutes protons and neutrons, and the two bind together to constitute the stable nuclei with which the universe can be said to taking shape.

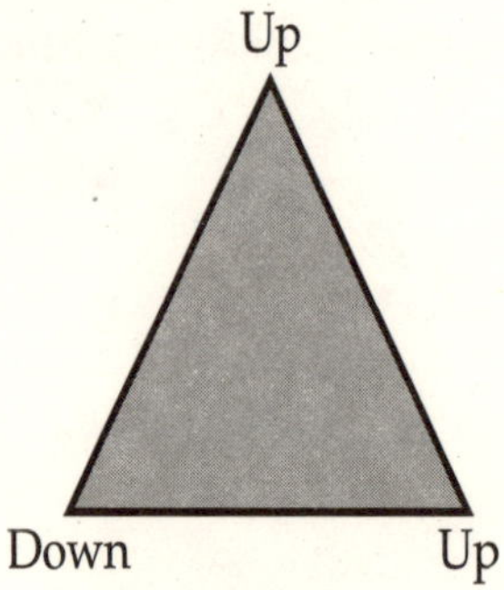

fig. 12: Proton

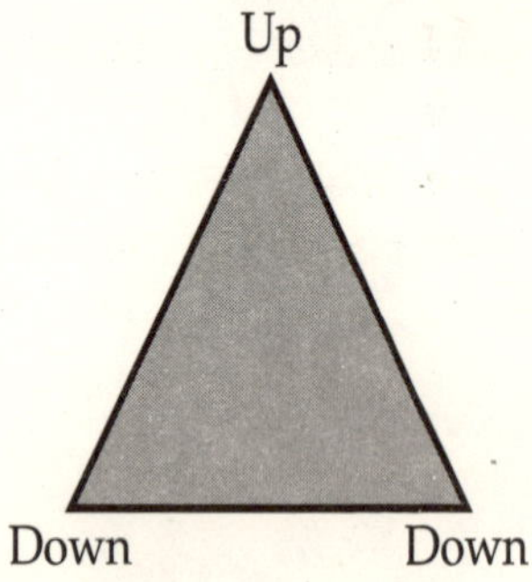

fig. 13: Neutron

[8] Dmitri Krioukov et al., "Network Cosmology", *Scientific Reports* 2, article no. 793, 16 November 2012. http://www.nature.com/srep/2012/121113/srep00793/full/srep00793.html

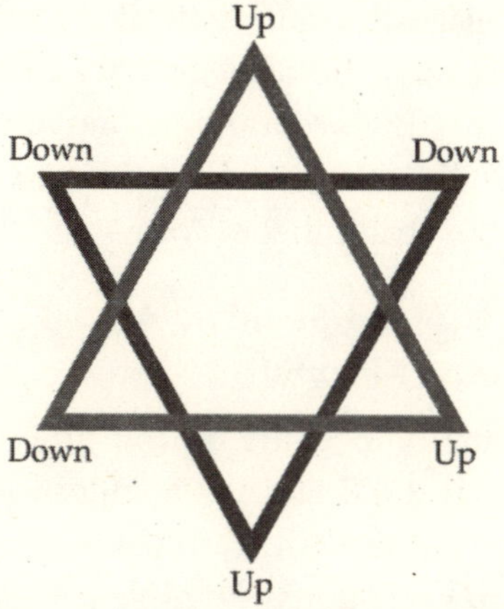

fig. 14: Nucleon

The nucleus itself can be expressed as a simpler version of Śrī-yantra with proton and neutron binding together.

It is also not surprising to note that a proton–neutron pair is found in abundance in the visible matter of the universe with significant presence of helium.

One can see how even at the level of biology, DNA is nothing but a helical structure, intermingling of one strand with its mirror image. Similarly, in the genetic code, genes are arranged in the triplet sets of codons. Up to the level of emergence of most complex life form, we find the continuous unfolding of same simple geometric design.

There is a lot of discussions going on about what after Standard Model, once Higgs Boson has been discovered? The challenges are still ahead as discussed above. Standard Model only explains less than 5 per cent of the universe. Moreover, Standard Model has not been fitted with the General Theory of Relativity (GTR) so that gravitation can be properly explained. It operates at a different scale. While gravitation operates only at longer distance and huge mass, Standard Model applies only to quantum level and atomic distances. The votaries of string theory hijacked headlines for long in postulating how all the particles are made up of elementary strings and different particles are merely strings vibrating differently. But, there have been huge mathematical inconsistencies and presuppositions that have made the string theory to march a retreat.

Unifying Relativity and Standard Model Through Ṭimbukṭu Algebra!

In recent years, the boldest attempt to unify gravity and the other three forces or GTR and the Standard Model was taken by American surfer-physicist, Garrett Lisi in his exceptionally elegant paper, "An Exceptionally Simple Theory of Everything"[9] in 2007. The work has hogged limelight since its publication. But, one will be surprised to know that this unification could be attempted by Lisi only by following the concept of "triality". Lisi introduces his paper with some a priori notion like, mathematics corresponds with reality. In other words, reality must be encapsulated in mathematical models. For him, Standard Model and GTR are the best mathematical descriptions we have of our universe and only by accepting these two as guiding principles, one can attempt a beautiful unification. And exactly, this is what he achieved by deploying E8 Lie algebra (named after the nineteenth-century Norwegian mathematician Sophus Lie) and obtained an exquisite model of the fundamental structure of the universe. In his E8 theory, all forces and matter are described as the twisting of a single geometric object. The Standard Model propounds the geometric idea that every point in space–time has shapes attached to it corresponding to a different kind of particle. These are known as fibres and the space–time along with fibres that appear as sprout as a fibre-

[9] Garrett Lisi, "An Exceptionally Simple Theory of Everything", http://www.arxiv.org/abs/0711.0770 also see Garrett Lisi and J.O. Weatherall, "A Geometric Theory of Everything", *Scientific American*, 2010, **303**(6): 54-61.

bundle. It appears as the mud houses of Ṭimbukṭu in Africa with spikes coming out of the mud houses and old constructed pyramids. Every force has its own fibre-bundle. Lisi mentions how fibre-bundle of electromagnetic force consists of circles attached to every point of space–time. The electromagnetic wave can be said to be in progression through the "undulation of circles over space–time". Different kinds of twisting of fibres produce different particles.

He uses the notion of triality where each root after rotation takes to first triality partner and then to its second and back. The triality rotation produces an elegant formula of $T^3 = 1$. By using the triality rotation, he explains mathematically the three generations of fermions. E8 root system was first described by Thorodd Gosset in 1900. It is drawn in a beautiful geometrical figure. It is a polytope.

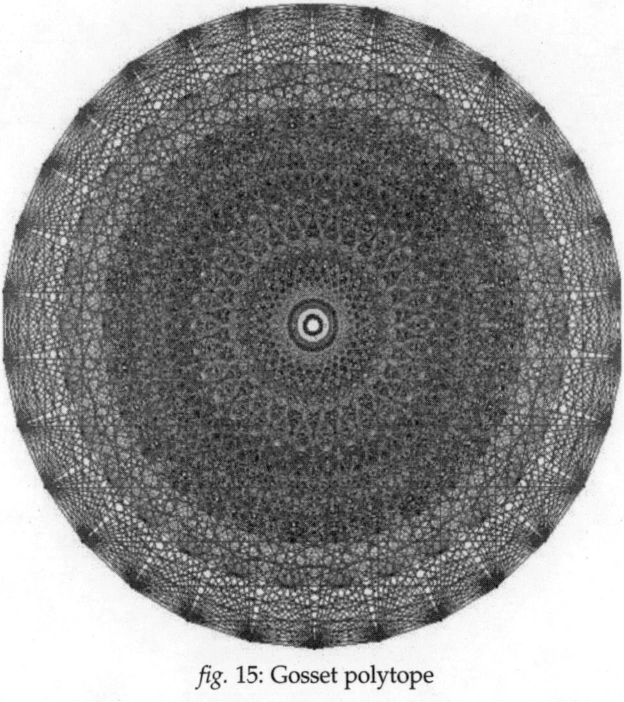

fig. 15: Gosset polytope

Lisi is the first to use it to attempt unification of two most elegant mathematical structures in physics. In the solution, each root of E8 corresponds to an elementary particle. Lisi could show how 222 elements in his algebra correspond to the quantum numbers of all gravitational and standard model field. In the E8 Lie algebra, the solution is 240 roots. Thus, Lisi is certain that missing 18 roots will correspond to new particles to be discovered in the experiments of high energy physics at LHC. Lisi's E8 polytope in eight-dimensional structures explains three generations of fermions related by triality. If one can stretch the imagination, the eight enclosures

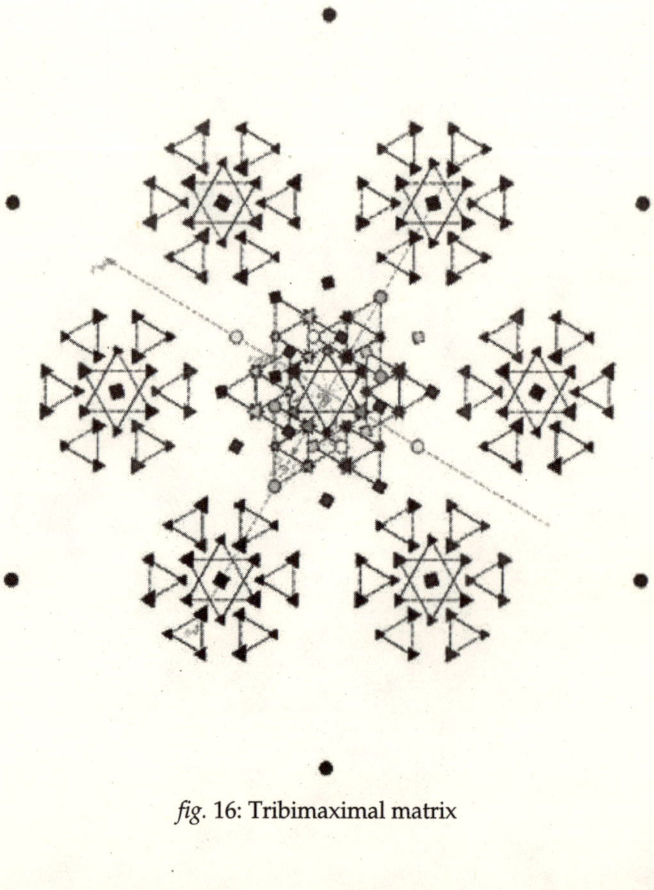

fig. 16: Tribimaximal matrix

in the geometrical figure of the solution appear very similar to Śrī-yantra which too has eight sheaths with the ninth as the merely central *bindu*. One can also observe how in the unifying model, there are triangles and upward and downward triangles intersecting to produce the simpler Śrī-yantra diagram as a hexagon; thus, in E8 root system, one can see how there are self-similar hexagons at the six vertices of two interesting triangles with vertices in opposite directions. Lisi has coined a term for his matrix — "tribimaximal" matrix — which is very much the description of Śrī-yantra also as it is the intersection of triad (tri) with its image (bi-) and producing maximal symmetry and self-replicating form.

SUSY as Grand Śrī-yantra

Weak Scale Supersymmetry (SUSY) is the most debated extension of the Standard Model. This aims to unify gravity with the three forces unified under the Standard Model. Popularly, the unification has been termed as SUSY. SUSY provides a symmetry between matter and forces, and predicts that for each known particle there is a "supersymmetric" partner. The generic prediction in SUSY is that every SM particle has a superpartner. Superpartners are mirror copies of the Standard Model under hidden interaction.

Though this doubles the number of particles with sparticles coming into picture, this brings unification and also anticipated to explain the dark matter and dark energy, since it is assumed that due to symmetry breaking, the sparticles gained greater mass than normal particles. Thus, the luminous matter composed of particles is only 4.6 per cent of the universe and remaining is composed of dark SUSY heavy particles.

Under SUSY, for every particle, there is a superpartner whose spin differs by 1/2. Thus, all standard model fermions have partners as SUSY boson and all standard model bosons have partners in SUSY fermions.

<table>
<tr><td colspan="2">Generation</td><td>I</td><td>II</td><td>II</td><td></td></tr>
<tr><td rowspan="4">Sfermion</td><td rowspan="2">Squarks</td><td>Sup
ũ</td><td>Scharm
c</td><td>Stop
t̃</td><td rowspan="4">Sbosons</td></tr>
<tr><td>Sdown
s̃</td><td>Sstrange
s̃</td><td>Sbottom
b̃</td></tr>
<tr><td>Sleptons</td><td>Sleptons
ẽ</td><td>Smuon
μ̃</td><td>Stauon
T̃</td></tr>
<tr><td></td><td>Selectron neutrino
$\tilde{\nu}_e$</td><td>Smuon neutrino
$\tilde{\nu}_\mu$</td><td>Stauon neutrino
$\tilde{\nu}_\tau$</td></tr>
</table>

Chart 2: SUSY model

Squarks are the superpartners of quarks and sleptons that of leptons.

The SUSY model can be geometrically represented as the full-scale Śrī-yantra. Śrī-yantra emerges after intersection of nine triangles, four facing upward and five downwards. The central triangle is equilateral triangle while others are isosceles. The whole geometric figure is contained within a circle. The largest up and down triangles' vertices touch the circumference. The up triangles correspond to Śiva and the down triangles the Śakti. The central *bindu* is the home to the source of creation — Tripurasundarī, the Goddess of Three Cities or Ṣoḍaśī, the sixteenth digit of immortality that pervades all aspects of universe without revealing herself. Within the innermost equilateral triangle, from the central dot emerges Vārāhī and Kurukullā, father-figure and mother-figure, respectively. The vertices of the central triangle is the home of three aspects of dynamic energy — Mahākālī, Mahāsarasvatī and Mahālakṣmī, corresponding respectively with the will, knowledge and action, or dissolution, consciousness and growth. The Śrī-yantra has unique mathematical properties like asymmetry at centre and symmetric neighbourhood. It produces secondary triangles that numbers forty-three. Thus, through the primary intersection of eight triangles with ninth at the centre, forty-three similar triangles multiply and produce an elegant geometric figure.

Śrī-yantra is the ultimate geometric principle of the universe. If Einstein believed how space-time relationship is merely a geometry and Standard Model Theory believes again in geometrical structure of the universe's make-up, SUSY, which combines the two, would also possess an elegant geometry. We have seen how by following the path of triadic logic, Lisi produced an elegant theory of everything with the E8 geometric figure resembling like a giant Śrī-yantra, without manifesting the triangular characteristics. But, Śrī-yantra is unique since with its forty-three secondary triangles and balanced ternary tree structure, it also explains the three generations of triadization.

Now let us consider four triangles of the fermions family. There will be four mirror triangles from the super fermions family. This adds up to eight primary triangles. I do not foresee the possibility of sparticles for Standard Model bosons. The

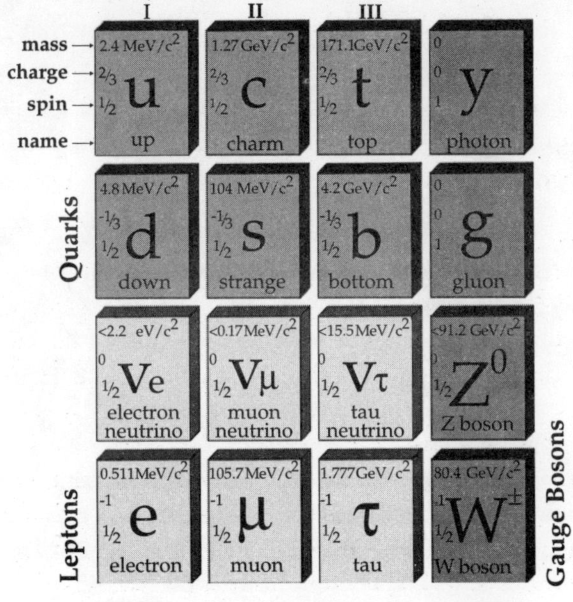

fig. 17: Three generations of matter (fermions)

neutalino and gluinos would be revealed as working of available force particles only. Inner ninth triangle will be independent with bosons — photon, gluon and W/Z boson-at three vertices mediating the force from the innermost core. At the centre can be the Higgs Boson as Ṣoḍaśī. Just as the central *bindu* creates Vārāhī and Kurukullā through Kāmakalā, primary Higgs Boson can be predicted to create its second- and third-generation resonances. While the central *bindu* Higgs Boson can be responsible for luminous matter, other two Higgs Bosons can be credited with dark matter and dark energy. SUSY model can be constructed as a giant Śrī-yantra. Each secondary triangle can correspond to different kind of interaction at the fundamental level. The Śrī-yantra model can also explain the oscillatory nature of the universe from quantum to cosmic level. It can also solve the hierarchy problem.

Recently a team led by Dmitri Krioukov in the work on network cosmology has hinted at a common law that governs the dynamics of complex networks as different as space–time, human brain and internet. In the research work published in the *Scientific Reports* in November 2012, the team based at the San Diego Supercomputer Center (SDSC) at the University of California, San Diego, concluded:

> Structural and dynamical similarities of different real networks suggest that some universal laws might accurately describe the dynamics of these networks, albeit the nature and common origin of such laws remain elusive. Here we show that the causal network representing the large-scale structure of space–time in our accelerating universe is a power-law graph with strong clustering, similar to many complex networks such as the Internet, social, or biological networks. We prove that this structural similarity is a consequence of the asymptotic equivalence between the large-scale growth dynamics of complex networks and

> causal networks. This equivalence suggests that unexpectedly similar laws govern the dynamics of complex networks and space–time in the universe, with implications to network science and cosmology.[10]

The scientists are now groping to discover the common law that applies to three levels of consciousness in the universe — universe itself with law-based thermodynamic intelligence, human beings with error-prone forgetful memory-based intelligence and machines with computational intelligence. The ubiquity of hexagonal structures, the Meru of Śrī-yantra, provides a glimpse to discover the hidden common law of organizing complex networks.

In Indian tradition, mirror analogy is what explains the unity and the multiplicity of beings simultaneously. Śrī-yantra, incorporates the reflection analogy into geometry and produces the multiplicity while maintaining the primary triangular characteristics of the constituent figures. It produces forty-three triangles which are produced through three generations of triadization and, amazingly, the experiments have confirmed the presence of only three generations of fermions. Śrī-yantra can be redefined as the cosmic principle in which an object with its triadic nature self-reflects and intersects with its reflection to produce plurality while retaining the originality as well as the unity. The whole cosmos now appears to be a living whole from terascale to humanscape.

---

10 Krioukov et al., n. 8.

7

Śrī-yantra
Footprints from Kaṭrā to Paris

GEOMETRIZATION of knowledge is in vogue. This is the hallmark of transmodern turn, an epistemic shift in global consciousness. I have been quite excited to see how geometrical structures are being explored from tiniest level to cosmic level. Albert Lautman (1908-44), a French mathematician–philosopher, discovered the "primacy of geometric synthesis" over that of the "numerical" analysis. The rise of combinatorial geometries which deal with combinations and arrangements of geometric objects and with their properties has added to the major shift in mathematics. More the communication of information and transaction of goods in a globalized market are deepening, the aesthetic aspects concerning packing, covering, colouring, folding, etc. are seizing the best minds to expand frontiers of new geometry. Study of spatial pattern formation in chemical and biological systems has arrived. Alan Turing had predicted forty years back how a system of reacting and diffusing chemicals could spontaneously evolve to spatially complex pattern from an initially uniform state after minor perturbations. Search for Turing structures in chemistry has led scientists to discover now the black-eye patterns, self-replicating spots and so on.

Similarly, genomics itself has been geometrized under the able guidance of Andras J. Pellionisz. He is trying to geometrize neuroscience also and synthesizing fractal geometry with such biological dimensions. In recent years, scientists from Laboratory of Molecular Sciences, University of South California, have discovered DNA triangles and self-assembled hexagonal tiling. The team described that while existing DNA self-assembled structures use helices as linear elements, they created non-linear helices from triangular complexes which stick at vertices.[1] The arrangement of triangles in hexagonal structures appears as if two triangles, with an upward and downward vertices intersect. This is exactly what forms the first basic structure of Śrī-yantra.

Star of David as Meru of Śrī-yantra

Śrī-yantra is drawn from nine triangles, four pointed upward and five pointed downward, that intersect and interlock to form forty-two small triangles around a central small triangle. But, the first drawing is made of two triangles intersecting to form a hexagon. These are the biggest primary triangles. Left to itself, the hexagonal star (*ṣaṭakoṇa*) is the Lakṣmī-*yantra* in Indian spirituality, closely related with the Goddess of Śrī-yantra whose one aspect is the goddess of prosperity,

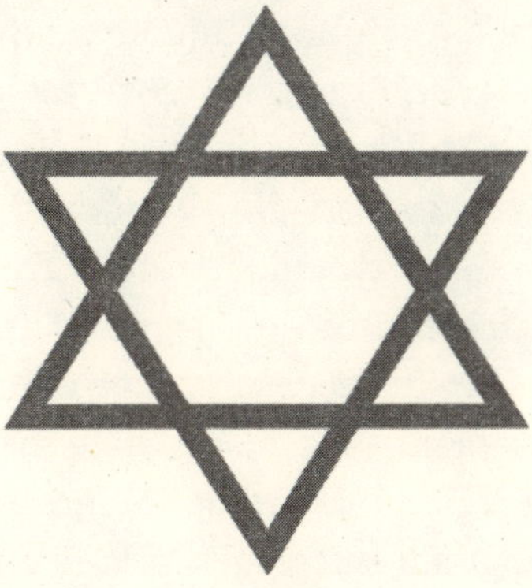

[1] Nickolas Chelyapov, Manoj Gopalkrishnan et al., "DNA Triangles and Self-Assembled Hexagonal Tilings", *Journal of the American Chemical Society*, 2004, **126**: 13924-25.

Mahālakṣmī. The triangle pointing upwards represents Śiva, male principle, and the triangle with apex downward, as the Śakti principle. The interlocking of two principles manifests the universe.

Tirumūḷar in his *magnum opus* on Tantra *Tirumantiram,* written in the seventh century, places the six-pointed *yantra* as the *yantra* of Tripura-Bhairavī (chapter 5 of Tantra 4).[2] For, Tirumūḷar, the star-shaped *yantra* is Śrī-yantra. But, I would put the same as the Meru of Śrī-yantra, the foundational structure of Śrī-yantra.

It is surprising that the hexagon formed by the interlocking triangles is also an auspicious symbol in the semitic culture. The Star of David is the symbol of Judaism. The trinity stands for the relationship among body, soul and spirit. While, we are witnessing geometrization of sciences, there is a parallel process of trinitization of knowledge brought through Peircean revolution.

Śrī-yantra: Secret of Memory

In 2012, a new research on memory encoding by a team of scientists has caused a sensation among neuroscientists. Stuart Hameroff et al. have done an extensive work on quantum consciousness. The team discovered the secret of memory encoding after working on the paradox that even though, synaptic receptors and channel protein are transient, being synthesized and degraded in the protein life-cycle, memories do last lifelong. They tried to discover where does memory restore and yet remain able to regulate synaptic plasticity. The team finally discovered that memory is encoded and processed in hexagonal microtubule lattice within the nerve cells. Turing patterns are found in biological systems across scale — from micro to mega. Critical neurons representation

[2] Tirumūḷar, *Tirumantiram: A Tamil Scriptural Classic,* Madras: Ramakrishna Math, 2002.

maps are organized hexagonally and grid cells in cortex arrange in hexagonal patterns. Thus, hexagonal pattern is seen in human brain at varying scales. The team proposes that "scale-free" implies self-similar information pattern repeating at different spatial and temporal scales and like fractal, these are very durable. They suggest that microtubules can generate Turing patterns that operate at multiple scales to regulate biological systems through scale-free information patterns.[3]

We often find hexagonal structures in biology like a honey-bee comb. Hexagons provide one of the best packing structures. But, there can be other reasons also pertaining to coherence intensity of hexagonal Turing structures. This might be the reason for ubiquity of hexagon in esoteric rituals world across.

Sacred Network in Paris

Chris Hardy, in her path-breaking work, *The Sacred Network: Megaliths, Cathedrals, Ley Lines, and the Power of Shared Consciousness* (2011), astounds readers with her unveiling of structure of Paris City:

> Whole ensembles of buildings were fitting into vast structures based on sacred geometry. To give you an idea: a large golden rectangle, which has the Obelisk as a center, extends from Etoile plaza to Châtelet plaza. Moreover, this golden rectangle is surrounded by a hexagon sharing the same center and being marked by important churches and avenues. Nested within both the golden rectangle and the hexagon, and having the same node, the Obelisk is a magnificent masterpiece of sacred geo-architecture.[4]

---

3 Travis J. Craddock, Stuart Hameroff et al., "Cytoskeletal Signaling: Is Memory Encoded in Microtube Lattices by CaMKII Phosphorylation?", *PLoS Computational Biology*, 2012, **8**(3): 1-16.

4 Chris H. Hardy, *The Sacred Network: Megaliths, Cathedrals, Ley Lines, and the Power of Shared Consciousness*, Rochester: Inner Traditions/ Bear & Company, 2011.

Hardy has been traversing the ancient cities and sites to measure the cosmo-telluric lines which influence human consciousness. She stumbled upon one in the city of Paris and discovered the hexagon, which occurs in sacred geometry worldwide:

> Another exceptional geometrical and symbolic design is the St John the Baptist's Pyramid. A large triangle is formed by three of the five churches dedicated to St John the Baptist. The inner node of this triangle is . . . the Obelisk. Both the western church and the triangle's center are on Paris' main east–west axis. The eastern side of the triangle goes through Saint-Sulpice Church (built above an ancient Isis temple), then passes in front of Carreau du Temple — part of the medieval headquarters of the Knights Templars' worldwide order. Another line in this structure runs into the prominent St Denis Church, and connecting St Denis to the three St John churches creates a pyramidal shape. The symbolical richness of the whole St. John's Pyramid is astounding.[5]

She goes on to postulate massive geostructure of Śrī-yantra within Paris[6] after examining the hexagon. I would not term it as Śrī-yantra, but yes, this is one of the foundational frameworks of Śrī-yantra.

Hardy develops the hypothesis:

> Giant telluric waves, undulating vertically and linked to the geomagnetic field of earth, create a network of crisscrossing lines all around earth. The megaliths builders had understood that the points at which these waves crisscross each other had a tantamount effect on consciousness.[7]

---

5 Chris H. Hardy, *The Sacred Network: Megaliths, Cathedrals, Ley Lines, and the Power of Shared Consciousness*, Rochester: Inner Traditions/ Bear & Company, 2011, p. 7

6 Ibid., pp. 229-30, 235-36.

7 Ibid., p. 4.

There is an excellent scientific study on telluric currents, published under the title, *The Earth's Electric Environment* (1986) by the Geophysics Committee under the aegis of National Academy of Sciences.

Louis J. Lanzerotti of AT&T Bell Laboratories and Giovanni P. Gregori of Istituto Di Fisica Dell'Atmosfera, Rome, explain telluric currents in the following words:

> Telluric currents consist of both the natural electric currents flowing within the earth, including the oceans, and the electric currents originating from man-made systems. Telluric currents could also be considered to include geodynamo currents, i.e. the electric currents that are presumed to flow in the earth's core and are responsible for the generation of the "permanent" geomagnetic field. This review excludes geodynamo considerations from its purview. They are produced either through electromagnetic induction by the time-varying, external-origin geomagnetic field or whenever a conducting body (such as sea water) moves (because of tides or other reason) across the earth's permanent magnetic field. Both causes produce telluric currents, which, in turn, produce magnetic fields of their own — fields that add to the external origin geomagnetic field and produce a feedback on the ionosphere current system.[8]

The team does catalogue the work on responses of living species to electromagnetic fields produced by telluric currents. These include the induced currents in a tree produced by geomagnetic

---

[8] Louis J. Lanzerotti and Giovanni P. Gregori, "Telluric Currents: The Natural Environment and Interactions with Man-made Environment" in Geophysics Study Committee, Geophysics Research Forum, Commission on Physical Sciences, Mathematics and Resources, National Research Council (eds.), *Studies in Geophysics: The Earth's Electrical Environment*, National Academy of Sciences, 1986, pp. 212-50.

fluctuations and the use of magnetic fields for orientation by aquatic bacteria and by migrating birds. Magnetite crystals have been reported as isolated from a sinus in the yellowfin tuna. Enhanced DNA synthesis has been reported for human fibroblasts exposed to magnetic-field fluctuations with frequencies and amplitudes similar to many geomagnetic occurrences.[9]

Therefore, Hardy is not wrong in postulating the impact of cosmo-telluric current over human consciousness. She postulates that "megaliths" people must have had the

> gift of seeing and sensing these cosmo-telluric lines — a gift that enabled them to gather a whole body of knowledge about the influence their flows and crossings had on human consciousness — namely they trigger a shift to a heightened and more spiritual state of consciousness.

It is upon same sites for millennia that sacred temples and monuments have been built. She further argues that the telluric impact becomes stronger at those points where there is a hexagonal structure created by the presence of upward and downward energy triangles. She claims that every sacred site is an AG site. A-spot is the triangle having an upward apex like temples, domes, steeple above ground and, G-spot as the triangle having a downward apex like caves, sources and rivers which are underground. When both are at the same place, it is a high telluric current zone and the place becomes a sacred spot. In two-dimensional schemata, it will be a hexagon and in three-dimensional schemata an octahedron is formed which is diamond shaped, eulogized so much as *vajra* in Hinduism and Buddhism.

She describes the churches and cathedrals, mega structures of Paris, by pursuing her cosmo-telluric hypothesis and

---

9 Louis J. Lanzerotti and Giovanni P. Gregori, op. cit., p. 249.

provides an answer to the continuing relevance of same spot for the generation as scared or special centres.

Cosmo-telluric Lines and Mā Vaiṣṇo Devī Shrine

Mā Vaiṣṇo Devī shrine is unique. There is a cave up in the mountain and there is water stream inside the cave. Stream in a mountain cave creates double-level of energy — it gushes forth and it also descends from top. So, it has both the properties of ascending and descending energy. This is a perfect AG spot. But, more interesting, this is the sacred spot with scale-free trinity structure. The shrine is situated in the region of three adjacent mountain peaks (Trikūṭa). The cave itself has three sacred stone-emanation. Now, the government has built two more tunnels for smooth flow of pilgrims. This has created a three-tunnel structure to the holy spot. The cosmic energies appear to be in perfect trinitarian harmony. No doubt, a stable hexagon of energy persists inside the shrine. Since the adjoining mountains do have mines where magnetite deposits have been found at Kaṭrā-Panthal area, the huge deposit of magnetite and the trapping of lightening energy within the particular mountainous topology may enhance cosmo-telluric currents in the region. With the location of holy *piṇḍī*s inside the cave, a powerful combination of forces attains a stability that profoundly effects human consciousness and may cause entrainment thereby causing long-lasting impact over pilgrim's psyche. Thus, the visit to shrine for the first time makes a pilgrim a regular visitor for it induces euphoria and one longs for the same experience again and again.

Pilgrimage to the sacred Trikūṭa mountains in the state of Jammu & Kashmir is extremely popular for every Indian *tīrtha-yātrī* (pilgrim). More than eight million devotees visit the holy cave in the Śivālik range, almost 60 km away from Jammu every year. The importance of Mā Vaiṣṇo Devī can be gauged from the fact that it is being duplicated and widely disseminated.

The connection with the Vaiṣṇo Devī shrine is often indicated by its setting among snow-capped mountains, particularly among the three peaks of Trikūṭa.[10]

Most of the pilgrims begin their journey from Kaṭrā and there is a 13-km mountain trek to Bhawan where the holy cave is situated. Popular *darśana* sites include Bāṇagaṅgā, Darśanī Darwājā, Caraṇa Pādukā, Ardhakuṅwārī, Bhawan and the Bhairoṅ Temple. But, the first *darśana* has to begin from Kaul Kandoli at Nagroṭā. There is Deva Māī which is the sacred site for second *darśana*. Here Vaiṣṇo Devī revealed her cosmic self to Paṇḍit Śyāmidāsjī, the fourth generation of Paṇḍit Shridhar, who discovered the caves after getting guidance in a dream.

[10] Georgana Foster and Robert Stoddard, "Vaishno Devi, the Most Famous Goddess Shrine in the Siwaliks" in Rana P.B. Singh (ed.), *Sacred Geography of Goddess in South Asia*, New Castle upon Tyne: *Cambridge Scholars*, 2010, p. 121.

In the triadic thinking, number 9 recurs. I have discussed how number 9 is significant in the construction of Śrī-yantra. Śrī-yantra being a representation of human body with nine holes and nine bodily constituents like phlegm, sweat, blood and bone has nine intersecting triangles.

Durgā, the Mother Goddess who is worshipped during the national festival of Daśaharā, has nine forms symbolizing eight directions in space and the ninth as the great centre. There are nine planets in Hindu cosmogony, eight planets and ninth, the sun as the centre and source of power to other eight planets. Surprisingly, the recurrence of this structure assumes nature of fractality of dynamic system.

Mā Vaiṣṇo Devī's posters are similar to Durgā, only the three mountain peaks in the background posit the difference. In the myth/legend/narrative about Mā Vaiṣṇo Devī, number 9 recurs. There are nine places for *darśana*. Mother was nine-year old when the first divine spark was manifested. To avoid the evil gaze of the tāntric Bhairava, she hid herself in the cave at Ardhakuṅwārī for nine months. This cave is also known as Garbhajūna (womb-cave) signifying nine month of being in Mother's womb. Mā Vaiṣṇo Devī created another opening by her trident at the other end of the cave. This is allegory for opening of womb and play of three *guṇa*s (*sat*, *rajas*, *tama*s) that govern the wheel of existence.

There is connection between the semiotics of Śrī-cakra, the symbolic matrix of the cosmos and Mā Vaiṣṇo Devī of Trikūṭa. The name of Vaiṣṇavī as one related to Lord Viṣṇu appears in the *mantra*s of Śrī-yantra. Vaiṣṇavī is the fourth among the eight Mātṛkās, the great mothers of phonemic emanations. Hence, she represents the intersection of the four-part *pada* structure (3 + 1) and eight-layered reality (ninth is the central pulsating dot).

Tripurasundarī, the Goddess of Śrī-yantra, is in the form of Ṣoḍaśī (sixteen-year old beautiful maiden). She is represented in the sonic universe by certain alphabets. The rosary of alphabet is the *ṣoḍaśākṣarī mantra* (sixteen-letter *mantra*). She is said to reside in the Trikūṭa (chapter 10 of *Śrī-Tattva-Cintāmaṇi*, verse 118).[11] Trikūṭa in Tantra stands for three *kūṭas* (codes/rosary of seed alphabets/secret *mantra*). Those are Vāgbhava Kūṭa, Kāmrāja Kūṭa and Śakti Kūṭa representing the goddess of knowledge, prosperity and power (Mahā-Sarasvatī, Mahā-Lakṣmī and Mahā-Kālī).

The Trikūṭa mountain where the shrine of Goddess Vaiṣṇo Devī is located has three adjacent peaks. Trikūṭa does mean semantically "three peaks". This is the polysemic acausal relationship so prevalent in the Indian culture. In the sacred cave, three *piṇḍī*s represent Mahā-Sarasvatī, Mahā-Lakṣmī and Mahā-Kālī. Mā Vaiṣṇo Devī is believed to be the combination of all three great goddesses similar to Tripurasundarī. Interestingly, Tripurasundarī has been named "Vaiṣṇavī" in *Śrīlalitā Sahasranāma* (verse 166). The connection of Śrī-cakra worship and Mātā Vaiṣṇo Devī shrine is yet to be fully explored. But, one thing is certain that in the liberalizing India, the duplication of two connected things has grown manifold. Both are not merely cultural icons, but also the manifestation of a triadic geometry.

It may be Paris or Mā Vaiṣṇo Devī shrine, geometry holds the key to understand the fascination that human mind has for such sacred and special spots. But, with so powerful effect over consciousness, I would prefer to be a recurrent pilgrim to Mā Vaiṣṇo Devī shrine rather than to Paris!

---

[11] Chintamani Bhattacharya, *Śrī-Tattva-Cintāmaṇi*, Calcutta: Metropolitan Printing and Publishing House Limited, 1937; Also in *Śrī Lalitā Sahasranāma Stotram*, verse 118.

8

Bhārata Mātā

Map and Śrī-yantra

Source: http://www.columbia.edu/itc/mealac/pritchett/00routesdata/1800_1899/congress/bharatmata/bharatmata.html

ANNA Hazare's agitation and Baba Ramdev's protests in Delhi resurfaced patriotic fervour. The magnificent image of Bhārata Mātā was on display at the podium. The slogan of "Bhārata Mātā kī Jai" reverberated across India. Even in newsroom studios, protest leaders whenever retorted to a battery of silly questions from the news channel anchors, the reply usually was intermittently interrupted by the slogan shouting of "Bhārata Mātā kī Jai", "Vande Mātaram".

The year 2012 was the year of regeneration of patriotic spirit. The carriers are again the age-old trusted slogans of Bhārata Mātā. National debate about "Bhārata vs. India" is tilting in favour of "Bhārata". Bhārata stands for the non-English speakers, peasants, labourers, students and youth, technivists and the young Indian diaspora, whereas India has become emblematic of the crony capitalists, media crooks and crony leadership. While the imagery and slogan of Bhārata Mātā have emerged as the most potent binding spirit for the regeneration of patriotic virtue, it is appropriate to look into the sacred history of Bhārata Mātā.

India's Imagined Sacred Landscape

India is a sacred land. Benedict Anderson's model of "nation state" as imagined community[1] has made scholars to deconstruct the very idea of India. There was a coterie of historians under subaltern school whose sole objective was to denationalize India, while there are few globalization experts who claim to defragment India's border and to unify the fragments with wider trans-Indian region.[2] But, a counter-

---

1 Benedict Anderson, *Imagined Communities: Reflections on the Origin and Spread of Nationalism*, London: Verso, 1991.

2 William van Schendel, "Geographies of Knowing, Geographies of Ignorance: Jumping Scale in Southeast Asia", *Development and Planning D: Society and Space*, 2002, **20**: 647-68.

school, which is more influential than either of the two, has begun to argue that India's identity is rooted in its imagined sacred landscape, in its pilgrimage routes and the strategy of duplication. Diana Eck, David Kinseley, Rana P.B. Singh, Ravi P. Singh, John M. Malville, Sumathi Ramaswamy and Anne Feldhaus are some of the scholars who have put sacred landscape at the heart of Indian identity.

Indian geography has been described in various Purāṇas as well as *Mahābhārata.* The Tīrtha-yātrā-Parva in the Vana-Parva of *Mahābhārata* contains description of India's sacred geography. *Brahmāṇḍa Purāṇa* is an encyclopaedia. Apart from the Purāṇic descriptions, ancient Indian astronomers were also cartographers in their own way. They had the knowledge of Roma (Rome), Java, Sri Lanka, Tibet and the knowledge was used in calculating the calendrical time. One has to just flip through the ninth-century writer Rajaśekhar's work[3] to realize the advanced knowledge about territorial geography. But, the credit for establishing the continuing tradition of pilgrimage across four *dhāma*s that mark the four corners of this scared territory goes to Śaṅkarācārya (eighth century CE). The pilgrimage system and the mythologies intermingled neatly to weave the fabric of "sacred landscape".

Eck generates a grammar of signification in the "imagined landscape" of India in the recent work, *India: Sacred Geography,*[4] largely taken from Anne Feldhaus's work, *Connected Places: Region, Pilgrimage and Geographical Imagination in India* (2003).[5] The latter work is based upon Feldhaus' extensive work on

---

3 Sadhana Parashar, *Kāvyamīmāṁsā of Rājaśekhara,* Delhi: D.K. Printworld, 2000.

4 Diana Eck, *India: A Sacred Geography,* New York: Harmony Books, 2012.

5 Anne Feldhaus, *Connected Places: Region, Pilgrimage, and Geographical Imagination in India,* New York: Palgrave Macmillan, 2003.

pilgrimages in Maharashtra. She has been arguing for many years that the cosmos as well as the land of India are pictured as organic whole and a sacred geography. The living landscape in India is full of signification. There have been networks of pilgrimages across the nation which are the *tīrtha*s that is believed to help in the "crossing over". These places themselves have non-terrestrial origin and believed to be either *svayambhū* as with the *jyortirliṅga*s and the case of appearance of Rāmalallā idol at Ram-Janmabhoomi in the year 1949; or to have descended (*avataraṇa*) like the sacred river Gaṅgā. Eck finds that the identity of India is rooted in living landscape that is constructed through pilgrimage networks. Finally, she generates a grammar of shaping of Bhārata as a scared landscape.

Such work on India's cultural geography and the conception of India as a geobody tracing back to the earliest times when the *tīrtha-yātrā* system ensued has affected a paradigmatic shift. The Western and Westoxified Indian intellectuals always parried India as an artificial construct a la' British empire. But, now the mainstream academics have come to accept India as an integrated sacred landscape. The source of unity amidst linguistic, regional and topographic diversities lies in the collective sharing of this sacred landscape that characterized Hinduism.

Idea of India is not a modern construct but merely resonates the ancient idea of Bhārata. India is not the cartographic map, it is the sacred Bhārata, the Mother Goddess, Bhāratī dotted with sacred landscape and enlivened by the people and the pilgrims.

Cartography of India

Indigenous "maps" were based on various *avataraṇa* myths and Purāṇic geography. The first modern map of India was drawn by d'Anville, a French in 1751-52. But, the most popular map was created by James Rennell whose *Map of Hindoostan* (1788)[6] was very comprehensive. He was the Surveyor General of Bengal and published the *Bengal Atlas* in 1779.

Manoshi Lahiri has produced a wonderful collection of the maps of India in her recent book, *Mapping India* (2012).[7] She has compiled the visual history of the creation of modern India. It is evident from the detour of the work that in spite of the rise and fall of empires and the shift of capitals, India has remained, very nearly, the land bordered by the Himalayas in the north, the Indian Ocean in the south and great rivers on either side. There is a continuity and something underneath the collective imagination springing from the geography that has kept India united and largely peaceful internally.

Before Indian nationalists learnt to cartograph India, the cosmography of the sacred landscape was done by placing the sacred sites in a cow's body. Thus, Banaras's pilgrimage centres can be seen to form the body of the cow. The image of cosmic cow (Kāmadhenu) is one of the most powerful surviving symbols. *Puruṣa* is like the cow and the four Vedas, the four nipples in the udder that provide milk of wisdom. I assume that the first mapping of territory by Indians as a reaction to colonial mapping would have been in the form of a cow. The territory was assumed as Gaumātā (Mother Cow).

Why do I posit this view? Because, the Hindu revivalism and national movement coalesced around the symbol of cow. Swami Dayananda Saraswati, the founder of Ārya Samāj,

---

[6] James Rennell, *Memoir of a Map of Hindoostan; or the Mogul Empire*: with an introduction, illustrative of the geography and present division of that country: and a map of the countries situated between the head of the Indus and the Caspian Sea (1788), available at www.ia700504.us.archive.org/8/items/memoirofmapofhin00renn/memoirofmapofhin00renn.pdf

[7] Manoshi Lahiri, *Mapping India*, Delhi: Niyogi Books, 2012.

established the first Gorakshini Sabha in 1882. But, when in 1886, the Allahabad High Court ruled that the cow was not a sacred object in accordance with the newly-introduced IPC (Section 295), there was a strong Cow Protection Movement.[8] The desacralization of the cow was the main reason for massive popular support against British rule as well as the Muslims. The communal riots spread across Bhojpur and Shāhabad, Ayodhyā and Varanasi.

The cow as the symbol of Mother India was turning counter-productive. The solution was soon found. The image of Bhārata Mātā with a modern cartographic map of India in the background was created to channelize the political movement of emancipation from the colonial rule.

Bhārata Mātā

Kirin Chandra Banerjee is credited with creating the title character of a dispossessed Mother in the play, "Bhārata Mātā" that was first performed in 1873.[9] Bhārata Mātā was the source of inspiration for the all-time patriotic composition "Vande Mātaram" and appeared in Bankim Chandra Chatterjee's novel *Ānandamaṭh*, in 1882. This caused the stirring of national imagination. In the year 1904/1905, she appeared under the name Baṅga Mātā (Mother Bengal) in Abanindranath Tagore's painting of a four-armed, saffron-clad Beṅgālī woman holding the four gifts of the Motherland to her children — *anna–vastra–śikṣā–dīkṣā* (food, cloth, education and spiritual salvation) in her four hands.[10]

8 Jackie Assayag, "The Body of India: Geography, Ritual, Nation", *Etnografica*, 1997, **1**(1): 39.

9 Zo Margaret Newel, *Picturing the Goddess: Bazaar Images and the Imagination of Modern Hindu Religious Identity*, Ph.D. Dissertation, Graduate School of Vanderbilt University, Nashville, Tennessee, 2011, p. 226.

10 Debashish Banerjee, *The Alternate Nation of Abanindranath Tagore*, →

In 1905, she was eulogized as the Bhārata Mātā, probably upon Sister Nivedita's advice. Sister Nivedita herself wrote a piece, *The Spirit of the Motherland* (1906). The image began to be mechanically reproduced and generated in a kind of "visual patriotism".[11]

Bhārata Mātā, painting by Abanindranath Tagore, 1905

Subramaniam Bharati (11 December 1882 – 11 September 1921) popularized the idea of Bhārata Mātā in the Tamil region with his powerful poetries and writings. On 20 April 1907

→ New Delhi: Sage, 2010, Debashish Banerjee is the great-grandson of Abanindranath Tagore. The original painting of Bhārata Mātā is kept safely with the Rabindra Bharati Society, Kolkata.

11 Sumathi Ramaswamy, *The Goddess and the Nation: Mapping Mother India*, Durham and London: Duke University Press, 2009, p. 49.

Bharati published a Map of India on Indian New Year in his magazine *Intiya*. Again, when he escaped to Pondicherry, he continued to popularize the image of Bhārata Mātā standing across the map of India. The image travelled across the borders. In Geneva, a magazine financed by Bhikaji Cama began publication. The title of the magazine was *Bande Mataram: Monthly Organ of Indian Independence*. Lala Lajpat Rai started a journal called *Vande Mataram* from Lahore. On 7 August 1906 the *Bande Mataram* daily journal was started by Bipin Chandra Pal and later became the mouth-piece of Sri Aurobindo's political vision. The researchers can explore meeting of two great minds, Sri Aurobindo and Bharati, who infused passion for Bhārata Mātā while living contemporaneously in Pondicherry.

Indian nationalists brought a unique fusion after the query by Rabindranath Tagore that "no one can give up his life for a Map".[12] They anthropomorphized the map form of India and cartographed the gendered body of Mother India.[13] Bhārata Mātā merged with Indian territory. The modern form of popular Bhārata Mātā image is credited to Roopkishore Kapur (1893–1978). Finally, a temple was built for Bhārata Mātā in the spiritual centre of Indian civilization, Banaras where map of undivided India is placed in the background. The temple was built by Babu Shiv Prasad Gupt and inaugurated by Mahatma Gandhi, in 1936.

Sumathi Ramaswamy writes in her book that "the anthropomorphization of earth as sentient female and as Pr̥thvī is as old as Hinduism. . . ."[14] David Kinseley, famous for his work on Indian goddesses, states:

---

[12] Newel, n. 9, p. 220.

[13] Ramaswamy, n. 11, p. 36

[14] Ibid., p. 102.

> The fundamental conviction that the earth itself, or the Indian subcontinent itself, is a goddess, indeed, that she is one's mother, pervades the modern cult of Bhārata Mātā (Mother India).[15]

Bhārata Mātā is not a mere nationalist construct as argued by some. Indian collective memory in the form of *kathā, māhātmya,* Purāṇas always viewed the territory as a geographic entity which is coextensive with the goddess's body and sanctified by *avatārs* and *avatar*-entities like the river Gaṅgā and the hilltops.

What is surprising is the gendering of the territory of Bhārata. The geography of Bhāratavarṣa derives its name from the legendary emperor Bharata. But, rather than Bhāratavarṣa emerging as a Fatherland, the female form of Goddess Bhārata Mātā came to represent the territory of Bhāratavarṣa. This has to do with the geophilosophy of India.

There is always a lingering cartographic anxiety among us, after the partition in 1947. We survived thousands of years of external aggression and retained the collective imagination about our sacred territory. It was the British who brought the accurate cartography that led to amputation of India's geo-body. Therefore, maps are the surfaces of our strategic tension with Pakistan, China, Bangladesh. The maps produce paranoia among us. It is the Bhārata Mātā image that provides hope and succour since it represents the continuity, survival and sustainability of our landscape. Thus, during the time of national crisis, every Indian automatically raises his/her hands and sings "Vande Mātaram" and "Bhārata Mātā kī Jai". This springs from the collective unconscious, the symbolic ocean

---

15 David Kinseley, *Hindu Goddess: Vision of the Divine Feminine in the Hindu Religious Tradition,* Berkeley: University of California Press, 1986, p. 181.

of our imagination. It is the de-Indianized locals whose heart and soul never throbbed for this sacred territory who feel ashamed of joining the patriotic fervour.

Bhārata Mātā is the goddess of patriotism. We are her devotees, but there are very few temples devoted to her. She instills in us the patriotic virtue, but we never worship her at home, like we do with the posters of other gods and goddesses. There has been a recent attempt to expose "subterfuge of antiquities"[16] behind the emergence of Bhārata Mātā idea and to take out the venerable spirit from this deity of patriotism. This can have debilitating impact on our unity which derives the gluing power from the sacred imagination. It is no body's case that Bhārata Mātā is an anthropomorphic image of Indian territory and a cartographic form of an image. The cartographic representations show Bhārata Mātā's body either emerging from or coextensive with Indian territory.

Sumathi Ramaswamy characterizes Bhārata Mātā as a

> new and unusual mother/goddess [with a] complicated entanglement in the Indian nation's attempts to create for itself a visible and tangible form over the course of a century that began in the 1880s.[17]

She questions the garb of antiquity in which Bhārata Mātā has been presented to Indian followers and describes her as

> a tangled product of charged encounters between the new and the old and of a fraught and conflicted modernity that is India's late colonial and post-colonial experience of history.[18]

---

16 Quoted in Ramaswamy, n. 11, p. 55. For details see Sudipto, Kaviraj, *The Unhappy Consciousness: Bankimchandra Chattopadhyay and the Formation of Nationalist Discourse in India*, Oxford: Oxford University Press, 1995, p. 13.

17 Ibid., p. 2.

18 Ibid.

Ramaswamy argues that Bhārata Mātā is less a modern manifestation of Devī than a nationalist response to the problem articulated by Tagore in the maxim: "No one can give up his life for a map". Ramaswamy argues that Hindu reformers attempted to conceal the recent origins of their religious and national vision "by resorting to all manner of subterfuges of antiquity". Ramaswamy maintains:

> [I]t is a pictorial analysis that is most revelatory of the extent to which her devotees cover Mother India in the garb of antiquity. So much so that it is commonplace for her followers — and some scholars — to be taken in by the subterfuge and assume that she is one among the many time-honoured goddesses of the region. Yet she is not one, and even the subterfuges of antiquity to which her pictures resort are unable to shake off the tell-tale traces of her novelty and modernity. . . .[19]

It is the shallow reading of India's cultural past which leads Ramaswamy to propose an ungrounded argument.

Bhārata Mātā and Lalitā Tripurasundarī

Bhārata Mātā emerged from the evolving form of the Tripura goddess. The cult of Mahā-Tripurasundarī and the Śrī-Vidyā is the sheaf that binds India's different traditions. Śrī-Vidyā worship is the highest worship among both the Vedic and Āgamic traditions. It is thus the hinge that mediates the two strands of Indian tradition — right-hand and left-hand. Śrī-Vidyā tradition is also the ritualization of triadism inherent in Indian civilization. There are three levels of worship — *sthūla* (gross), *sūkṣma* (subtle) and *parā* (transcendental). One can see how in the case of Bhārata Mātā, she is worshipped as idol, as the cartographic map and then as the patriotic spirit. Just like Śrī-Vidyā, where there is another triad of *yantra–mantra–tantra*,

---

19 Quoted in Ramaswamy, n. 11, p. 55.

Lalitā Tripurasundarī, a nineteenth-century painting (*Source* : http://en.wikipedia.org/wiki/File:Lalita_ _The_Goddess_Tripurasundari.jpg)

the Bhārata Mātā case is characterized by the slogan, "Vande Mātaram", the map is a homologic resonance to Śrī-yantra with its abstract symbolism and the image of Bhārata Mātā itself appears to be the image of Tripurasundarī. Just as Śrī-yantra is the seat of Goddess Tripurā (Lord of Three Cities), cartographic map is the seat of Bhārata Mātā. Śrī-yantra is covered by a bhūpura, a rectangular boundary. The map of Bhārata is enclosed within a rectangular boundary.

Sadhu V. Rangarajan, the founder of Bhāratamātā Temple near Bangalore, puts up a strong argument to establish the connection between Śrī-yantra and the Śakti *pīṭhas*, which constitute the body of the Sacred Goddess Bhārata Mātā.[20]

20 Bhārata Mātā Mandir, Bangalore; "Bhārata Mātā, Mother India, or Bhāratāmbā is the national personification of India as a mother goddess." http://www.sribharatamatamandir.org/word/

He quotes Rostislav Rybakov, former director of the Institute of Oriental Studies in Moscow that why do many Russians doing research on Śrī-cakra.

The few adventurous explorers are trying to fit in the fifty-one Śakti *pīṭha*s over fifty-one points of the Śrī-cakra. If one places a diagram of Śrī-cakra and a map of pre-Partition Bhārata, the dots of Śrī-cakra approximately superimpose over the Śakti *piṭha*s. Thus, Śrī-cakra (*yantra*) morphologically resembles a cartographic map. Interestingly, when the British were creating an atlas which had to be the Map of India, they conceived South Asia as a "single space structured by a common geometric framework". And this framework was the triangulation. Mathew Edney terms triangulation as the cartographic panacea in his work, *Mapping an Empire* (1990).[21] It was the leadership of George Everest, the head of Great Trigonometric Survey and William Bentick that triangulation survey was conducted during 1831-43 and India's cartography emerged. The territory was subdivided into triangular regions, much as Śrī-yantra appears as the triangular *kṣetra*. Everest formed a grid of chains of triangles dependent on

21 Mathew H. Edney, *Mapping an Empire: The Geographical Construction of British India (1765–1843)*, Chicago: Chicago University Press, 1990, pp. 17-39.

backbone of a Great Arc running through Dehra Dun, for a coherent image of India.

If it was a tough task for the British cartographers to arrive at an Indian way of imagining the Indian territory, it was quite easy for the nationalists to merely substitute modern map for the Śrī-cakra and Bhārata Mātā for Lalitā Tripurasundarī. It resonated well with ancient thought structure and made huge appeal since the image of Bhārata Mātā was rooted in the geophilosophy of India.

Bhārata Mātā is shown holding four gifts in her four hands for the children of sacred territory — Bhārata. These are: book, rosary, grain, cloth. Compare this with the iconography of Tripurasundarī who also bestows gifts to her children. One can also see the presence of lion in the iconography of Bhārata Mātā and Tripurasundarī.

Map of GTS (1870)

In Tantras, there are two different traditions — Kālīkula and Śrīkula. While Kālīkula focuses on the destructive aspect of the Mother Goddess, Śrīkula is identified with the propitiation of the prosperity-goddess. Bhārata Mātā clearly falls in the second category. Kālī worship picked up in Bengal prior to the propagation of Gaṇeśa-Pūjā initiated by Tilak in Maharashtra. The popularity of Kālī-Pūjā in Bengal is credited to the nationalists. Bhārata Mātā represents the generative aspect of Śakti. The Śrīkula tradition was chosen. Bhārata Mātā gives boon to her children, famous four boons of *śikṣā–dīkṣā–anna–vastra*. But, one is tempted to ask as to when the Beṅgālīs intensified Kālī worship as a mode of protest against colonial administration and Kālī worship became the mobilizing force for the politicizing *bhadraloka*, why did Bhārata Mātā image not follow the Kālīkula trajectory, since the first picture and songs emerged from Bengal only?

Some scholars like Zo Margaret Newel have tried to establish Bhārata Mātā as a modern manifestation of Bhūdevī. Newell emphasizes:

> The modern Hindi words translated as "patriotism" — *deśaprema*, *deśabhakti*, or *svadeśabhakti* — combine the concepts of *deśa*, "country" (Sanskrit *deśa*), with concepts of love (*prema*, *bhakti*), with *bhakti* having specifically religious connotations.[22]

But, I find this to be far-fetched. The elaborate iconography and the song by Bankim Chandra Chatterjee that inspired the painting by Abanindranath Tagore (1905) contains the source of inspiration. The evolution of the image in the next three decades further adds to the idea that Bhārata Mātā concept did not emerge from forgotten, Vedic deities like Bhūdevī. Rather, it was the then prevailing practising tradition that spurred the concept of Bhārata Mātā.

[22] Newel, n. 9, p. 225.

Let us read carefully Bankim's immortal song, "Bande Mataram". Here is excerpts from appropriate translation by Keshab Bhattarai,

You are indeed the ten-handed Durgā Goddess,
you are the goddess of wealth, Kamalā or
Lakṣmī, residing on the lotus,
you are the bestower of (power of) speech and
knowledge — Goddess Sarasvatī, I pray to you.
I salute you O pure unmatched Goddess Kamalā.
You are blessed with water resources,
blessed with plenty of fruits,
Salutations (to you), O Mother!

You are peaceful, kind, pleasant and beautiful.
O Mother earth, nourisher, salutations.
Salutations (to you), O Mother! Vande Mataram. — para 4

"Bande Mātaram" song in Sanskrit.

वन्देमातरम्

सुजलां सुफलां मलयजशीतलाम्
शस्यश्यामलां मातरम् ।
शुभ्रज्योत्स्नापुलकित यामिनीं
फुल्ल कुसुमित द्रुमदलशोभिनीं
सुहासिनीं सुमधुर भाषिणीं
सुखदां वरदां मातरम् ।। १ ।। वन्दे मातरम् ।

कोटि-कोटि-कण्ठ-कल-कल-निनाद-कराले
कोटि-कोटि-भुजैर्धृत-खरकरवाले,
अबला केन मा एत बले ।
बहुबलधारिणीं नमामि तारिणीं ।।
रिपुदलवारिणीं मातरम् ।। २ ।। वन्दे मातरम् ।

तुमि विद्या तुमि धर्म,
तुमि हृदि तुमि मर्म

त्वं हि प्राणा: शरीरे
बाहुले तुमि मा शभि,
हृदये तुमि मा भभि,
तोमारई प्रतिमा गडि
मन्दिरे-मन्दिरे मातरम् ।। ३ ।। वन्दे मातरम् ।

त्वं हि दुर्गा दशप्रहरणधारिणी
कमला कमलदलविहारिणी
वाणी विद्यादायिनी, नमामि त्वाम्
नमामि कमलां अमलां अतुलां
सुजलां सुफलां मातरम् ।। ४ ।। वन्दे मातरम् ।

श्यामलां सरलां सुस्मितां भूषितां
धरणीं भरणीं मातरम् ।। ५ ।। वन्दे मातरम् ।

Vande Mātaram

sujalāṁ suphalāṁ malayajaśītalām
śasya śyāmalāṁ mātaram
śubhrajyotsnā-pulakita yāminīṁ
phulla kusumita drumadalaśobhinīṁ
suhāsinīṁ sumadhura bhāṣiṇīṁ
sukhadāṁ varadāṁ mātaram | | 1 | | *vande mātaram*

koṭi-koṭi-kaṇṭha-kala-kala-nināda-karāle
koṭi-koṭi-bhujairdhrata-kharakaravāle,
abalā kena mā eta bale |
bahubaladhāriṇīṁ namāmi tāriṇīṁ
ripudalavāriṇīṁ mātaram | | 2 | | *vande mātaram*

tumi vidyā, tumi dharma
tumi hr̥di, tumi marma
tvaṁ hi prāṇāḥ śarīre
bāhule tumi mā śakti,
hr̥daye tumi mā bhakti,
tomāraī pratimā gaḍi
mandire-mandire mātaram | | 3 | | *vande mātaram*

tvaṁ hi durgā daśapraharaṇadhāriṇī
kamalā kamaladalavihāriṇī
vāṇī vidyādāyinī, namāmi tvām
namāmi kamalāṁ amalāṁ atulāṁ
sujalāṁ suphalāṁ mātaram | | 4 | | *vande mātaram*

syāmalāṁ saralāṁ susmitāṁ bhūṣitāṁ
dharaṇīṁ bharaṇīṁ mātaram | | 5 | | *vande mātaram*

Thus, Bankim's Mother (Bankim did not use the word, Bhārata but merely Mātaram — Mother in the sense of mother of territory) has three aspects — warrior aspect of Durgā, wisdom aspect of Sarasvatī and prosperity aspect of Lakṣmī. The great goddess with three aspects inspired the song of Bankim Chandra Chatterjee. But, this is the Great Goddess, Rājarājeśvarī — Śrī Mahā-Tripurasundarī — whose three aspects are Mahā-Kālī, Mahā-Lakṣmī and Mahā-Sarasvatī. Though, the Kālī tradition was popular in Bengal, Bankim expressed the Śrīkula aspect of the warrior Goddess in the form of fair-complexioned Durgā. It is also important to note that Bankim had earlier composed his novel, *Durgesh-Nandini* (1865) that also had the etymological root "Durgā", decades before the publication of *Ānandamaṭh* (1882). But, looking at the subtler level, it is clear that Bankim had in his mind the three aspects of the Goddess as "*icchā* (desire), *jñāna* (wisdom) and *kriyā* (action)" represented through the image of Lakṣmī, Sarasvatī and Durgā, respectively. Lalitā Tripurasundarī, herself, is looked upon as a divine manifestation of Durgā or Pārvatī, as per the views of historian of religion, V.R. Ramachandra Dikshitar.[23] The interchangeability of Durgā and Lalitā Tripurasundarī is further evident from the fact that during the Daśaharā festival in October, special prayers are offered to both, Durgā and Lalitā Tripurasundarī. People worship Śrī-yantra in house altars during Durgā-Pūjā as it is

[23] V.R. Ramachandra Dikshitar, *The Lalita Cult* (1942), rpt., Delhi: Motilal Banarsidass, 1991, p. 1.

believed to be the seat of Lalitā. On Vijayadaśamī, it is considered auspicious to carry sugar cane to homes. Lalitā is also represented in pictures as holding sugar cane. We will explore how the concept of Mahā-Tripurasundarī and Bhārata Mātā interweaves into each other.

Bankim Chandra Chatterjee and Goddess Durgā

Bankim Chandra Chatterjee (1838–1911) was born to Durgā Devī. This might be a reason for him to invoke Durgā as mother frequently since it also gave expression to his real life. He appears to be enamoured with the Śakti worship which was quite prevalent in Bengal at that time. One can just recount two contemporary Śāktas — Bāmakhepa of Tarāpīṭha and Ramakrishna Dakṣiṇeśvara. His writings reflect his own quest to unravel the cult of goddess. In his famous novel, *Kapala-kundala* (1866), the central character is a woman, Kapala Kundala, who was a companion of the fierce Kāpālika. One can also discover the inspiration behind his greatest composition, *Ānandamaṭh*. It was the *saṁnyāsī* (ascetic) rebellion of 1760-70s against the British and their allies which forms the central theme of the work. *Saṁnyāsī*s defeated the British in CE 1766 at Dinhata. *Saṁnyāsī*s and *fakīr*s were first to give jolt to the British supremacy within a decade of the Battle of Plassey which granted British the *dīwānī* rights over Bihar, Bengal and Odisha. The *saṁnyāsī*s consisted of two groups — Mardānā *fakīr*s and Daśnāmī *akhāḍā*s. Daśnāmī *sādhu*s propitiated Goddess Durgā and some even followed the Śri-Vidyā ritual. With his deep exploration and own instinct, Bankim might have realized that the patriotic fervour among these *saṁnyāsī*s came from Goddess Durgā, who could manifest in multifarious forms to protect her children. This made him to compose the "Bande Mataram" song for the Mother India form of Durgā.

When Abanindranath Tagore painted the picture of the Baṅga Mātā (1905) which was later renamed Bhārata Mātā;

the inspiration had come from the "Bande Mataram" song. Bhārata Mātā is depicted in simple saffron cloth without jewellery, but keeping her four arms full with gifts for her children. The saffron-draping inspiration can be traced to the theme of *saṁnyāsī* rebellion in *Ānandamaṭh* and iconographic simplicity again to the fact that the *saṁnyāsī* rebellion took place during the times of worst famines. The Mother Goddess could not shine in jewellery when her children were suffering due to the wrong policies of the British.

When the image started to be reproduced, a lot of modifications were carried out before coming into the present form. These modifications were neither the construction of any "colonial period" nor the by-product of modern technology. Rather, these were in sync with the age-old social memories and Indian geophilosophy. A poster titled "Mahā-Kālī" was printed from the Ravi Varma Press, Bombay. On the right is depicted Mother Sarasvatī who holds a book and a *mālā* (garland), while Lakṣmī is on the far left with lotuses and by *dāna* (bestowing gifts) gesture. The central figure is Mahā-Kālī. Below her feet sits Gaṇeśa, identified as her son by the trident which he holds. Here one can clearly see the concept of Tripurasundarī and the identification of Tripurasundarī with Pārvatī, mother of Gaṇeśa. Later, more posters emerged in which Durgā/Kālī was thoroughly homologized with Mother India. Zo Margaret Newel Dhas done a fantastic work showing the iconographic evolution from the three goddesses to the Bhārata Mātā, covering the map of India.

Historian of religion, Kinseley suggests that

> the fundamental conviction that the earth itself, or the Indian subcontinent itself, is a goddess, indeed, that she is one's mother, pervades the modern cult of Bhārata Mātā (Mother India).[24]

---

[24] Kinseley, n. 15, p. 181.

Another interesting thing is pointed out by Kinseley in his masterpiece, *Hindu Goddess*, is that Lalitā Sahasranāma (Thousand Names of Lalitā) calls the goddess with many names signifying territoriality like Kṣetrasvarūpā (no. 341 — she whose body is territory), Bhūmarūpā (no. 666 — she whose form is all existing things on the surface of earth, Bhūmi). *Devī Bhāgavata Purāṇa* calls the earth the Devī's loins, ocean as her bowl, mountain as her bones, rivers as her veins, trees as her body hair, sun and moon as her two eyes. Pṛthvī as territoriality is worshipped as goddess by the Ṛgvedic sages. Pṛthvī is eulogized as Indrāṇī in Pṛthvī-Sūkta of *Ṛgveda*, and Lakṣmī or Śrī or Bhūdevī. Thus, there is strong correlation between Śrī Lakṣmī, the geographical land as well as auspiciousness. What I have suggested about the evolution of Bhārata Mātā from the Lalitā Tripurasundarī concept gets fortified with the unlayering of various philosophical–religious texts.

India's territoriality is superimposed with the imagination of sacred sites. The body of Goddess Umā is believed to have fallen at fifty-one places sanctifying those places as the Śakti *pīṭha*s and sanctifying the whole nation. Recently, Eck has compiled her thirty-year long research on India's sacred imagination and published the book, *India: Sacred Geography*. Though, she also maps *cāra dhāma*s, seven holy cities, twelve *jyotirliṅga*s, it is the aspect of the Śakti *pīṭha*s that gives the territoriality an overarching unity. Like the territory, the goddess nurtures her children. Thus, it is the Bhārata Mātā that emerged as an iconographic representation and not the Bhārata as father, even though the name of the land Bhārata was derived from the legendary king Bharata.

Bhāratī is a Vedic Goddess and often hymns are sung for her in *Ṛgveda*. She is one of the three beautiful goddesses, other two being Sarasvatī and Ilā. This is an interesting episode in India's cultural history that in spite of the existence of Bhāratī as goddess and Bhārata as the legendary male forefather, the paradoxical nomenclature of Bhārata Mātā evolved. Subramaniam Bharati who exhorted the theme of Vande Mātaram and the worship of Bhārata Mātā, being a male adopted the feminine nomenclature of "Bhāratī". Bhāratī has emerged as a surname for Indian males, while Śrī, which was meant to address Goddess Lakṣmī, is now prefixed as honorific before male names. The movement of categories across gendered mass itself is a fascinating story to unravel.

Nationalists often exhorted the people with the storyline from *Mahābhārata* to describe their struggle against the British as *dharma-yuddha*. But, in spite of the term, "Bhārata" being associated with masculinity, the mother figure emerged with the same name. This has to do with India's geophilosophy.

Geophilosophy of Bhārata Mātā

Geophilosophy is the drive of "earthly thought". Thinking is rooted in a grounded relation to the earth. Geophilosophy signifies this-worldly perspective that includes all kinds of landscape. In the simplest term, it is the geography that determines philosophy. It is the holy places and the battlefields, the pattern of mountains and the terrain which become the conditions of history and thinking. Philosophy cannot escape its relationship with the territory from where it emerged. Though Nieztsche is credited as the father of geophilosophy, in recent years after the critical development of the concept by French philosophers Deleuze and Guattari, geophilosphy has entered the wide arena of thought. Reza Negarestani's speculative realism is the latest branch to emerge from this ever-growing field.[25]

---

[25] Reza Negarestani, "Globe of Revolution: An Afterthought on Geophilosophical Realism", 2012 (extended version of paper) written for Dark Materialism, Kingston University, London, 12 January 2011; available at http://archive.org/details/aaaaarg-32071.

Extending the geophilosophical ruminations over India, one is surprised to find how India is the home to the "triadistic" thinking (which new synthetic philosophers are pursuing on the path laid down by Charles Peirce).[26] This has to do with the peninsular geography. The perfect traingular projection with the Himalayas that limit northern boundary like a lunar crescent has influenced India's philosophy. *Prakṛti* is considered to be of *tri-guṇa*s — *satoguṇa, rajoguṇa* and *tamoguṇa*. Now, the entire Indian thought structure is encapsulated in 3 + 1 thinking, where the first three categories concerns the world of immanence and fourth is the category. It is like the three dots of the triangle that form the sides with a central dot as the transcending point. Many Indologists have pointed out this feature with respect to the *puruṣārtha* system, caste system and *varṇāśrama* system. But, the philosophy had its pinnacle in the Trika Śaivism and Tripura Śāktism. Triads became the determining aspects of reality from micro to transcendental level. Similarly, the moon became the pinnacle of attainment. Just as the Himalayas appear to be superimposed over the lower peninsula and a middle body, the moon signifies the highest manifestation. From Buddha to Tantras, from Vedic Soma rituals to lunar supremacy in determining the extant rituals, the moon hovers over like an overarching presence in the Indian thought and practice.

What surprised the ancient man was the geometrical shape of generative structure of the woman. This has the shape of a triangle. For the Indian mind, it was easy to connect the triangular shape of female generative organ and the shape of

---

26 Charles S. Peirce, *Collected Papers*, Cambridge: Harvard University Press 1931; also see Fernando Zalamea, "Peirce's Continuum: A Methodological and Mathematical Approach", 2005 http://acervopeirceano.org/wp-content/uploads/2011/09/Zalamea-Peirces-Continuum.pdf

the territory. It could homologize the two. India became a sacred goddess. The whole territory undergoes radical anthropomorphization in imagination. The cult of Lalitā Tripurasundarī is the storehouse of the practice of triadism with its three aspects — gross, subtle and transcendental; with three ways of ritual — *yantra, mantra* and *tantra*; and with three traditions — *kāḍi, hāḍi* and *khādi*. If one sees the image of Bhārata Mātā, one will be astonished to find that not only she is the synthesis of the three goddesses — Mahā-Kālī, Mahā-Sarasvatī, Mahā-Lakṣmī like Tripurasundarī, she also holds a trident. The flag is triangular. The whole image is in tricolour. The part of the map that appears is only the triangular lower part. And when is the Bhārata Mātā Day? It is the *akṣaya tṛtīyā* . . . another category of 'third'. It is celebrated on the third day of the bright fortnight of the lunar month of Vaiśākha (Śukla Tṛtīyā). The reason again is interesting. The sun is exalted in Aries, the moon is exalted in Taurus. Since the three celestial bodies (*piṇḍa*s) — sun, moon and earth — are in a multidimensional relationship, it is assumed that the earth is in exaltation only on the third day of this conjunction. Thus, whole persona of Bhārata Mātā appears to be merely an extension of Tripurasundarī. This is the underlying reason for Indians to defend Kashmir from foreign intervention so aggressively, since Srinagar is the city of Lalitā Tripurasundarī as narrated in *Brahmāṇḍa Purāṇa*.

Trans-modern Synthesis

Many post-ists from post-modernists, post-colonialists and post-structuralists bandwagon would cry foul with the arguments. But, they must keep in mind that post-modern fragmentation in thinking is over. The thinking has left the particularized, fragmented domain. It is a networked society and connectedness is the fundamental characteristic of the emerging episteme. The analytical perception has sought asylum from the new emperor, the synthesis. Now is the trans-modern turn of synthetic philosophy, sheafification of different criss-crossing trajectories of knowledge. The philosophers are trying to establish synthesis between different fields. Fernando Zalamea's synthetic philosophy, Reza Negarestani's speculative realism and Jean Petiot's neurogeometry are becoming the trendsetters for the revolution in new knowledge. Herein is reproduced an excerpt from the Colombian mathematician and synthetic philosopher Zalamea's recent work, *Synthetic Philosophy of Contemporary Mathematics*:

> . . . the knowledge of mathematical processes advances itself by means of a series of iterations in correlative triadic fields [*ámbitos*]: differentiation–integration–invariance, eidos–quidditas–arkhé, abduction–induction–deduction, possibility–actuality–necessity, locality–globality–mediation. Advanced mathematics invokes this incessant "triangulation", the most striking reflection (as much technical as conceptual) of which perhaps appears in the notion of sheaf. A fact of tremendous importance in contemporary mathematics is the necessity of situating oneself in a full thirdness and not reducing it (not "degenerating it", Pierce would say) to secondnesses or firstnesses. In the analytic modes of understanding, however, thirdness disappears because accomplished [*realizado*] (classical) analysis is basically dual, in the style of either . . . or . . . exclusions à la Benacerraf. This means that the apparatus of analytic vision finds itself intrinsically limited in observing the functioning of advanced mathematics, if it considers them on its own, independently of any synthetic contrast. A pendular combination of the analytic and the synthetic, the differential and the integral, the ideal and the real seems to be the epistemological road [*camino*] to follow. Observe in passing [*en camino*] that, on a "meta-epistemological" level, what is needed is a precedence of the synthetic, not the analytic, in order to allow flows, oscillations and gluings between analytic and synthetic sub-fragments on lower levels. A "sheafification" in comparative

> epistemology requires — as we have seen in the generic analysis of the notion of sheaf — first prescinds [*prescisar*] notions of neighbourhood, covering and coherence, before passing to possible [eventual] gluings. A neighbourhood [*vecinidad*] between epistemological perspectives requires us to postulate before all else a certain commensurability between them; here, we explicitly position ourselves against the supposed incommensurabilities between "paradigms" (Kuhn), which, at least in mathematics, rarely occur [*se dan*]. In this context, an epistemological neighbourhood should bring together [*acercar*] the different perspectives whether in their methods (for example, the "synthetic" method applied to a realist) or idealist stance.[27]

Contemporary transmodernist thinkers have drifted back onto a triadistic ontology for synthetic turn in thinking. But, the Indian mind, which, due to geographical reason, has developed a neural geometry that looks at the thing with triangular perspective, is already adept in dabbling with triadistic categories of thinking. If the triangulation generates synthetic approach and a sheaffing mechanism, Indian mind did the same with this sacred territory. Bhārata Mātā is the product of millennia of sheaffing of a triangular perspective towards the world — historical, ahistorical and trans-historical. Those who are still glued in the analytic binary tradition espoused under Andersonian perspective on nationalism are getting decomposed into an academic compost.

In the future iconographic evolution, artists might opt for Śrī-yantra as the seat of Bhārata Mātā which is the most appropriate diagrammatic representation of Indianness through sheaffing of triangular spaces. Śrī-yantra is the condensed Hinduity, the pure crystalline form of imagination about Indian territory.

---

27 Fernando Zalamea, *Synthetic Philosophy of Contemporary Mathematics*, tr. Z.L. Fraser, Falmouth, UK: Urbanomic Sequence Press, 2013.

9

Pleading for a New National Flag

WHAT does the national flag represent? Is the national flag merely an insignia to symbolize the sovereignty of a modern nation state? Is it merely the master site for the production of nationalism? Can the national flag be manufactured without considering the history of the people and the emotive attachment with the symbol? Sister Nivedita put these issues for the first time so succinctly in her article, "The Vajra as a National Flag" (1909):

> For, a banner is at once a benison and a menace, a consecration and a rallying-cry. It is as an altar, at whose foot, whether for assault or defence, men's lives are freely offered up. Generations come and go. New combinations arrive and vanish, but that for which national symbol stands — that ineffable union of *jana–deśa–dharma* for every which people fight — remains for ever, simple and steadfast as eternity, mirrored in the fugitive minds of its myriad worshippers.[1]

Adopting the National Flag

India adopted the national flag through a resolution unanimously on 22 July 1947. A nine-member ad hoc committee on the national flag was constituted on 23 June 1947 under the chairmanship of Rajendra Prasad. The other members were: Abul Kalam Azad, C. Rajagopalachari, Sarojini Naidu, K.M.

---

1 Sister Nivedita, "The Vajra as a National Flag", in *The Complete Works of Sister Nivedita*, Kolkata: Advaita Ashrama, 1999, p. 170.

Panikkar, K.M. Munshi, B.R. Ambedkar, S.N. Gupta, Frank Anthony and Sardar Ujjal Singh.

FLAG COMMITTEE REPORT

The committee received various suggestions from across the undivided India. It was a time of communal flare up and the majority community as well as other minorities were debating for their existential question through the proposed designs for the national flag.

V.D. Savarkar sent a telegram from Bombay on 7 July 1947 suggesting

> . . . The standard of Hindustan must be *bhagwā* — ochre-coloured. . . . The *carkhā* too must be replaced by a *cakra* (wheel) or any other symbol signifying progress and strength.[2]

But, the ad hoc committee decided on 14 July to retain the Purna Swaraj flag of 1931 with a minor change by replacing the *carkhā* with Aśoka's *dharmacakra* on the centre of the white stripe. The sample of national flag prepared by Badr-ud-Din Tyabji was approved on 17 July 1947, and two samples of the national flag, one in silk and another in *khādī*, were placed before the Constituent Assembly on 22 July 1947.

Pandit Jawaharlal Nehru introduced the motion. The motion is reproduced herein:

> Resolved that the national flag of India shall be horizontal tricolour of deep saffron (*kesarī*), white and dark green in equal proportion. In the centre of the white band, there shall

---

2 Sekhar Chakrabarti, *Quest for a National Flag for India*, Part XVII "National Flag of Independent India-1947", 22 July 2010. http://flagstamps.blogspot.in/2010/07/quest-for-national-flag-for-india-part_22.html (last accessed on 1 December 2012). Also see, Sekhar Chakrabarti, *The Indian National Flag UnfurledThrough Philately*, New Delhi: Niyogi Book, 2012.

> be a wheel in navy blue to represent the *carkhā*. The design of the wheel shall be that of the wheel (*cakra*) which appears on the abacus of the Sārnāth, Lion Capital of Aśoka. The diameter of the wheel shall approximate to the width of the white band. The ratio of the width to the length of the flag shall ordinarily be 2 : 3.[3]

Nehru eloquently declared that glow and warmth which he felt at the moment of presenting resolution sprang from history, "the concentrated history of a short span in a nation's existence".

But, clearly the then leaders did not have a clue to the concentrated history of the civilization, caught as they were in the warp of communal frenzy. The whole debate upon the resolution revolved around communal interpretations, even though Nehru tried to steer the misunderstanding around the symbolism. Nehru had to admit that many people wrongfully believe that some part of the national flag represents this community or that. Nehru clarified that the symbolism of the national flag had nothing to do with the separate communities, but only to evoke the spirit and tradition of the nation. Nehru said:

> We thought of a flag which would in its combination and in its separate parts would somehow represent the spirit of the nation, the tradition of the nation, that mixed spirit and tradition which has grown up through thousands of years in India. So, we devised this flag.[4]

Nehru also spoke at length about India's spiritual tradition with an immemorial past, which he conveyed was reflected in the national flag.

The resolution referred to *carkhā* in the centre of the white strip being symbolized by *cakra* of the Aśoka's Lion Pillar at

---

[3] *Constituent Assembly Debates*, vol. IV, 22 July 1947. http://parliamentofindia.nic.in/ls/debates/vol4p7.htm

[4] Ibid.

Sārnāth. *Cakra* is merely a synecdoche, since the *carkhā* design used in the Purna Swaraj flag was constituted by two parts, a wheel (*cakra*) and a triangle of string. It is understood that Mahatma Gandhi was not happy with this substitution in the national flag, but finally the will of the Constituent Assembly prevailed.

Nehru gave a bizarre justification for substituting *cakra* for *carkhā*. It is the appearance of symmetry. Nehru stated:

> The symbol on one side of the flag should be exactly the same as on the other side. Otherwise, there is a difficulty which goes against the rules. Now, the *carkhā*, as it appeared previously on this flag, had the wheel on one side and the spindle on the other.[5]

Nehru stated that wheel is a symbol of India's ancient culture. But, he did not elaborate upon the enunciation. He obfuscated the debate with the achievements of Aśoka and India's glorious past as an international centre.

Obviously, Nehru was not harping on "condensed history of India" or even hoary spiritual past that existed in variegated form from time immemorial. He was fascinated with the recent discovery reported in the English newspapers and reports and like his contemporary, cut off from the stream of Indian spiritual tradition which was being practised by the toiling masses.

Aśoka's Lion Pillar at Sārnāth was discovered only in 1905 by British archaeologists led by F.O. Oertel. The history of Aśoka was forgotten from Indian mind and could be rewritten only after the marvellous work of the orientalist, James Prinsep (1799–1840). Prinsep was the founding editor of the *Journal of Asiatic Society* and he carried a series of results between 1836-38 after deciphering the Brāhmī script. It was Prinsep who explored the historical sources about Aśoka. Close on the heels,

---

5 *Constituent Assembly Debates*, vol. IV, 22 July 1947. http://parliamentofindia.nic.in/ls/debates/vol4p7.htm

the history of Buddhism, which was long forgotten in India, was being brought to light. Brian Houghton Hodgson, a civil servant in Bengal from 1820s onwards, collected Mahāyāna Prajñāpāramitā texts from Nepal. He donated these manuscripts to the Asiatic Society libraries in France, India and Britain. French orientalist, Eugene Burnouf used some of Hodgson texts and published first introductory history of Indian Buddhism, *Al'histoire Du Buddhisme Indien V1* (1844). Edwin Arnold, the Principal of Deccan College, Poona, wrote biographical work on Buddha in verse under the title *Light of Asia* in 1879. Sir Alexander Cunningham, the father of the Archaeological Survey of India (ASI), unveiled heritage sites like the Bharhut *stūpa*, Sārnāth, Sāñcī and the Mahābodhi Temple.

Mahābodhi Temple in Bodh-Gayā became a rallying point for international campaign for the preservation of Buddhist heritage at Bodh-Gayā under the leadership of Mathew Arnold. Soon, Anāgārika Dharmapāla (1864–1933) came from Ceylone and settled in Calcutta for establishing a global Buddhist mission. He began to work tirelessly for the preservation of Bodh-Gayā and established a network of Buddhists in Burma, Ceylon and Siam. He founded Mahabodhi Society in Calcutta in 1891. Bodh-Gayā and Buddha caught the urban Beṅgālī imagination.

Girishchandra Ghosh, a noted dramatist, wrote a play *Buddhadev Charit* based on Arnold's *Light of Asia*. It was staged in 1885 and later published in 1887. Nabinchandra Sen (1847–1909) wrote a biography in verse, *Amitav* (1895) imitating Mathew Arnold's work. It became customary for the Beṅgālī *bhadraloka* to go on pilgrimage to Bodh-Gayā. Leading lights of Bengal and the Asianist circle members like Swami Vivekananda, Rabindranath Tagore, J.C. Bose, Sister Nivedita, Kakuzo Okakura, Anand K. Coomaraswami visited Bodh-Gayā in their quest to understand Indian civilization.

It is clear that the *cakra* inserted in the national flag taken from the Lion Pillar of Sārnāth did not spring from the living Indian tradition. The rediscovery of Aśoka, Buddha and *cakra* was only half a century old and in no way stood for the continuity of Indian civilization, a theme upon which Nehru harped time and again while seeking unanimous support for the resolution on the national flag.

In fact, there were three amendments to be moved against the resolution, but the somber mood of the Constituent Assembly and eloquent speech by Nehru and Sarojini Naidu led to an unanimous adoption of the national flag.

H.V. Kamath, the member from Central Province and Berar, was the first to move the amendment which read as follows:

> That the following new para be inserted in the motion: That inside the *cakra* in the centre of the white band, the *svastika*, the ancient Indian symbol of Śāntam, Śivam, Sundaram, be inscribed.[6]

Kamath withdrew the resolution after seeing the national flag. But, Kamath was more forthcoming with his insight:

> I thought that this flag, being the flag of our new Indian Republic, of Bhāratavarṣa, should adequately symbolize our ancient culture, the culture of our spirit, the spirit which has animated our sages and our seers, which gave the message of Śāntam, Śivam, Sundaram to the world, the message of peace, the peace not merely of stillness, not merely a passive peace, but a dynamic peace that passeth all understanding, the peace of which the great Vālmīki has sung (*samudraiva gambhirye dhairyeca himavaniva*). I thought, Sir, if the *svastika* be inscribed inside the *cakra* it would along with the *dharmacakra* of Aśoka fittingly symbolize our ancient culture, that is to say, the esoteric and exoteric aspects of

---

6 *Constituent Assembly Debates*, vol. IV, 22 July 1947. http://parliamentofindia.nic.in/ls/debates/vol4p7.htm

> our culture. The *dharmacakra* symbolizes the esoteric and the *svastika* symbolizes the exoteric aspects. But, Sir, I have now seen the flag and I find that it is somewhat hard to fit the *svastika* into this *cakra*. It would look cumbersome because of the design of the *cakra*.[7]

The *svastika* as a symbol was more pervasive and part of everyday life of Indians unlike the *dharmacakra* of Lion Pillar which was rediscovered only four decades back. Since, Kamath realized that it would look clumsy and cumbersome if the *svastika* was inserted in the wheel, he withdrew the amendment.

The debate in the Constituent Assembly brings to light the manner in which the issue of national flag was viewed. Basically, the whole debate remained limited to the question of colour and *cakra* vs. *carkhā*. There was no discussion about either the shape or the size or the symbol that represented Bhāratavarṣa's continuing tradition in both aspect — material as well spiritual.

Seth Govind Das, a member from Central Province and Berar, clarified that saffron was not the colour of the Hindus as misconstrued by many. Though, the Peshwās and Rājpūts used saffron dress and saffron ensign, saffron was not the colour of the older times. He narrated how in the times of *Mahābhārata* there was no question of colour. It was what kind of symbol was being used. The flag flying over the chariot of Arjuna had the symbol of Hanumān and Karṇa's flag had the symbol of the elephant. Seth Govind Das could take the discussion into India's living history as well as mythical past unlike Nehru who deployed various strategies to deflect attention from a debate on the symbol of India's "condensed history that signify both material as well spiritual realm".[8]

---

7 *Constituent Assembly Debates*, vol. IV, 22 July 1947. http://parliamentofindia.nic.in/ls/debates/vol4p7.htm

8 Ibid.

Seth Govind Das's reference to *Mahābhārata* and clarification that ancient Indian flags did not have specific colours was an important intervention. Indian flags were marked with the distinctive insignia that those carried and not the colour to which the whole debate on the national flag was focused. *Mahābhārata* mentions how the battlefield saw flags of different colours with different symbols. Arjuna's chariot had *kapidhvaja* (monkey), Bhīṣma's flag had *tāḍi* (*Palmyra palm*) leaves and five stars, Kr̥pa's flag had the sign of a bull. Similarly, one can compile different kinds of ancient flags mentioned in *Mahābhārata* based on the plant and animal signs — a wild boar on Jayadratha's flag, lion tail on Aśvatthāmā's flag, a bow on Droṇa's flag, a cobra on Duryodhana's flag, golden *karṇikara* tree on Abhimanyu's flag, pair of *mr̥daṅga* on Yudhiṣṭhira's flag, a lion on Bhīma's flag, a swan (*haṁsa*) on Sahadeva's flag, a donkey (*gr̥ddha*) on Ghaṭotkaca's flag, elephant chain on Karṇa's flag, elephant on Śalya's flag, peacock on Vīrasena's flag, band of jackal on Alāyudha's flag and crocodile on Pradyumna's flag. Kr̥ṣṇa, an incarnation of Viṣṇu, carried Garuḍa in his flag. Such flags continued to be used by the kings and the emperors. Uma Prasad Thapaliyal has brought to light the tradition of *dhvaja*s in India in his work, *The Dhvaja, Standards and Flags of India.*[9]

Aśoka used *cakra-dhvaja* to represent the Buddhist concept of *cakravartin* (*cakra* + *vartan* — turning of wheel). The greatest Indian conqueror Samudragupta used *garuḍa-dhvaja* (eagle sign in the flag) during his conquests and has been found depicted on gold coins. The Coḷa, Pāṇḍya and Pallava kings had tiger, fish and bull signs in their flags. Even in the twentieth century, the custom of using the image of an animal or a plant in their flags did not disappear. The Kingdom of Laos had a red flag,

---

9 Uma Prasad Thapaliyal, *The Dhvaja, Standards and Flags of India: A Study*, Delhi: B.R. Publications, 1938.

Flag of the Kingdom of Laos

with a white three-headed elephant (Erawan) in the middle. Erawan is the Thai name of Indra's mythic white elephant, Airāvata.

When the Constituent Assembly debates were taking place, most of the members were aware about *garuḍa-dhvaja* of Samudragupta for the invitation cards in Hindu marriages carried the Sanskrit *śloka* eulogizing *garuḍa-dhvaja*.

> *maṅgalam bhagvān viṣṇu maṅgalam garuḍa dhvajaḥ*
> *maṅgalam puṇḍarikākṣo maṅgalāya tanno hari . . .*

> May auspiciousness be unto God Viṣṇu, May auspiciousness be unto the one who has the Garuḍa symbol, in flag. May auspiciousness be unto the Lord with lotus-like eyes, Hari is the abode all auspiciousness.

But, Seth Govind Das could not point out the commonality among all these flags. All such flags were non-quadrilateral in shape. The *kapidhvaja* of Arjuna's chariot or the Peshwa's flag, the flag of *saṁnyāsī*s thronging the spiritual congregation of the *kumbha* or the flags fluttering over temples, Śakti *pīṭha*s, trees, stones or even in the courtyard of Hindu houses where flags are hoisted on the eve of Rāmanavamī each ninth day of the bright half (*śukla-pakṣa*) of the lunar month of Caitra, the flags used atop sūfī shrines, all these are remarkably similar in shape. The triangular shape of indigenous *dhvaja*s, *jhaṇḍā*s, and *patākās* pervade Indian territory in terms of history and space.

Chaudhuri Khaliquzzaman, the Muslim League member from the United Provinces, argued succinctly that "a country's flag symbolizes its ideals and its aspirations, both moral and spiritual".[10] But he could not retrieve an emblem for the flag which symbolized both moral and spiritual ideals and aspirations and which should have been handed on from generation to generation. Naturally when the national emblem of a great civilization was being agreed upon, the criteria should have been what Sister Nivedita had put up in the very first paragraph of her inspiring essay, the "Vajra as a National Flag" (1909):

> When we look at all that a national banner means, we see the utter impossibility of manufacturing or devising such an emblem. It can grow up only out of the heart and history of the people. . . . For, while this symbolism cannot be imparted piecemeal to those outside the circle of the enthusiasm, it can and must be handed down from generation to generation, and province to province.[11]

Saiyid Mohammad Saadulla , the Muslim League member from the province of Assam, in fact recognized common ground in the saffron colour which many were imbuing only to the Hindu community. Saadulla mentioned:

> India is very well noted for her spiritual attainments. Everywhere it is admitted that India has got a great spiritual message to send out to the different countries of the world. The saffron, as is well known, is the colour of all those people who live the spiritual life not only among Hindus but also among Muslims. Therefore the saffron colour should remind us that we should keep ourselves on that high plane of

---

10 *Constituent Assembly Debates*, n. 3.

11 Sister Nivedita, n. 1, p. 163.

> renunciation which has been the realm of our *sādhus* and saints, *pīrs* and *paṇḍits*. I therefore welcome the inclusion of this colour in the flag.[12]

In fact, Saadulla supported the inclusion of *cakra* in place of *carkhā* upholding the *cakra* as a religious emblem and that it was not fair to dissociate India's social life from the religious environments.

Similarly, Jaipal Singh, a tribal member from Bihar, was very blunt in stating his facts. He traced the pride associated with hoisting flags to non-Aryan indigenous roots. Jaipal Singh rightly stated that *ādivāsīs* had been the first to hoist flags and to fight for their flags. And that

> year after year, in *melās*, *jātrās* and festivals in Chota-Nagpur, whenever various tribes with their flags enter the arena, each tribe must come into *jātrā* by a definite route by only one route and no other tribe may enter the *melā* by the same route. Each village has its own flag and that flag cannot be copied by any other tribe.[13]

It is only in recent decades that the cultural historians and anthropologists have begun to seriously study this aspect of symbols in fostering unity and identity among various communities which Jaipal Singh stated with rustic musings. Raymond Firth identified the flag as a "master symbol" in both primitive societies as well as contemporary societies, serving as "instruments of expression, communication, knowledge and control".[14] The flag as a symbol has very high emotive value and usage in maintaining unity among a community howsoever small or large it may be.

---

12 *Constituent Assembly Debates*, n. 3.

13 Ibid.

14 Raymond Firth, *Symbols: Public and Private*, New York: Cornell University Press, 1973.

Extreme Hindu view was expressed by Pandit Govind Malaviya during the debates in the Constituent Assembly. He expressed in no unambiguous terms that red colour is the colour of the Hindus and the green represents the Muslim community. But, he added that even green colour can be interpreted as Hindu colour as green is the colour of the planet Mercury. He mixed up gemology with vexillology while formulating a heraldic symbol for the nation. He conflated Buddhist *dharmacakra* with *sudarśana cakra* of Viṣṇu and thence with the conception of *avatāra*. In fact, he even declared that the *avatāra* is amidst them.[15]

The parochial and particularistic outlook of some of the participants debating the national flag was appalling. Lakshminarayan Sahu from Orissa compared the three colours of the flag, with the three images inside the temple of Jagannātha. It is what he spoke:

> Lord Jagannātha represents the blue colour, Balarāma represents the white and Subhadrā Devī represents the yellow colour, with Lord Jagannātha and Balarāma on either side of Subhadrā Devī, in a way defending the womenfolk.[16]

The concluding speech was given by the Nightingale of India, Sarojini Naidu. Her speech reflected more on her personal anguishes suffered while attending international programmes because India possessed no flag; rather than speculating for a truly national emblem for the country with a cosmopolitan past. She described about how she felt on the day when peace was signed at Versailles after the World War, then a peace celebrations at New York where flags of forty-four nations fluttered without the flag of Free India and thence in Berlin while attending an international conference with women representatives from forty-two nations. She expressed how

15 *Constituent Assembly Debates*, n. 3.

16 Ibid.

the greatest anguish came when in the Asian Relations Conference held in Delhi in 1947 (23 March to 2 April), Tricolour was excluded as it was merely the Congress flag.

Naidu spoke so much about the international conferences, foreign visits and the personal sense of humiliation because India lacked a flag in such gatherings. But, she herself admitted that the august Assembly was adopting a symbol which was not in the veins of people. Though, Nehru in his opening address spoke highly about Aśoka and the reason for picking up the *cakra* from Aśoka's Lion Pillar in Sārnāth, Naidu stated her ignorance about Aśoka. Naidu commenced her speech as follows:

> I was especially reminded by the people that sit behind me from the Province of Bihar that it was at the risk of my life and seat in their province, should I forget to mention that this flag, so willingly and proudly accepted today by the House has for its symbol the *dharmacakra* of Aśoka, whom they claim (I do not know with what historical veracity) to be a Bihārī![17]

It is clear from her version that not much historical facts were known about Aśoka during those times. In fact, as discussed earlier, the Lion Pillar was excavated only in 1905. It is also amusing to see how Sarojini Naidu who belonged to Hyderabad, and represented the province of Bihar, had to succumb to the parochial perspective towards the national flag. In fact, the whole debate was community-centric and colour-centric. There was nothing substantial in discussions regarding retrieving the banner of Indianness which grew "out of heart and history of the people" and which encapsulated both the material and spiritual ideals of the homeland. The Princely States were appalled at the way the Congress flag was imposed as the national flag. In July 1947, the Mahārājā of Bikaner wrote to Rajendra Prasad suggesting that the representatives of

---

17 *Constituent Assembly Debates*, n. 3.

Indian states should also be nominated to the Flag Committee.[18] There was no attempt to infuse into the national flag an eternal symbol that has been handed over from generation to generation. The national flag which was neither rooted in living tradition, nor imbued with the holistic perspective lacks the criteria to be a symbol for India as a nation state.

Quest for the National Flag

All ancient cultures deployed their flags as a banner for communicating a shared destiny. Indian civilization, ancient as it is, and replete with the diversity of spiritual and material paths, has witnessed an elaborate flag culture. Hoisting flag is an essential part of a ritual, both for the householders as well as the renunciate *saṁnyāsī*s. *Saṁnyāsī*s carry ochre-coloured flags with staff on their shoulders. In each congregation or consecration for a sacred and auspicious space, the flags are raised. The colours of the flag may vary from white, red or saffron, but one thing is invariable, i.e. shape. Thus, the evolution of flags in India to encapsulate the esoteric as well exoteric aspect has to pass through the dialectic of variance/invariance. There never was monopoly over hoisting of flag in Indian tradition. Each householder was free to hoist a sacred flag in his courtyard or to offer flags to the *iṣṭa*-deities in the temples. The liberal flag culture that prevailed in Indian culture has not been studied by the culture experts and there is a tendency to see the origin of national flag only from the time that the political activists raised the demand for "own flag" for political mobilization during the freedom struggle.

Writing history of flag was never an easy task. The first long elaboration of the Indian national flag was done by Arundhati Virmani in her book, *A National Flag for India: Rituals,*

18 *National Herald*, 21 June 1947 cited in Arundhati Virmani, *A National Flag for India — Rituals, Nationalism and the Politics of Sentiment*, Ranikhet: Permanent Black, 2008, p. 257.

Nationalism, and the Politics of Sentiment (2008). But, she has ignored the hoary past of flag in India and links the quest for the national flag to the British attempt to have a separate Indian flag to represent India during the ritual of "monarchical succession".[19] After Queen Victoria's death on 23 January 1901, Edward VII's coronation on 9 August 1902 was succeeded by the "public debate on appropriate symbols for the British nation and her dominions".[20]

Virmani reproduces the letter written by a retired British civil servant William Coldstream in May 1902, and sought to enquire about proper sanctioning of any flag or heraldic blazon for India to "embody the idea of the unity of India with the British Empire".[21]

But, the Indian attempt to rally the nation under a common national flag began soon after the end of unsuccessful first war of Independence in 1857. In 1883, a national flag appeared on the front cover of a book written by Srish Chandra Bose, *Indian National Songs and Lyrics* in 1883. The flag design consisted of the symbol of the sun. Virmani is certain that "this flag was paraded in Lahore by the members of Indian National Society founded same year".[22]

Raj Narayan Bose (1826-99), maternal grandfather of Sri Aurobindo prescribed "lotus" to be the national symbol in his book *Bridhya Hindoo-r Asha* (*An Old Hindu's Hope*) written in 1888. The first attempt at designing a national flag came from the Irish disciple of Swami Vivekananda, Sister Nivedita (Margaret Nobel, 1867–1911). While she visited Bodh-Gayā in the company of physicist J.C. Bose and Rabindranath Tagore

19 Virmani, *A National Flag for India*, p. 10.

20 Ibid., p. 11.

21 Ibid., p. 12.

22 Ibid., p. 46.

in 1904, she was seized with the *vajra* (thunderbolt) sign of Buddhism. The *vajra* flag was prepared by the students of Nivedita Girls' School at Calcutta and displayed for public view at the Indian National Congress exhibition in December 1906.[23] The flag was square in shape, red in colour and carried the symbols of *vajra* in the centre. On both sides of the *vajra* flag was written "Vande" and "Mātaram" in Bengali and 108 *jyotis* (flames) in the outer periphery. Sister Nivedita in her article "The Vajra as a National Flag" (1909), described to persuade the public to accept *vajra* as an emblem in the national flag for whole of India.

First national flag was hoisted in Calcutta on 7 August 1906, in the Parsee Bagan Square (Green Park). The flag was composed of three horizontal strips of red, yellow and green. There were eight lotuses in the top strip, the lower strip had the images of the sun and the moon, and Vande Mātaram was written in Hindi in the middle strip.

The first national flag

On 22 August 1907, Madame Bhikaji Cama unfurled the national flag while attending the International Socialist Congress in Stuttgart, Germany. It was a tricolour of green, saffron and red with one lotus flower in the middle of the top strip, Vande Mātaram in the middle and in the red portion below there was a crescent on one side and the sun on the other. The top strip had only one lotus, but it had seven stars denoting *saptarṣi*.

23 Sister Nivedita, n. 1, p. 166.

The national flag raised by Madame Bhikaji Cama in 1907 in Stuttgart, Germany

During the Home Rule Movement, Pingali Venkayya from Musilpatam founded an Indian Flag Mission in 1916. He wrote a booklet in 1916, *A National Flag for India* in which he published twenty-four illustrations of his proposed flag models. This also included the *vajra* flag as proposed by Sister Nivedita. There were illustrations of the Himalayas, Buddha, Airāvat,

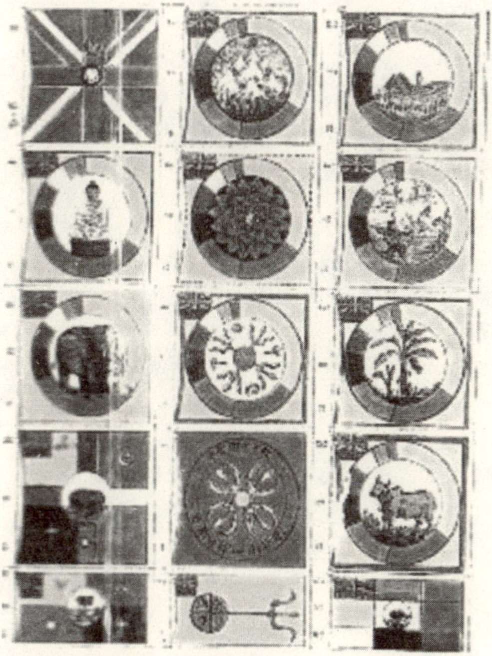

Pingali Venkayya's design, 1916[24]

24 Reproduced in Virmani, n. 18, p. 83.

lotus, trident of Śiva, bull, swan, bow and arrow. But, Venkayya's designs were rejected by Mahatma Gandhi. The tropes from India's rich and variegated cultural pool became a thing of the past. Venkayya retired from politics and was never again invited for any Congress activity.

But, the emblems from India's cultural treasure were soon rejected from the creation of national flag once the Swaraj flag, influenced by Mahatma Gandhi was designed in 1921. The Swaraj flag was tricolour and contained the symbol of *carkhā* in the middle stripe. It was raised for the first time at the Ahmedabad Congress in 1921. Writing in *Young India* on 14 April 1921, Mahatma Gandhi provided the accounts of how he was the father of the Indian national flag. *Carkhā* was introduced by Gandhi. The tricolour also lost the spiritual significance. The flag itself appeared trifurcated in terms of composition symbolizing a triple India. The flag no longer appeared cosmopolitan but marred by the vision of particularism through representation of colours. A scholar has commented over this tragic dilemma:

> Gandhi's comments on the flag in terms of the communal or religious significance of each of its colours point to a general dilemma of Indian nationalism that would increasingly occupy centre stage: How to proclaim national unity without erasing sub-national diversities of religion, language, region, or caste.[25]

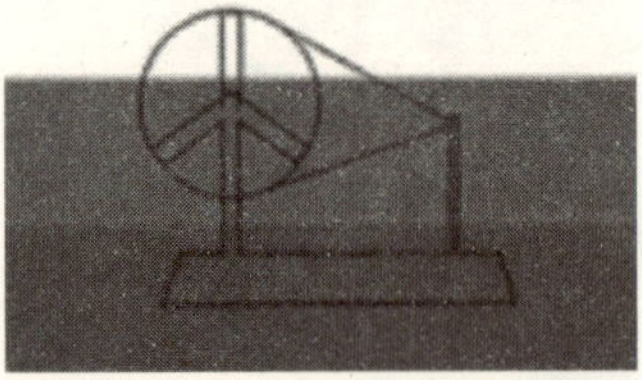

Mahatma Gandhi's flag, 1921

---

[25] Srirupa Roy, "A Symbol of Freedom: The Indian Flag and Transformations of Nationalism, 1906–2002", *Journal of Asian Studies*, 2006, **65**(3): 503.

The flag was popularized across the nation along with the mass political ritual of spinning *carkhā*. The two resonated. When a ban was imposed after the flying of the Swaraj flag in Jabalpur in 1923, Nagpur Flag Satyagraha was launched. The flag itself became the means of national mobilization.

Congress flag, 1931

The quest for the national flag, based upon spiritual symbolism, faded and the space was occupied by the partisan organizations to deepen their political support from the masses. What was merely a Swaraj flag became the Congress flag after the report of the National Flag Committee presided over by Sardar Vallabhbhai Patel was presented on 5 August 1931. It went back on the colour scheme of the three colours in a sequence used by Madame Cama but instead of Vande Mātaram in the centre, inserted *carkhā*. Thus, the flag was a hybrid of the Gandhi flag and the colour scheme of Madame Cama minus the spiritual symbolism infused into Stuttgart national flag. It was the same Congress flag which was accepted as the national flag by the Constituent Assembly by spinning a short substitution of image of *cakra* from the Iron Pillar at Sārnāth in place of *carkhā*. Though, *carkhā* remained the signified for the signifier *cakra*. Nehru argued that *cakra* as wheel is also present in *carkhā* and in one way *cakra* was transformed into a synecdoche. This national flag was manufactured by the political leadership for mass mobilization and did not spring from the heart of the people and the history of the nation. When the flag was presented by Hansa Mehta on behalf of the "Flag Presentation Committee" consisting of all the women members of the Constituent Assembly as a gift from the women of India, one thing was never noticed. The national flag of Bhārata Mātā lacked symbolism of half of India. There was no space designated for women in the scheme of a flag whose creed was stated to be non-violence and peace.

Triangular Flag for India

Since the time Swaraj flag was created by Mahatma Gandhi, the whole debate on the national flag revolved around what colour would represent which community. Hardly any debate took place on the size and shape of the flag. The advent of national flag in India did not occur in the vibrant socio-political space of symbolic richness. India has been a land of variegated flags in the forms of *dhvaja, jhaṇḍā, patākā*. All of these had a triangular shape and resonated well with the public consciousness since triadic thinking is at the root of Indian civilization. In the previous chapter, I have argued how the triadic thinking has a geophilosophical root in India's triangular geography. In fact, the popularity of the Swaraj flag of 1921 or the Congress flag of 1931 was due to this misplaced resonance of triadness. The public accepted *tiraṅgā* as it appealed to their own structure of speculative thinking. The tricolour contained the image of the *carkhā*, which appeared as a fusion of a triangle and a wheel. The shape of triangle is formed by the yarn joining the wheel with the spindle.

Should not a triangular *tiraṅgā* be much suited to Indian consciousness? Shouldn't the national flag be unique that encapsulate "condensed imagination of a civilization"? Should not the national flag spring from the pre-existing tradition of a community and not appear to be overtly manufactured? In fact, vanishing of Venkayya was a major blow to the project of designing a national flag commensurate with national ethos and extant consciousness.

A triangular national flag should not be viewed as merely an attempt by the Hindu majority to impose a partisan religious orientation. The triangular flag should not be seen as merely the flag that Rāma carried in the narrative of the great epic *Rāmāyaṇa* or the Rājpūts and the Marāṭhā carried while resisting the Mughal hegemony.

The Mughals also paid respect to the triangular flags and did not view it as a Hindu or a Muslim flag. It was Hindustānī flag and used the shape in their own flags. Virmani traces the usage during Mughal period:

> Muhammad Shah, the Mughal emperor, presented a flag to the French forces under Governor-General Joseph Dupleix in 1742. This was triangular like the Mughal standards and dotted with golden pomegranates surrounding a sun on a white background.[26]

The Indian National Congress and Mahatma Gandhi neither took into account the existing culture of using triangular flags nor were considerate towards the then princely states which too formed inherent part of India. There were five princely states with twenty-one-gun salute — Mysore, Gwalior, Baroda, Hyderabad and Jammu & Kashmir, and three of these states had at one time or another a triangular flag or its combination in the royal flag.

Aldo Ziggiotto, an Italian vexillologist, has studied the flags of Indian principalities and published the book, *Vessillologia dell'India: Paese principensco e feudale* (1998) (*Vexillology of India: Feudal and Princely States*).[27] The book reveals the popularity of triangular-shaped flags across the Indian principalities even during the British regime.

---

26 Virmani, n. 18, p. 43.

27 Aldo Ziggiotto, *Vessillologia dell'India — Paese principensco e feudale* (*Vexillology of India: Feudal and Princely States*) Issue 6 of la rivista marittima/supplemento, ISSN 0035-6964 (Lucca, Italy: Rivista Marittima) (1998). Also available on http://flagspot.net/flags/in-princ.html (last accessed on 1 December 2012)

Baroda was founded in 1730 by the Marāṭhā General Pilaji Rao Gaekwad, and the state banner was saffron-coloured, common to the whole Marāṭhā confederation. It had two triangles fused into one such that the vertices remain separate.

The flag of Baroda (*Source*: Aldo Ziggiotto (1998))

Similarly, the kingdom of Gwalior, like other principalities of Marāṭhā confederacy, carried the saffron flag. Saffron triangular flag with a swallowtail was the flag of the army of Gwalior in 1726.

The Mysore state's origin can be traced to Haider Ali and his valiant son, Tipu Sultan, the Tiger of Mysore. The flags carried the image of a tiger. But, one of the flags carried by the army of the Mysore state was a perfect isosceles triangle with golden border.

The flag used by the army of Mysore state (1782-99) (*Source*: Aldo Ziggiotto (1998))

Even other major princely states lower in the hierarchy than the twenty-one-gun salute, like Udaipur–Mewāṛ, Dewās Jr. & Sr., Koṭāh displayed triangular flags with religious motif like Hanumān carrying the Droṇagiri mountain. The State of Koṭā had a perfect triadic flag. Three triangles fused with the

The flag of Udaipur–Mewāṛ (*Source*: Aldo Ziggiotto (1998))

The flag of principalities of Dewās Jr. & Sr.
(*Source*: Aldo Ziggiotto (1998))

The flag of Koṭā, a princely state of Rājputānā, Rajasthan
(*Source*: Aldo Ziggiotto 1998))

red plain background and Lord Hanumān as emblem reverberated powerful spiritual and civilizational influence.

It was this disillusionment with Mahatma Gandhi's Swaraj flag that in 1925, when the Rashtriya Swayamsevak Sangh (RSS) was founded in Nagpur by K.B. Hedgewar, the triangular saffron flag (*bhagavā dhvaja*) was accorded the status of *guru*. The political gatherings involved the salutation before *bhagavā dhwaja*, both at the beginning and the end of the programme. In 1939, V.D. Savarkar, in his presidential address to the twenty-first session of the Akhil Bharatiya Hindu Mahasabha held at Calcutta, declared that

> the *kuṇḍalinī kr̥pāṅkr̥ta geruā* flag (saffron flag blessed with the *kuṇḍalinī* energy) shall be the flag of the Hindu nation.[28]

The triangular flag in no way is communal and it is surprising that the leaders of the freedom struggle failed to debate the possible non-quadrilateral shapes for the national flag. Virmani writes:

[28] Virmani, n. 18, p. 262.

> There were comparatively few voices reclaiming a revival of the oriental tradition of triangular flags. Those who did so pointed to their use by both Muslim states and Hindu kingdoms.[29]

The Qing empire of China had a triangular flag with the image of a dragon as the emblem (Ketu in Indian tradition) on the flag.

The Qing flag (1862-90)[30]

The triangular flag was characterized by a blue dragon on plain yellow background, with a red pearl at the upper left corner. This is also counted as the first national flag of China (Yellow Dragon Flag or *Huáng lóng qí*). Since yellow has been the royal colour of Chinese emperors and the first emperor of China was known as the Yellow emperor, the yellow background suggested the uninterrupted continuity of the royal tradition. The dragon was a symbol of imperial power and strength. The red is the auspicious colour in China. The red pearl connoted prosperity and wealth. Thus, the Qing flag symbolized together the strength, continuity and prosperity.

At present, there are dozens of nations that have triangle in their national flags. The Philippine national flag has a white equilateral triangle with three stars symbolizing equality and fraternity in its rectangular flag.

---

29 Virmani, n. 18, p. 135.

30 Source: Wikipedia, http://en.wikipedia.org/wiki/Flag_of_the_Qing_Dynasty (last accessed on 1 December 2012).

The national flag of the Philippines

The triangle is contained in the flag of the following nations: Bahamas, Comoros, Djibouti, Cuba, Czech Republic, Equatorial Guinea, Guyana, Eritrea, Palestine, Mozambique, Jordan, Puerto Rico, the Philippines, Sao Tome & Principe, Sudan, Vanuatu, Zimbabwe, Bosnia and Herzegovina, Nicaragua, and South Africa.

But, currently the only triangular national flag is found in the Himalayan nation of Nepal. The flag was adopted on 16 December 1962. It is a combination of two triangles.

The national flag of Nepal

Within India also, triangular flags are being used by various political and cultural organizations. Shiv Sena has adopted the flag used by Śivājī. In 2012, when Sadhvi Uma Bharati launched her campaign for protecting the Gaṅgā River from pollution, the flag of the political campaign under the banner of Ganga Samagra Yatra, was in triangular shape. The flag caught the imagination of public since the shape and design resonated the phylogeny of civilizational emblems.

The flag of Shiv Sena

The flag of Ganga Samagra Yatra (2012)

The current Indian flag was created by viewing the nation as merely a sum of part-communities and not as the iconic signifier of the Indian territory. The national flag must be unique and it should reflect the common wisdom and hope for the teeming millions. The *tiraṅgā* flag is no more unique with exactly similar looking flag having been adopted as the national flag of Niger.

The national flag of Niger

But, the Niger flag is not an imitation of the Indian flag. It emerged out of the geographical conditions of the country. In a way, it is the reflection of the geophilosophical imagination of the Niger's indigenous leadership. The national flag of Niger is not just a national flag but also a geographic depiction of Niger. The three strips represent three major environmental regions of Niger. The orange at the top represents the Sahara in the north of the country; the white in the middle represents the savannah in the centre and the green at the bottom represents the fertile regions of southern Niger.

Thus, the Indian national flag is no longer unique and in an age of globalization, it is necessary to have a unique new flag that represents India in matter and spirit.

New National Flag with Śrī-yantra Emblem

I have elaborated in previous chapters how Śrī-yantra is the abstract and condensed signifier of Indian thinking. Śrī-yantra itself is merely a geometrical object and unlike the various symbols proposed during the last two centuries or being used at present. Śrī-yantra as an emblem in the new national flag will resonate with the heart, philosophy, territory and history of India. There is no reason to discard a non-quadrilateral flag as the national flag. In fact, a triangular flag will be akin to widely used flags in social as well as private occasions. India is a civilizational unity not by the power of the modern state, but by the march of pilgrims for centuries criss-crossing the nation. *Yātrās*, as they are known, are carried under the banner of triangular *jhaṇḍā*. Thus, a triangular flag will also cater to the spirit of oneness.

Śrī-yantra is an interlocking bunch of triangles which appears mysterious, and yet is aesthetically pleasant to look at. Śrī-yantra has lateral symmetry, a choice referred by Nehru while arguing against *carkhā* as the emblem. Śrī-yantra is an emblem of connectivity itself and hence a great symbol to represent the mutual connectivity in a variegated territory. Śrī-yantra also represents India's great cosmopolitan past. Śrī-yantra moved offshore to Java and Bali, Champa and Sriwijaya. Śrī-yantra is the common thread between India's two great traditions of Vedas and Āgamas. Śrī the prefix used in Śrī-yantra, is used as a universal honorific and welcomed by Indians irrespective of religious affiliation and mark for respect, auspiciousness and prosperity. Śrī-yantra is a graded design which is polysemantic and the whole is revealed only through graded revelation. This provides the viewer an opportunity to ponder over its significance, meaning and pattern. Only such a symbol can hold the past and future of such a diverse nation together. Śrī-yantra with its rhythm, connectivity and hierarchical geomtery is akin to non-sonoric optical refrain, what Deleuze and Guattari visualized as an ideal territorial motif.

Sthaneshwar Timalsina, Professor of Religious Studies at San Diego State University, who specializes in studying consciousness in Asian philosophy, tāntric visualization and cognitive engineering, argues how *yantra*s and *maṇḍala*s used in south Asian religious tradition are in fact mnemonic devices. He argues in a recent paper presented in a conference:

> Multiple research studies on human cognition have established that visual images are powerful devices for enhancing memory. Following these studies, the interaction of images with each other effectively consolidates retention. It has also been established that bizarre images remain in memory for a longer time than merely pleasant, aesthetically appealing images, landscapes for example. . . . One study suggests that spatialization is twice as effective in recollecting multiple items. It has also been found that retrieval of memory is easier if its organization follows a systematized framework. Tāntric images are comparable to cognitive maps that integrate information acquired through various perceptual modes, and studies on tāntric images can further expand our understanding of spatial cognition and vice versa.[31]

With organized and aweful image, a person can "activate in his short-term memory the cosmologies and philosophies cultivated over a longer period of time".[32] Śrī-yantra being a complex visual image organized in a geometric pattern will be an apt emblem to induce the recollection of civilizational memory and the territorial integrity. Śrī-yantra is an apt cognitive attractor for the citizens.

Verily, Śrī-yantra represents the *kuṇḍalinī* energy in each one of us. It is this discovery of endless source of ceaseless

---

31 Sthaneshwar Timalsina, "Mnemonics, Image Compression, and Tantric Visualization", 2012 accessed on 1 December 2012 at https://www.facebook.com/sthaneshwar.timalsina/posts/108687295956801

32 Ibid.

creativity and strength inherent in each of us and yet remaining unharnessed which is India's unique contribution to the mankind. Śrī-yantra symbolized the strength, spiritual salvation as well as material prosperity. Śrī-yantra is the matrix of invariance and variability and thus mediates continuity amidst change, permanence amidst transitory and momentary phenomena. Śrī-yantra also is the site for mediation between science and humanism. It reveals the significance gradually. It is a mnemonic device that aids in memorizing a complex ritual, but it also operates as the index of the Śakti that is being propitiated. Śrī-yantra is the complex fusion of the computational intelligence of machines and error-prone human intelligence. Śrī-yantra is the geometry of a triadic universe. Śrī-yantra is the ultimate design of the universe.

Śrī-yantra represents the Mother and all the women of India. It will not be a one-time affair like Hansa Mehta getting an opportunity on behalf of the women of India to merely present the national flag for hoisting on the eve of the declaration of Independence.

I have discussed how the Meru of Śrī-yantra is the interlocking of a triangle with its mirror image. This sign has been in use for fostering the unity since time immemorial. In fact, it was widely used in the Mughal architecture and paintings. The image has been inscribed at the main entrance of the magnificent Humayun Tomb.

Entrance of the Humayun Tomb, Delhi

When the Mughals under Bābur conquered Delhi in CE 1526, they made the Purana Qila as their administrative centre. The entrance gate of the Purana Qila still carries the sign of the Meru of Śrī-yantra. Sher Shah, an Afghan commander, defeated Humayun in the battle and occupied the Purana Qila complex. He built a mosque which is still well maintained. The mosque has plenty of designs of Meru of Śrī-yantra. Therefore, it has to be assumed that the Muslim rulers appropriated the Śrī-yantra's core for legitimizing their rule. Purana Qila complex is stated to be situated over the ruins of Indraprastha, the first city of Delhi during the Mahābhārata period. Indraprastha is stated to be the capital from where Pāṇḍavas ruled. There is still a Pāṇḍava era Bhairoṅ Temple adjacent to the Purana Qila. Near the complex is the Siri Fort area which derives the name from "Śrī". There are only few places in India named with the prefix Śrī. Srinagar in Kashmir is considered the site of foremost place as it is believed to be the capital of the deity of Śrī-yantra. Cultural historians are yet to explore the popularity of Śrī-yantra and its cult during the advent of the Mughals in and around Delhi and the awe the geometric image caused among the foreign rulers.

The critics might object that the Śrī-yantra is a religious image. I have described in detail how Śrī-yantra is much more than an object of Hindu religious worship. Śrī-yantra is the ultimate fruit of geophilosophical imagination of India. The Mughals adopted it, the Himalayan cultures adopted it, the people in extreme east in Tripura adopted it. It is an amulet for common masses and the philosopher's stone for sages and *paṇḍit*s. It is an auspicious symbol that provides hope for material prosperity and the dawn of wisdom.

The critics should also keep in mind that the emblem in the national flags need not be a desacralized object. The flag of Israel includes two blue stripes on white background with a Star of David in the centre. The Star of David is a common symbol of Israelites from ancient period.

The flag of Israel

It is interesting that the leaders of the Indian freedom movement never opposed the Union Jack on the ground of being communal.

The Union Jack was established by proclamation of James VI and I of Scotland and England with following command:

> By the King: Whereas, some differences hath arisen between Our subjects of South and North Britain travelling by Seas, about the bearing of their Flagges: For the avoiding of all contentions hereafter. We have, with the advice of our Council, ordered: That from henceforth all our Subjects of this Isle and Kingdome of Great Britaine, and all our members thereof, shall beare in their main-toppe the Red Crosse, commonly called St. George's Crosse, and the White Crosse, commonly called St. Andrew's Crosse, joyned together according to the forme made by ourheralds, and sent by Us to our Admerall to be published to our Subjects: and in their fore-toppe our Subjects of South Britaine shall weare the Red Crosse onely as they were wont, and our Subjects of North Britaine in their fore-toppe the White Crosse onely as they were accustomed.
>
> —James VI and I, *Orders in Council: Official Creation of the Union Flag*, 1606[33]

---

[33] Arthur Charles Fox-Davies, *The Art of Heraldry: An Encyclopaedia of Armory*, London: Bloomsbury Books, 1904, p. 399.

The Union Jack

The Union Jack and the Israeli flag have clearly religious motifs in their national flags. But, never has same been ridiculed on the ground of being communal. For a national flag, what matters is that the emblem must echo the heart and mind of the people. Śrī-yantra as an emblem in a triangular national flag retaining the tricolour will be unique and also represent the soul and territory of India.

I propose a simple flag incorporating India's triadic destiny. Creative artists can improve upon such a template to devise a *truly* Indian flag that will encapsulate India's history and territory.

Proposed flag with Śrī-yantra emblem

Logo of Development Institute (MSME), Goverment of India

Indian government and State Government of Karnataka have appropriated Śrī-yantra as logo for various departments. Development Institute, Ministry of Micro, Small and Medium Enterprises (MSME), Government of India places national emblem and Śrī-yantra side-by-side. It is opportune time to bring Śrī-yantra into centrality of national consciousness. Verily, Śrī-yantra is India's ultimate refrain.

Conclusion

Avataraṇa of India's Past of Abundance

IN every rice field in Bali, there is a small shrine to Śrī Devī, the goddess of rice and fertility, whose roots can be traced to the tradition of worship of Śrī-yantra in India. It is believed that the presence of Śrī Devī makes rice grow, safeguards the paddy from the pest and provides sufficient water for the better yield. In Bali, farmers form Subak to manage water to irrigate their rice fields and to build the temple (Pura Subak) of Śrī Devī. But, in the name of the "Green Revolution", new agricultural technologies were introduced to radically increase rice production. After brief increase in productivity, the yield plummeted. The pests and vermins grew. The farmers sought the government to let them return to the traditional system of irrigation scheduling by the Pura Subak. Under the National Science Foundation Programme, Stephen Lansing was sponsored to examine the role of water temples in Balinese irrigation management in 1983. Lansing recommended the efficacious traditional method mediated through the Śrī Devī temples. Later, Lansing collaborated with ecologist/computer expert James Kremer to study the traditional Balinese agricultural system using computers to calculate the effects of various crop management scenarios. The simulation model, using historical rainfall data, concluded that the traditional water temple system was far more effective than the government's current policy. Lansing summed up his praise for the Śrī temple system of Bali in ensuring rich harvest for centuries in an excellent book, *Priests and Programmers: Technologies of Power in the Engineered Landscape of Bali.*[1]

India is still struggling to mitigate poverty and scarcity of resources for the billion plus population in spite of six decades of Independence. Who knows the miracle eagerly awaited by policy-makers might happen once the national flag designed and created by experts is replaced with another flag carrying the power of abundance of Śrī Devī represented through Śrī-yantra! Like the Balinese Śrī Devī temples in rice fields which guarantee abundant harvest, India will rise in abundance with the auspicious symbol of prosperity fluttering atop each household. This will be the people's flag, a true national flag obliterating traumatic memory of partitioned nationhood associated with the hoisting of national flag in 1947!

Jai Hind! Bhārata Mātā kī Jai!!

1 Stephan Lansing, *Priests and Programmers: Technologies of Power in the Engineered Landscape of Bali*, Princeton: Princeton University Press, 1991.

Bibliography

Āryabhaṭa, *Āryabhaṭīya*, ed. Kripa Shankar Singh, New Delhi: Indian National Science Academy, 1976.

Anderson, Benedict, *Imagined Communities: Reflections on the Origin and Spread of Nationalism,* London: Verso, 1991.

Assayag, Jackie, "The Body of India: Geography, Ritual, Nation", *Etnografica*, 1997, **1**(1): 39.

Banerjee, Debashish, *The Alternate Nation of Abanindranath Tagore,* New Delhi: Sage, 2010.

Bhārata Mātā Mandir, Bangalore; "Bhārata Mātā, Mother India, or Bhāratāmbā is the national personification of India as a mother goddess." http:/ www.sribharatamatamandir.org/word/

Bhattacharya, Chintamani, *Śrī-Tattva-Cintāmaṇi,* Calcutta: Metropolitan Printing and Publishing House Limited, 1937.

Boeyens, Jan C.A. and Demetrius C. Levendis, *Number Theory and the Periodicity of Matter*, Berlin: Springer Verlag, 2008.

Bonta, Mark and John Protevi, *Deleuze and Geophilosophy: A Guide and Glossary*, Edinburgh: Edinburgh University Press, 2004.

Bouchrey, Pascal, "Terrace Cultivation and Mental Landscapes in Southern Yunnan", in Marie Lecomte-Tilouine (ed.), *Nature, Culture and Religion at the Crossroads of Asia*, Hyderabad: Social Science Press, 2010, pp. 318-42.

Brooks, Douglas Renfrew, *Auspicious Wisdom: The Texts and Traditions of Srividya Sakta Tantrism in South India*, Albany, NY: SUNY Press, 1992.

Bruce, B. Janz, "The Territory Is Not the Map's Place, Deleuze and Guattari, and African Philosophy", *Philosophy Today* (Winter 2001), **45**(4): 395.

Casey, Edward S., "Between Geography and Philosophy: What Does It Mean to be in the Place-World?", *Annals of the Association of American Geographers* (2001), **91**(4).

———, "Cityscape and Landscape: Place and Site in Urban Life", special issue of *Sphinx* in 1998; Casey, Edward S., "Body, Self, and Landscape: A Geophilosophical Inquiry into the Place-World" in P. Adams, S. Hoelscher and K. Till (eds.), *Textures of Place: Exploring Humanist Geographies*, Minneapolis: University of Minnesota Press, 2001.

———, *Getting Back into Place: Towards a Renewed Understanding of the Place-World*, Bloomington: Indiana University Press, 1993.

———, *The Fate of Place: A Philosophical History*, Berkeley: University of California Press, 1997;

CERN press release, "Observation of a New Particle with a Mass of 125 GeV' CMS Experiment, CERN", 4 July 2012. http://cms.web.cern.ch/news/observation-new-particle-mass-125-gev

CERN, "Missing Higgs" available at http://public.web.cern.ch/public/en/science/higgs-en.html. CERN, The Standard Package available at public.web.cern.ch/public/en/science/standardmodel-en.html (last accessed on 4 December 2012); also see, Dave Fehling, *The Standard Model of Particle Physics: A Lunchbox's Guide*, Johns Hopkins University www.pha.jhu.edu/~dfehling

Chakrabarti, Sekhar, *Quest for a National Flag for India*, Part XVII "National Flag of Independent India-1947", 22 July 2010. http://flagstamps.blogspot.in/2010/07/quest-for-national-flag-for-india-part_22.html (last accessed on 1 December 2012).

Chakrabarti, Sekhar, The Indian National Flag Unflurled Through Philately, New Delhi: Niyogi Books, 2012.

Charles, Arthur and Fox-Davies, *The Art of Heraldry: An Encyclopaedia of Armory*, London: Bloomsbury Books, 1904, p. 399.

Chelyapov, Nickolas, Manoj Gopalkrishnan et al., "DNA Triangles and Self-Assembled Hexagonal Tilings", *Journal of the American Chemical Society*, 2004, **126**: 13924-25.

Chen, Yanguan, "Fractal Systems of Central Places Based on Intermittency of Space-filling", *Chaos, Solitons & Fractals*, 2011, **44**(8): 619-32, http://arxiv.org/ftp/arxiv/papers/1105/1105.0589.pdf.

Chisholm, Dianne, "Rhizome, Ecology, Geophilosophy", *Rhizomes*, **15** (Winter 2007). http://www.rhizomes.net/issue15/chisholm.htmlaccessed (last accessed on 1 December 2012).

Cook, Francis H., *Hua-Yen Buddhism: The Jewel Net of Indra*, University Park and London: Pennsylvania State University Press, 1977.

Craddock, Travis J., Stuart Hameroff et al., "Cytoskeletal Signaling: Is Memory Encoded in Microtube Lattices by CaMKII Phosphorylation?", *PLoS Computational Biology*, 2012, **8**(3): 1-16

Dahlquist, Allan, *Megasthenes and Indian Religion: A Study in Motives and Types*, Delhi: Motilal Banarsidass, 1996.

de Casparis, J.G., *Prasasti Indonesia* 2, Bandung: 1968, pp. 16ff.

Deleuze, Gilles and Felix Guattari, *A Thousand Plateaus: Capitalism and Schizophrenia*, tr. B. Massumi, London: Continuum, 1987.

Deleuze, Gilles and Felix Guattari, *What Is Philosophy?*, tr. Hugh Tomlinson and Graham Burchell, New York: Columbia University Press, 1996.

Dikshitar, Ramachandra V.R., *The Lalita Cult* (1942) rpt., Delhi: Motilal Banarsidass, 1991.

Eck, Diana, "The Imagined Landscape: Patterns in the Construction of Hindu Sacred Geography", *Contributions to Indian Sociology* (1988), **32**(2): 165-88.

Eck, Diana, *India: A Sacred Geography*, New York: Harmony Books, 2012.

Edney, Mathew H., *Mapping an Empire: The Geographical Construction of British India (1765–1843)*, Chicago: Chicago University Press, 1990.

Eugene, Walter, tr., *The Āryabhaṭīya of Āryabhaṭa*, Chicago: University of Chicago Press, 1930.

Evena, C.O. and J. Fudjack, *Consciousness: An Interdisciplinary Study* (1976) available at www.mentalstates.net consciousness.html

Farmer, Steve, John B. Henderson and Michael Witzel, "Neurobiology, Layered Texts and Correlative Cosmologies: A Cross-Cultural Framework for Premodern History", *Bulletin of the Museum of Far Eastern Antiquities* (Stockholm) (2000), **72**: 48-90.

Feldhaus, Anne, *Connected Places: Region, Pilgrimage, and Geographical Imagination in India*, New York: Palgrave Macmillan, 2003.

Firth, Raymond, *Symbols: Public and Private*, New York: Cornell University Press, 1973.

Flanagan, Patrick, How to Draw a Sri-yantra, 1991, http://www.sri-yantraresearch.com/Construction/Flanagan patrick_flanagan_method.htm

Formoso, Bernard, "A Terraced World for an Armoured Body: The Symbolism of Women Costumes Among the Yi of Yuan Yang, 2006", *Research in Anthropology and Aesthetics*, **37**: 89-106.

Foster, Georgana and Robert Stoddard, "Vaishno Devi, the Most Famous Goddess Shrine in the Siwaliks" in Rana P.B. Singh (ed.), *Sacred Geography of Goddess in South Asia: Essays in Memory of David Kinsley*, New Castle upon Tyne: Combridge Scholars, 2010.

Fudjack, John and Patricia Dinkelaker, "The Enneagram as Classic Double Mandala", April 1999. http://tap3x.net/EMBTI/j4selfcc.html (last accessed on 4 December 2012).

Ganguli, K.M. (tr.), *The Mahābhārata*, Calcutta: Bharata Press, 1883-96.

Gonda, Jan, *Change and Continuity in Indian Religion*, The Hague: The Mouton, 1965.

Gray, David B., *The Cakrasamvara Tantra: The Discourse of Śrī Heruka*, New York: American Institute of Buddhist Studies/Columbia University Press, 2007.

Griffith, Ralph T.H. (tr.), *The Hymns of the Rig Veda*, Benares: E.J. Lazarus, 1896.

Gunzel, Stephen, "Nietzsche's Geophilosophy", *Journal of Nietzsche Studie* (2003), **25**: 87.

Hameroff, Stuart, Travis J.A. Craddock and Jack A. Tuszynski, "Cytoskeletal Signalling: Is Memory Encoded in Microtubule Lattices by CaMKII Phosphorylation?", *PLOS Computational Biology* (March 2012), **8**(3): 1-16.

Hardy, Chris H., *The Sacred Network: Megaliths, Cathedrals, Ley Lines, and the Power of Shared Consciousness*, Rochester: Inner Traditions/Bear & Company, 2011.

Heidegger, Martin, *Poetically Man Dwells in Poetry, Language, Thought*, tr. Albert hofstadter, New York: Harper Collins, 2001 (repr.).

Huber, Tony, "Where Exactly Are Caritra, Devikota and Himavat?: A Sacred Geography Controversy and the Development of Tantric Buddhist Pilgrimage Sites in Tibet", in A. McKay (ed.) *The History of Tibet*, vol. II: *The Medieval Period: c. 850–1895 — The Development of Buddhist Paramountcy*, London: Routledge Curzon, pp. 392-424.

Juilesz, Bela and Ilona Kovacas (eds.), *Maturational Windows and Adult Cortical Plasticity, Proceedings*, vol. XXIII, Sante Fe Institute, Readings: Addison-Wesley, 1995.

Kinseley, David, *Hindu Goddess: Vision of the Divine Feminine in the Hindu Religious Tradition*, Berkeley: University of California Press, 1986.

Krioukov, Dmitri, et al. "Network Cosmology", *Scientific Reports* 2, Article number 793, doi:10.1038/srep00793 Published 16 November 2012_http://www.nature.com/srep/2012/121113/srep00793/full/srep00793.html

Kulaichev, Alexander Pavalovich, "Śrī-yantra and Its Mathematical Properties", *Indian Journal of History of Science*, 1984, **19**(3): 279-92.

Kumar, Niraj and C.N. Biak, "Zomi, Zomia, Nomadia: Landscape, Handicraft and Statecraft", 2011 http://epao.net/epSubPageExtractor.asp?src=manipur.Ethnic_Races_Manipur.Zomi_Zomia_Nomadia__Landscape_handicraft_and_statecraft_Part_1; http://ariseasia.blogspot.com/2011/09/zomi-zomia-nomadia-landscape-handicraft.html (last accessed on 1 December 2012).

Lahiri, Manoshi, *Mapping India*, Delhi: Niyogi Books, 2012.

Lansing, Stephan, *Priests and Programmers: Technologies of Power in the Engineered Landscape of Bali*, Princeton: Princeton University Press, 1991.

Lanzerotti, Louis J. and Giovanni P. Gregori, "Telluric Currents: The Natural Environment and Interactions with Man-made Environment" in Geophysics Study Committee, Geophysics Research Forum, Commission on Physical Sciences, Mathematics and Resources, National Research Council, (eds.), *Studies in Geophysics: The Earth's Electrical Environment*, National Academy of Sciences, 1986, pp. 212-50.

Lawrence, D.P., "Remarks on Abhinavagupta's Use of the Analogy of Reflection", *Journal of Indian Philosophy* (2005), **33**(5-6): 594.

Lieberman-Aiden, Erez et al., "Comprehensive Mapping of Long-Range Interactions Reveals Folding Principles of the Human Genome", *Science*, October 2009, **326**(5950): 289-93.

Lisi, Garrett, "An Exceptionally Simple Theory of Everything", http://www.arxiv.org/abs/0711.0770 also see Garrett Lisi and J.O. Weatherall, "A Geometric Theory of Everything", *Scientific American*, 2010, **303**(6): 54-61.

Locke, J., *An Essay Concerning Human Understanding* (1690), P.G. Nidditch (ed.), Oxford: Clarendon Press, 1975.

Mackay, Robin (ed.), *Collapse*, vol. VI: *Geo/philosophy*, Falmouth, UK: Urbanomic, January 2010.

Madhvananda, Swami (ed.), *Bṛhadāraṇyaka Upaniṣad* with the commentary of Śaṅkarācārya, Madhu Kāṇḍa, chapter 1.5.14, Almora: Advaita Ashrama, 1950, p. 225.

Masciandro, Nicola, "Becoming Spice: Commentary as Geophilosophy", *Collapse*, vol. VI: *Geo/philosophy*, 2010, p. 32.

Nakamura, Hajime, *Ways of Thinking of Eastern Peoples: India, China, Tibet, Japan*, Honolulu: University of Hawaii Press, 1964.

National Herald, 21 June 1947 cited in Arundhati Virmani, *A National Flag for India — Rituals, Nationalism and the Politics of Sentiment*, Ranikhet: Permanent Black, 2008, p. 257.

Negarestani, Reza, "Globe of Revolution: An Afterthought on Geophilosophical Realism", 2012 (extended version of paper) written for *Dark Materialism*, Kingston University, London, 12 January 2011; available at http://archive.org/details/aaaaarg-32071.

Newel, Zo Margaret, *Picturing the Goddess: Bazaar Images and the Imagination of Modern Hindu Religious Identity*, Ph.D. Dissertation, Graduate School of Vanderbilt University, Nashville, Tennessee, 2011, p. 226.

Nietzsche, Friedrich, *Thus Spake Zarathustra*, tr. Thomas Common, New York: Random House, 1954, pp. 6-7.

Nivedita, Sister, "The Vajra as a National Flag", in *The Complete Works of Sister Nivedita*, Kolkata: Advaita Ashrama, 1999, p. 170.

Pandey, G.S. (ed.), *A Study in the Mathematical Contributions of Varahamihira and His Heritage*, Shimla: Indian Institute of Advanced Study, 2010.

Parashar, Sadhana, *Kāvyamīmāṁsā of Rājaśekhara*, Delhi: D.K. Printworld, 2000.

Particle Data Group of Lawrence Berkeley National Laboratory (LBNL), Project History Under Supervision by Michael Barnett and Andria Erzberger. "The Particle Adventure", *Fundamentals of Matter and Force*. www.particleadventure.org/fermibos.html

Peirce, Charles S., *Collected Papers*, Cambridge: Harvard University Press 1931.

Pellionisz, Andras J., Graham Roy, A. Peter, Pellionisz and Jean–Claude Perez, "Recursive Genome Function of the Cerebellum:

Geometric Unification of Neuroscience and Genomics"; in *Handbook of The Cerebellum and Cerebellar Disorders*, ed. Mario Manto et al., New York: Springer, 2013, vol. 3, pp. 1381-1424.

Perez, J.C., "Codon Populations in Single-stranded Whole Human Genome DNA Are Fractal and Fine-tuned by the Golden Ratio 1.618", *Interdiscip. Sci.*, 2010, **2**(3): 228-40.

Petukhov, S.V. and Mathew He, *Mathematics of Bioinformatics: Theory, Practice and Applications*, New Jersey: Wiley, 2011.

Prakash, Satya, *Founders of Science in Ancient India*, New Delhi: The Research Institute of Ancient Scientific Studies, 1965.

Protevi, John, "Between Geophilosophy and Political Physiology", 3 October 2004. www.protevi.com/john/Geophilosophy.pdf (last accessed on 1 December 2012).

Protevi, John, *The Geophilosophies of Deleuze and Guattari*, Speech at November 2001 meeting of SEDAAG. www.protevi.com/john/SEDAAG.pdf (last accessed on 1 December 2012).

Ramachandra Rao, S.K., *The Tantrik Practices in Srividya*, Bangalore: Kalpatharu Research Academy, 1990, p. 179; also see S.K. Ramchandra Rao, *Srividya-Kosa*, Delhi: Sri Satguru Publications, 2005.

Ramanujan, A.K., "Is There an Indian Way of Thinking?: An Informal Essay", *Contributions to Indian Sociology* (1989), **23**(1): 41-58.

Ramaswamy, Sumathi, *The Goddess and the Nation: Mapping Mother India*, Durham and London: Duke University Press, 2009.

Rennell, James, *Memoir of a Map of Hindoostan; or, The Mogul Empire*: with an introduction, illustrative of the geography and present division of that country: and a map of the countries situated between the head of the Indus, and the Caspian sea. By James Rennell . . . To which is added, an appendix, containing an account of the Ganges and Burrampooter Rivers. London, Printed by M. Brown, for the author, 1788.

Roy, Srirupa, "A Symbol of Freedom: The Indian Flag and Transformations of Nationalism, 1906–2002", *Journal of Asian Studies*, 2006, **65**(3): 503.

Schendel, William van, "Geographies of Knowing, Geographies of Ignorance: Jumping Scale in Southeast Asia", *Development and Planning D: Society and Space*, 2002, **20**: 647-68.

Shastri, Lakshmana, *The Tantraraja Tantra*: Tantrik Texts, vol. VIII, ed. Arthur Avalon, London: Luzac, 1919.

Shastri, Mukund Ram (Pandit) (ed. with notes), *The Amaraugha Śāsana of Gorakhnātha*, Bombay: Research Department, Jammu and Kashmir / Nirnaya Sagar Press, 1918.

Shastri, Sitaram, *Kaula and Other Upanishads with Commentary by Bhaskar Raya*, Tantrik Texts, vol. XI, ed. Arthur Avalon, London: Luzac, 1922.

Singh, A.N., "On the Use of Series in Hindu Mathematics", in *Osiris: Studies on the History and Philosophy of Science and on the History of Learning and Culture*, The David Engene Smith Presentation Volume, ed. George Sarton, vol. 1, January 1936, Amsterdam: Swets & Zeitlinger N.V., 1969.

Sircar, D.C., *Studies in the Geography of Ancient and Medieval India*, Delhi: Motilal Banarsidass 1971.

Spinadel, Vera W. de, "The Metallic Means and Design", in *Nexus II: Architecture and Mathematics* (ed.) Kim Williams, Fucecchio (Florence): Edizioni dell'Erba, 1998, pp. 141-57.

Spinadel, Vera W. de, *The Metallic Mean Family and Renormalization Group Techniques*, 2000 available at http://www.tex.imm.uran.ru/tom6/spinadel/

Spinadel, Vera W. de, The Metallic Means Family and Art", *Journal of Applied Mathematics*, 2010, **3**(1): 53-64.

Stakhov, Alexey, *The Mathematics of Harmony*, Singapore: World Scientific Publishing Company, 2009.

Subramania Iyer, K.A. and K.C. Pandey (eds.) *Īśvarapratyabhijñā-vimarśinī of Abhinavagupta: Doctrine of Divine Recognition*, Delhi: Motilal Banarsidass, 1986.

Sudipto, Kaviraj, *The Unhappy Consciousness: Bankimchandra Chattopadhyay and the Formation of Nationalist Discourse in India*, Oxford: Oxford University Press, 1995.

Tagare, G.V., tr., *Brahmāṇḍa Purāṇa*, part I, Delhi: Motilal Banarsidass, 1983.

Tahta, Dick, "On the Geometry of the Śrī-yantra", *The Mathematical Gazette*, March 1992, **76**(475): 49-60.

Tegmark, Max, "Parallel Universes", in J.D. Barrow, P.C.W. Davies, and C.L. Harper (eds.), *Ultimate Reality: From Quantum to Cosmos*, Cambridge: Cambridge University Press, 2003.

Thapaliyal, Uma Prasad, *The Dhvaja, Standards and Flags of India: A Study*, Delhi: B.R. Publications, 1938.

Thivierge Jean-Philippe and Gary F. Marcus, "The Topographic Brain: From Neural Connectivity to Cognition", *Trends in Neurosciences* (25 April 2007), **30**(6): 251-59 [available on http://images.neuron.org/images/EdImages/Neuron/thivierge_oct25.pdf (last accessed on 1 December 2012)].

Timalsina, Sthaneshwar, "Mnemonics, Image Compression, and Tantric Visualization", 2012 accessed on 1 December 2012 at https://www.facebook.com/sthaneshwar.timalsina/posts/108687295956801

Tirumantiram: Tirumūḷar, *A Tamil Scriptural Classic,* Madras: Ramakrishna Math, 2002.

Tuan, Yi-Fu, "Geopiety: A Theme in Man's Attachment to Nature and to Place", in David Lowenthal and Martyn J. Bowden (eds.) *In Geographies of the Mind: Essays in Historical Geosophy in Honor of John Kirtland Wright*, New York: Oxford University Press, 1976, pp. 11-39.

Tuan, Yi-Fu, *Space and Place: The Perspective of Experience,* Minneapolis: University of Minnesota Press, 1977.

Virmani, *A National Flag for India: Rituals, Nationalism and the Politics of Sentiment*, Ranikhet: Permanent Black, 2008.

Wikipedia, http://en.wikipedia.org/wiki/Flag_of_the_Qing_Dynasty (last accessed on 1 December 2012).

Worster, Donald, *Rivers of Empire: Water, Aridity, and the Growth of the American West,* New York: Oxford University Press, 1985.

Yadav, B.S. and Man Mohan (eds.), *Ancient Indian Leaps into Mathematics,* Birkhauser: Springer, 2010.

Zalamea, Fernando, "Peirce's Continuum: A Methodological and Mathematical Approach", 2005; avialable at http://acervopeirceano.org/wp-content/uploads/2011/09/Zalamea-Peirces-Continuum.pdf

Zalamea, Fernando, *Synthetic Philosophy of Contemporary Mathematics*, tr. Z.L. Fraser, Falmouth, UK: Urbanomic Sequence Press, 2013.

Ziggiotto, Aldo, *Vessillologia dell'India — Paese principensco e feudale* (*Vexillology of India: Feudal and Princely States*), Issue 6 of La rivista marittima/Supplemento, Lucca, Italy: Rivista Marittima, 1998.

Zimmer, Heinrich, *Myths and Symbols in Indian Art and Civilization* (1946), ed. Joseph Campbell, Princeton: Princeton University Press, 1992, p. 147.

Index